The Art of
Strategic
Listening

PRACTICAL BOOKS FOR SMART MARKETERS FROM PMP

MARKET RESEARCH
The 4Cs of Truth in Communication:
  How to Identify, Discuss, Evaluate and Present Stand-out, Effective Communication
Consumer Insights 2.0:
  How Smart Companies Apply Customer Knowledge to the Bottom Line
Dominators, Cynics, and Wallflowers:
  Practical Strategies for Moderating Meaningful Focus Groups
Moderating to the Max!
  A Full-Tilt Guide to Creative, Insightful Focus Groups and Depth Interviews
The Mirrored Window: *Focus Groups from a Moderator's Point of View*
Religion in a Free Market:
  Religious and Non-Religious Americans—Who, What, Why, Where
Why People Buy Things They Don't Need

MATURE MARKET/ BABY BOOMERS
Advertising to Baby Boomers
After Fifty: *How the Baby Boom Will Redefine the Mature Market*
After Sixty: *Marketing to Baby Boomers Reaching Their Big Transition Years*
Baby Boomers and Their Parents:
  Surprising Findings about Their Lifestyles, Mindsets, and Well-Being
Marketing to Leading-Edge Baby Boomers
The Boomer Heartbeat:
  Capturing the Heartbeat of the Baby Boomers Now and in the Future

MULTICULTURAL
Beyond Bodegas: *Developing a Retail Relationship with Hispanic Customers*
Hispanic Marketing Grows Up: *Exploring Perceptions and Facing Realities*
Hispanic Customers for Life: *A Fresh Look at Acculturation*
Latinization: *How Latino Culture Is Transforming the U.S.*
Marketing to American Latinos: *A Guide to the In-Culture Approach, Part I*
Marketing to American Latinos: *A Guide to the In-Culture Approach, Part II*
The Whole Enchilada: *Hispanic Marketing 101*
What's Black About It?
  Insights to Increase Your Share of a Changing African-American Market

YOUTH MARKETS
The Kids Market: *Myths & Realities*
Marketing to the New Super Consumer: Mom & Kid
The Great Tween Buying Machine: *Marketing to Today's Tweens*

MARKETING MANAGEMENT
A Clear Eye for Branding: *Straight Talk on Today's Most Powerful Business Concept*
A Knight's Code of Business:
  How to Achieve Character and Competence in the Corporate World
Beyond the Mission Statement: *Why Cause-Based Communications Lead to True Success*
India Business: *Finding Opportunities in this Big Emerging Market*
Marketing Insights to Help Your Business Grow

The Art of Strategic Listening

Finding Market Intelligence through Blogs and Other Social Media

Robert Berkman

Paramount Market Publishing, Inc.

Paramount Market Publishing, Inc.
950 Danby Road, Suite 136
Ithaca, NY 14850
www.paramountbooks.com
Telephone: 607-275-8100; 888-787-8100 Facsimile: 607-275-8101

Publisher: James Madden
Editorial Director: Doris Walsh

Library of Congress Catalog Number:
Cataloging in Publication Data available
ISBN 978-09786602-7-7

Contents

Acknowledgements

I WANT TO EXPRESS my appreciation to my media studies colleague at The New School, Derek Tutschulte, who served as an invaluable research assistant for this book. Derek is a wizard in all things Web 2.0, (though like any good social media maven, he cringes at the buzzword). Derek served tirelessly as my online scout to ferret out just the best of the social media search and filtering tools, and did much of the background work and research for the entire discussion of RSS news reading in Chapter 12.

As always, thanks to my wife Mary, who read the full manuscript and lent her expert analysis and editing skills. Her insights, intuition and understanding of the big picture have always provided me with the clearest window for peering into the future.

PART 1

THE CONTEXT OF SOCIAL MEDIA

You can observe a lot just by watching.   —Yogi Berra

What is social media? How do blogs, YouTube, Facebook, and other forms of conversational media created by ordinary consumers all connect? Why is all of this important for market research and the success of your organization? And can this kind of "consumer-generated content" really be relied upon for credible market data so that you can better understand your customers, identify new customers, and spot emerging social and technology trends? Those are the questions that we'll address in this first section of the book, which places the notion of strategic listening online into a larger context. In addition to laying the groundwork for the practical research, filtering and evaluation strategies examined in the rest of the book, this first segment of *The Art of Strategic Listening* will also take a look at the ethics of monitoring bloggers and consumer conversation on the Web. I'll discuss some of the potential concerns and pitfalls that you need to know about when undertaking this kind of research, so that you can feel confident that the information gathering and monitoring you're doing online is going to conform to ethical principles.

CHAPTER 1

The Opportunity:
Blogs, Social Media, and Market Intelligence

WOULD you like access to near real-time market intelligence on your customers at no cost?

No doubt you would, and the fact is, you can.

At any given minute, millions of ordinary people around the globe are sharing opinions, concerns, and ideas; some are even documenting their day-to-day experiences and activities over the Internet. This is happening on blogs, web forums, newsgroups, podcasts, YouTube, social networking sites like Facebook, and on any of the other self-publishing sites and tools that collectively have come to be called *social media*.

Most—99 percent plus—of these conversations and "consumer-generated content" will not be substantive, nor relevant to your firm. But what you may not know is that a certain percentage *will* contain nuggets of conversation and content that represent true and invaluable market intelligence for your organization. And when you find substantive and relevant online conversations, you will be able to discover real actionable market information, such as:

- Whether your customers view your company and brands positively or negatively

- If your customers like or dislike your products, brands or services

- What your customers like or dislike about your products' capabilities and features

- What your customers think about your competitors and their products

- How your customers' preferences may be changing

- How new technologies and social change may be changing your target market

In other words, these online conversational sources can provide you with timely and authentic opinions and behaviors of your current customers, offer clues for identifying future customers, and can even provide insights as to where the whole market or industry may be headed.

This kind of information is what good market research is supposed to provide. There are some key reasons why Internet-based consumer conversations are different and noteworthy. They can be a source of unsolicited, authentic, and unvarnished opinions, and you can get these opinions in near real time. Furthermore, compared with spending months to launch a market research project, today there are many digital tools that make it possible for technology to do this work for you. Moreover, all of this information is available to any organization that knows how to efficiently tap into it. Let me give you a couple of examples of firms that in fact did just this.

Chicago-based U.S. Cellular Corp. is an example of one firm that did and an article in *The Wall Street Journal* highlighted its success. What the company needed to know was how its teenage customers were using their cell phones, and what sorts of concerns they were encountering on a day-to-day basis. But how could Cellular discover these young customers' current, authentic experiences? Could it have employees go and hang out with them in their homes and watch them make calls? While there are a few companies that do engage in ethnographic research and actually do send employees into the field to observe their customers as they use their products, for most businesses, that's not going to be a practical option.

So Cellular decided that it would do the next best thing to *physically* immersing itself in its teenaged customers' lives; it would immerse itself *virtually*. The firm decided that it could discover how teens really use their cell phones by finding and listening to selected discussions on the blogosophere. To carry out this virtual immersion project, the firm hired a blog-watching firm called Umbria, which applied its natural language processing software to parse and analyze blog conversations to figure out the age and demographics of the bloggers and then bring relevant conversations to the surface.

Cellular's approach paid off nicely, as the firm learned some valuable information. What it discovered was that many teenagers were unhappy and nervous regarding their cell phone use because they were getting too many incoming phone calls from their friends. Those incoming calls would quickly cause teens to use up their available minutes—and when that happened,

Mom and Dad often would step in and make their overly talkative child pay up and cover the difference. Informed of those real and unsolicited reports from the blogosphere, Cellular Corp. decided to introduce a new feature—an unlimited "call me" minutes plan, a strategy that would help meet the needs of this important market.

Another example of a company that strategically attended to—and took real action on—online consumer discussions was Cadbury Schweppes. In fact, it even took the step of rein-troducing a discontinued product based on consumer conversations it was alerted to taking place on the very hot social networking site, Facebook. (The use of social networking sites like Face-book is discussed in some detail in Chapter 11).

FIGURE 1.1

Cadbury discovered there was a pent-up consumer demand for its discontinued "Wispa" candy bar from the discussions occurring on Facebook.

Here's what happened. Facebook's members can do lots of socially ori-ented activities, and one of them is to create or participate in all sorts of niche groups on nearly literally any topic imaginable. Someone created a group that lamented the discontinuance of the firm's "Wispa" candy bar. Thousands of people joined the group, similar groups with the same theme were formed, and some members even created an online petition asking the company to bring the candy bar back. Cadbury listened to all this carefully, decided that it showed that there was enough passion and interest in the marketplace to support bringing the product back, and did so. The firm was quoted as stat-ing that it was the first time "that the power of the Internet played such an intrinsic role in the return of a Cadbury brand."

Cellular and Cadbury's experiences illustrate how, with the right strategies, digital tools, and knowledge, you can effectively use social media to conduct a form of instant market research. It is important to note that U.S. Cellular decided to hire out its blog analysis job, and indeed this is one of the options available to you. I will examine the pros and cons of taking this route in Part 2 of this book. But it's also true that, you can do much of this work yourself, for no fee at all.

This book will serve as a practical guide on how you can do this strategic listening *effectively, efficiently,* within ethical boundaries, and at virtually no cost. But while it's true that all this online conversation is out there for you to tap into and obtain valuable near real-time market intelligence, online strategic listening is also filled with challenges. These range from practical management issues like deciding whether to contract out the work to a social media-monitoring vendor, as Cellular did, or to do it yourself. There are research and data analysis challenges, which mostly relate to how to filter out valuable, credible, and relevant conversations from the noise and chatter.

There are ethical considerations as well, related to matters like privacy, authenticity, and deception. Because the ethical guidelines are particularly important, I'll address these in Chapter 5 at the end of Part 1. Those ethical considerations should serve as a framework for you as you learn and integrate the practical tips, tools and strategies for effectively listening and analyzing blogs and other forms of social media, as explained throughout the rest of the book.

WHAT IS SOCIAL MEDIA?

A Glossary of Terms

Social media, or consumer-generated media or consumer-generated content is a term that's used to describe any kind of text, image, audio, or video clip that is uploaded to the Internet by ordinary people, and can be easily shared and located by other people. Social media is different from the articles, programs and broadcasts created by professional journalists, photographers, broadcasting networks, or by authority figures and experts that have a special privilege or position that makes it more likely that they will have an automatic audience. Just as we've heard that the Internet has allowed everyone to be their own publisher, today it's also allowed everyone to be their own audio or video broadcasters as well.

Social media is realized on the Internet in a wide range of formats. Written or textual forms of social media are typically found on blogs, web forums, email discussion lists, message boards, and consumer reviews and complaint sites; photographs are displayed as images on Flickr or other image sharing sites; audio broadcasts are created as podcasts; and consumers who create video clips can upload them on YouTube, or other video sharing sites.

There are a lot of overlapping terms and jargon in the social media field, and you'll be encountering several of these in this book. Below then is a quick and selected glossary of the most important terms, sites, and jargon that you need to know in order to understand the various components of social media. I've also included marketing terms, and social media sites that you'll come across in the book.

Aggregator: A site or software that collects content from multiple sources, e.g., a news aggregator. Sometimes RSS "news readers" (see *news reader*) are also called aggregators.

Astroturfing: An attempt by an organized group to spread a predetermined message, but to do so in a manner that makes each message appear authentic and original. Astroturfing has been done by companies, political parties, and special interests trying to get their message out and make their views known.

Buzz Marketing: A marketing strategy to create awareness and interest about a product, service, or company by trying to get its message spread from person to person. Recently buzz marketing efforts have been directed towards blogs, Web sites, discussion groups and other discussion forums on the Internet (see also *word-of-mouth marketing*).

Citizen journalism: Reporting that's done by ordinary persons not trained or experienced as professional journalists.

WHAT IS SOCIAL MEDIA? (CONT.)

Co-Creation: The process whereby companies and consumers work together, typically remotely online, to design, modify, or plan existing or future products for the firm (see also *crowdsourcing*).

Collaboration: The sharing of information and working together that's become a hallmark of Web 2.0 and the guiding principle of Wikipedia, (see also *wisdom of crowds, crowdsourcing*).

Consumer-Generated Content (CGC): Any kind of text, audio, or video created and/or uploaded to the Internet by ordinary people.

Consumer-Generated Media (CGM): Similar to consumer-generated content. Typically, though, the term CGM is used to describe content that is more akin to media, while CGC is used to describe a simple blog post, an uploaded photograph, a piece of text, etc.

Crowdsourcing: A term used by companies where they enlist large groups of ordinary people to work remotely with the firm to share information, discuss, and try to work out design, feature, and other problems and issues for the firm, and assist in "co-creation" activities.

del.icio.us: The most popular social bookmarking site (see *social bookmarking*).

Digg: A social news site that surfaces the most popular news and blog postings by permitting its members to submit stories that other members can vote on. The items with the most votes are displayed at the top of Digg's listing.

Facebook: Currently the fastest growing social networking site (see *social networking site*).

Flickr: A very popular social network for sharing and tagging images for other community members (see *tags*).

Folksonomy: A term used to describe a practice whereby ordinary users create informal tags (see *tagging*) to describe a piece of content. The term "folksonomy" is a variation of the word taxonomy, which describes the controlled index terms created by librarians and professional indexers.

Forum: A place on the Web, typically associated with an existing Web site, where people can talk about and share views on a specific topic of interest.

ListServ: The very first email mailing list discussion software, developed back in 1984 (see *mailing list*).

Mailing List: An email based discussion group.

Mashup: The combining of digital information, data, or programs to create something new. The word has roots in the Jamaican sound system culture that means destroy. Mashups can

WHAT IS SOCIAL MEDIA? (CONT.)

be derived from and include songs, film trailers, videos, or applications. HousingMaps is an example of an application mash up that resulted from combining Google Maps and CraigsList housing ads; and there are content mashups that are just the recombining of digital video and music.

Meme: An idea that spreads quickly among many people on its own. Memes can spread quickly on blogs and other forms of online social media and their popularity often has to do with a social commentary and/or lampooning of society and culture using irony or sarcasm. Memes often tap into a cultural zeitgeist.

Natural Language Processing (NLP): A subfield of artificial intelligence relating to the ability of computers to recognize and understand the meaning of ordinary language.

Networked journalism: Another term for citizen journalism, proposed by the popular blogger and journalism professor Jeff Jarvis.

News Feed: Frequently updated content (text, audio, or video), typically created in the RSS standard (see *RSS*) syndicated by bloggers and other content providers so Internet users with a news reader (see *news reader*) can receive regular updates of new content and postings

News Reader: A piece of software that permits users to collect and read RSS or other syndicated news feeds from blogs or other frequently updated sites. A news reader allows users to aggregate and manage website feeds, and parses site's feeds' content into segments for easy consumption

PayPerPost: A firm that acts as a middleman so companies can pay bloggers to blog about their company or products. There are other lesser known firms that also work to pay bloggers to write about their products. The practice is considered ethically questionable or downright unethical by many.

Podcast: An online radio show that can be listened to via portable media players (like an iPod), a cell phone, or on a PC. Often users will subscribe and listen to the content via a syndicated feed on a news reader.

Post: An individual entry on a blog or the act of posting a blog entry itself.

RSS: A content syndication format or subset of XML used to categorize content. RSS can tag content as a summary, headline, or an enclosure (attached audio/video). In addition to RSS, "ATOM" is another XML format with slightly different ways of tagging/naming content. RSS is used by blogs, consumer video sites and other sites on the Web that have frequently updated content as the means to distribute their latest postings.

WHAT IS SOCIAL MEDIA? (CONT.)

Sentiment Detection: The capacity by some natural language processing software programs to detect whether a particular section of text is primarily positive or negative in its overall tone. Sentiment detection is a feature promoted by several vendors that sell a blog monitoring product.

Social Bookmarking: The process whereby web users save and share their favorite or recommended URLs. There are many social bookmarking sites, the most popular one is del.icio.us. Social bookmarking sites form a community around bookmarks as users can save and add comments to their own bookmarks and share them with the community. Community members can also monitor others' bookmark feeds via an RSS reader.

Social Media: Blogs, wikis, digital videos or any other kind of textual or multimedia forms of media and typically generated by ordinary consumers. A hallmark of social media is that it is designed to be easily shared, be collaborative, openly accessible and easily retrieved by others on the Internet or via other digital platforms.

Social Networking Site: A site where persons can find, communicate, and discuss common interests with persons they already know or have found through the site's networking capabilities. Popular social networking sites include Facebook, MySpace, and Linked-In.

Splog: A fake blog that has no substantive content but is only spam. These blogs publish meaningless content automatically, in an effort to garner web traffic from search engines.

Strategic Listening: In this book's context, strategic listening refers to the activity of paying close attention to selected online discussions of targeted consumers and Internet users in order to detect and understand their product and service preferences, concerns, needs, and understand possible future needs and behaviors. The goal of strategic listening is to be more fully informed in a proactive anticipatory manner in order to do a better job in anticipating emerging social and industry trends and better serve current and future customers.

Tagging: The activity of adding a word or phrase to a piece of text, audio, video or any other content as a way to identify and describe it. Tagging is a grassroots, bottom up approach to indexing content, and can make it easier for other persons to more easily locate digital information.

Technorati: A search engine specializing in indexing blogs and other forms of consumer-generated media.

WHAT IS SOCIAL MEDIA? (CONT.)

Trackback: An indication on a blog that another blogger has linked to a particular post.

Trend: A meaningful change. Unlike a fad, which is short lived, a trend emerges out of some underlying cause, builds over time, has staying power, and is long lasting.

Twitter: A free social networking "micro blogging" service that permits users to send brief notes and entries to other Twitter members over the Internet and on digital devices.

USENET: An early format created on the Internet that enabled online discussion groups and that preceded the Web. USENET groups are still active and can be searched via "Google Groups."

Vlog: A video based or oriented blog

Web 2.0: A term used to describe the evolution of the web from its original static, one way form (Web 1.0) to its current, more interactive two way medium. In Web 2.0, users are not only readers and recipients of information and media, but can also create and distribute their own content and various forms of media. Web 2.0 is sometimes used to refer to more user friendly design principles, such as the use of whitespace and friendlier fonts on a webpage to make the page more legible, and the automatic updating of content that refreshes without requiring the download of a new, static webpage.

Wiki: A type of software that permits multiple persons to remotely collaborate on the same document and make changes to the document without anyone else's consent. The most popular and well known wiki is the online encyclopedia, *Wikipedia*.

Wisdom of Crowds: A belief or perspective that under the right conditions, large groups of ordinary people can make better decisions and act smarter than a single person can, even if that single person is an expert.

Word-of-Mouth Marketing: A type of marketing that is considered particularly effective, where one person tells friends, colleagues, or other people of a positive experience with a company, product, or service. Some companies try to facilitate word-of-mouth marketing over the web by engaging in "buzz marketing" (see *buzz marketing*).

YouTube: A site where anyone can upload his or her own digital videos, and search or subscribe to videos made by others. YouTube is owned by Google.

Who Needs to Pay Attention to Social Media?

Businesses, of course, want to know how they are being viewed in their market, and need to keep up with larger social trends that indicate how their industry may be changing. But getting timely insight into customers' authentic opinions, and keeping up with social and technological changes in one's wider environment is not only for corporations and private firms. It is also important for non-profits, governments, universities and almost any other entity that has a customer base or serves the public.

As for who in an organization needs to pay attention to social media, this book is geared primarily to people who gather information and conduct research. That includes market researchers, analysts, planners, special librarians, business development persons, competitive strategists, and others who are responsible for discovering what their organization's customers and others are saying and doing. However, following and tracking social media on the Internet impacts a much wider range of organizations and business functions than those doing research. While not a focus in this book, the following functional areas also need to pay close attention to blogs and other forms of social media:

Communications/Public Relations

The blogosphere presents an opportunity to get instant, unmediated, and unvarnished reactions to an organization's recent announcements, developments, and newest product releases, and this, of course, is of vital interest to public relations and corporate communications professionals.

There are several specific ways that public relations and corporate communications professionals could effectively make use of conversation on blogs and other social media. They can evaluate the success of a public relations campaign in terms of its coverage; test out new ideas for a campaign; understand different media to target new campaigns; identify influential bloggers and communicators to ensure that they receive press and other informational material; and better understand their consumers' lingo and world view to target future marketing and PR campaigns.

Competitive Intelligence

Competitive intelligence professionals need to monitor the competitive landscape around their industry, understand various key forces, identify strengths and weaknesses of their firm vis a vis its competitors, and be alerted to early warnings of threats and opportunities on the horizon. If CI professionals can effectively tap into monitoring blogs and other social media they would get a sense of consumers' views of competitors and competing products and thereby do a better job in identifying new and emerging threats.

Reputation Management

The reputation management function recognizes that a firm's reputation is an actual asset that needs to be protected and those that work in that discipline need to pay close attention to what's being said about their organization in the media, and increasingly, on the Internet. Social media is particularly important in the reputation management area, since, as Nielsen BuzzMetrics' Peter Blackshaw aptly put it in one of his web essays, those messages and forms of media are out of the control of the organization's public relations department. What is written or posted on the Web "leaves a digital trail." It stays there and can be linked to by others, and turn up in a future Google search.

Those who work to maintain their organization's reputation need to monitor conversations on blogs and social media to discover if a crisis is brewing that needs attention, to identify misinformation that needs to be corrected, and to monitor developments during an actual crisis.

Product/Service/Brand Management

Brand and product managers also need to stay closely in tune with what people on the Internet are saying about the firm's products. Are people saying good things? Are they commenting positively on some of the product's features, but dislike others? Are consumers pining for some other feature or benefit that the product is not delivering? Among the reasons that product and brand managers monitor and analyze blogs and other social media are: to obtain customer reaction and feedback, to discover if the product is meeting their needs, to ensure that niche markets are being served appropriately, to discover complaints and problems, to evaluate the effectiveness of customer service, and to discover unusual uses of the product or service.

Marketing

It's long been known in marketing that the very best way to get new customers is via that all powerful word-of-mouth recommendation. When one person tells a friend, family member, or acquaintance about a positive experience he or she had with a company or product, that relationship-based referral is worth more than almost any kind of advertisement or promotion that the firm itself could have created. As Harvard Professor David B. Godes put it, word-of-mouth "allows you to get some information about the underlying value without actually buying the movie ticket or buying the book or, what is more costly, reading the book." ("Economic Scene: For those who live by buzz, it's important to know who's doing the talking," Virginia Postrel, *The New York Times,* October 9, 2003).

Whereas historically this kind of word-of-mouth referral happened offline in the physical world, increasingly it is happening online, mainly on sites where consumers and ordinary people can talk freely. That means blogs, web forums, consumer complaint sites, and other discussion-based formats. It certainly behooves marketers to know what kind of Internet-based word-of-mouth is occurring that relates to its firm, products, competitors, and so on.

*An aspect of word-of-mouth that I treat separately in this book is the effort by some firms to **consciously create** online buzz by signing up consumers to talk up their products to their friends and associates, sometimes offline, but increasingly online, through bloggers. This activity raises various ethical issues and considerations discussed later in the book.*

In addition to these functions and positions, there are also specific industries and fields where paying attention to social media is particularly important. While I believe that this kind of information is valuable for all disciplines and industries, there are some, which the blog tracking vendor MotiveQuest calls "high involvement 'passion' categories" where it is particularly valuable. Industries where people regularly and passionately discuss products and services online include, for instance, automobiles, computers, electronics, health care, entertainment, media, and telecommunications.

What You'll Find in this Book

Here's a quick overview of what you'll find in this book. Although monitoring blog conversations and social media is critical for a wide range of business functions, this book's focus will be on the value of social media for business research type applications. So it will be of particular relevance to market researchers, planners, market analysts, librarians, and anyone else who needs to find and filter conversations, to better understand current customers, to identify new customers, and to surface key issues and emerging trends in the market.

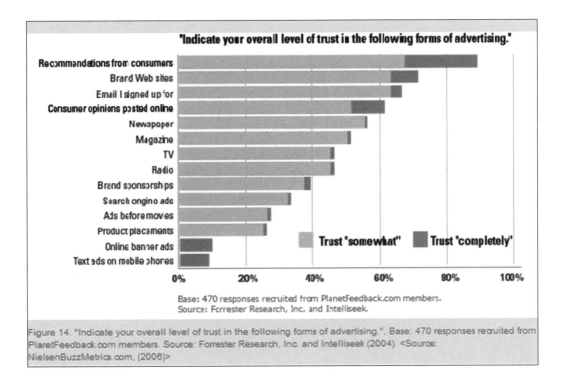

Figure 14. "Indicate your overall level of trust in the following forms of advertising.", Base: 470 responses recruited from PlanetFeedback.com members. Source: Forrester Research, Inc. and Intelliseek (2004). <Source: NielsenBuzzMetrics.com, (2006)>

Here's how this book works. I've categorized the book into three parts. The five chapters that compose Part 1 serve as an introduction to social media and describes how paying close attention to these new media forms can help you serve your current customers better, identify potential future customers, and better spot emerging consumer and social trends. This overview section also examines the different types of social media, explain the basic premise behind what counts as a trend and examines the critical matter of credibility: that is, can you really believe what you read on blogs and other social media and conversational sites? The final chapter in Part 1 is devoted to the matter of ethics: what are the considerations you need to attend to and keep in mind when you decide to use social media as your source for market intelligence?

Parts 2 and 3 get into the practical matter of making all this happen, and provide specific instructions, advice, strategies and tips on how to begin effectively gathering data from the social Internet.

In Part 2, you'll learn about one option available to you for gathering this kind of information: contracting out the research task to a third party. Chapter 6 addresses the pros and cons of taking this route, and provides advice on how the blog monitoring vendors differ and how to choose the right one.

FIGURE 1.2

Trusted Forms of Advertising

Recommendations from other people, or word of mouth, is the kind of advertising that consumers say they trust the most

Because many of these blog and social media monitoring vendors promote their ability to apply software to automatically detect the tone or "sentiment' of what it finds, Chapter 7 is devoted just to that topic, and takes a critical look at the capabilities and accuracy of sentiment detection software. Chapter 8 examines a couple of other alternative approaches that vendors take to helping organizations understand consumers' online. That includes firms that purport to measure blog *influence*, and others that create a private "hosted community" where you can run your own online virtual focus group.

Part 3 is the critical hands-on, do-it-yourself section. Here I tell you how you can use a wide range of Internet search engines, news aggregators, buzz trackers and other Internet based tools and sites to find the most relevant consumer content, filter our the unreliable and trivial conversations, and zero in on just the market intelligence of direct importance to your organization. Chapter 9 focuses on what you can do on Google; and Chapter 10 on the blog and social media search engine Technorati. In chapter 11, I'll examine a whole host of other sites and sources that provide market intelligence from social media. These include web-based forums and discussion groups, audio/video search sites, and social networking sites like Facebook. Because organizations that need to monitor social media generally want to set up automated mechanisms to keep them alerted automatically, the next chapter, Chapter 12, focuses specifically on how to set up email and RSS alerts as a way to efficiently stay up to date on keywords, phrases, bloggers, and conversations that you want to pay close attention to.

There are some sites and tools on the web that purport to automatically spot the latest and hottest terms, discussions, blogs, and overall "buzz" on the Net. The question is how and if these can be used as reliable market intelligence. Chapters 13 and 14 examine these buzz tracking tools, and offer tips on how to make sense of what they uncover.

Part 3 also provides a specific methodology for spotting significant trends, as well as what I call the "key conversations" online that are most likely to provide the most insightful discussions. I also provide specific tips on determining whether what you've read on a blog is accurate, knowledgeable, and believable, and whether you can assume what you find is representative of a larger population.

I add a few words at the end of Part 3 on some of the really big picture issues on social media and market research: how much of the current focus on blogs and social media is just hype? What are some of the biggest cautions and problems in relying on this kind of information for marketing purposes? And where might all this be headed?

Finally, there are three appendices: Appendix A is a listing of sites and tools on the web that can make your online research job more effective and productive; Appendix B is a selected list of recommended books, sites, and other resources for doing research with social media; and Appendix C is a list of the URLs of all the key websites mentioned in the book, organized by chapter.

To those of you who are reading the digital version of this book, you will see that all the sites and online tools are hotlinked, so you can just click on the link to open a page within your browser so you can view the site itself, and do so without losing your page in the book. You will also see some text with a special icon: Clicking on it will retrieve an online tutorial, movie, screencast, or other multimedia or special site I found and liked, and feel would enhance your understanding of whatever topic is being discussed.

Now let's take a look at the rise of social media within the context of market research, attending to your current customers, and understanding emerging trends.

This icon is for readers of the digital version only. Click on it to retrieve an online tutorial, movie, screencast, or other multimedia or special site that will enhance your understanding of the topic at hand.

Strategic Listening: A Key to Success

Although this book focuses on a variety of new media and digital technologies, its basic premise is based on an old and established principle: for any organization to be successful, it needs to be customer-centric, and to be customer-centric, an organization must understand the importance of listening.

Being customer-centric means more than, say, adding, "be responsive to our customers" or "survey our customers to find out how they like us" as another goal to the year's planning meeting. Instead, a focus on understanding customers and their desires becomes part of the very essence of the firm. The organization's core mission is to know and serve its current and future customers so that everything that grows out of that mission is a reflection and extension of that customer-centric orientation. In the classic formulation by author and management guru Tom Peters, you don't merely satisfy your customers, you "delight" them. You probably know one or two small stores close to where you live that consistently "delight" you when you visit, and you are probably aware that these outfits intimately know and understand the experience that you and its other customers want.

Many of the most successful firms have this kind of laser beam focus on their customers. Examples of larger companies and organizations that have built a reputation over the years for knowing and satisfying their customers include, for instance:

- Starbucks
- Target
- Apple
- Toyota
- Harley-Davidson
- Netflix
- Burton Snowboards

- L.L.Bean
- Intuit
- Google
- Southwest Airlines
- Virgin Atlantic
- Whole Foods Market
- Trader Joe's

As is clear from the list above, the size, industry, products, and image of each of these companies varies enormously, but they all have at least one common trait: a near obsessive attention to understanding their customers.

As noted earlier, that's what U.S. Cellular tried to accomplish—to understand its customers by listening. And it didn't just listen but did so deeply and "strategically." This meant that it went to a place where its customers were chatting and conversing—the Internet—and then it specifically worked to discern the *important* messages from all the noise, and put what it learned to effective use.

Traditional Strategies and Methods for Listening

What are people saying about your organization? What do they like or dislike? How are they using your products or service? What problems have they encountered? Why did they choose your firm over a competitor or vice versa? What are some of their problems or concerns where a new product or feature can be of help?

Traditionally, organizations of all types have employed a variety of tried and true methods for soliciting this kind of information. Depending on the discipline and department desiring the information, standard approaches have included:

- **Traditional market research techniques**
  This would include the use of quantitative-oriented data-gathering meth-

odologies like surveys and polls (conducted either in person, by mail or phone, or more recently, on the Internet); or the use of syndicated market data from major data collection firms like Simmons Market Research Bureau or NPD. Traditional market research has also included qualitative approaches such as the use of focus groups or direct interviews.

- **Secondary library and online research**
  Here information about customers and trends is located via standard library and other traditional research techniques. Typical sources would include trade journals, off-the-shelf research reports from third party market research and industry analyst publishers; consulting other professional literature; and searching professional business, government databases (SEC, Census) or fee-based online services like Dialog, Factiva, or Lexis-Nexis; or conducting keyword searches on an Internet search engine.

- **Empowerment of front line/salespeople**
  Smart companies have empowered those employees who have the most direct interaction with customers to be attuned to their needs, problems, concerns and questions, and then capture that information and relay it back to marketing or other parts of the company that can use it to better serve their customers.

  Peter Francese, the demographics and consumer markets expert who founded *American Demographics* magazine, is an independent demographer living in Exeter, New Hampshire. Francese says that he defines a "company that listens" as one where the top person in the organization makes "a part of the strategy of the corporation to constantly listen to its customers." He adds, "When it's not a strategy, then you have a bunch of people in a so-called market research department that send out questions, create unreadable reports, and have a budget." And, he says, "These reports are dull and get ignored, so the people that run the organization don't pay attention to them." Listening that leads to being more customer-centric needs to somehow be embedded as a core principle and practice for the organization as a whole.

  Companies that are successful strategic listeners employ varying strategies, but Francese says that one of the most important aspects is to ensure that those front-line people—those who are closest to and have the most intimate and frequent interaction with customers—are trained to pay attention and listen, are empowered to take action, and then pass what they learn back up the line so that upper management is aware of what they found out.

Francese highlights Starbucks as an example of a firm that's done an especially good job of empowering its front-line workers. He described how Starbucks made sure that its baristas pay close attention to the total experience their customers have while in the store. In this way, Starbucks management could be sure that it stayed on top of any special issues, problems, or changes in the needs of its customers, and could quickly make whatever adjustments were necessary in order to better serve its clients. As an example, Francese explained how one day a barrista noted that a hearing impaired customer was not able to participate in the way Starbucks informs its customers that their specialty drink is ready—by announcing the person's name. So the barrista did the obvious thing, if you are trained to pay attention: he put up a handwritten sign.

Another example of a firm that's a good listener is Trader Joe's, the specialty grocery store that's become popular among many urban professionals (the store has been called a "Wal-Mart for yuppies"). The firm has instituted a wide range of strategies to get customer feedback that occurs in a natural setting, and not via the more traditional and artificially set up focus groups. For instance, employees on the retail floor are encouraged to assist customers in sampling foods, getting feedback, and passing it along to buyers.

- **Establishment of "Listening Posts"**
  Some far-sighted firms create what are called "listening posts" in locations strategically identified as places where current and potential customers gather, as a way to carefully discern what shoppers were doing, asking, and talking about when browsing or using products. For example, Yamaha was reported to have set up listening posts in music stores to get a better handle on what music enthusiasts were looking for when doing their shopping.

Today so much of what people are saying and doing is available quickly and for free on the Internet. Management expert and consultant Oren Harari, who teaches at the Graduate School of Business at the University of San Francisco Harari says that for those involved in strategic listening, paying attention to these online places where consumers are chatting is "absolutely essential" as a way to get closer to the customer.

Some Background

Let's now take a closer look at the rise of blogs and other forms of social media where you can find consumers. Because blogs, as explained a little later in this chapter, are probably the most important form of social media for market intelligence purposes and are a primary focus of this book, I'll focus here on the blogosphere.

The Rise of the Blog

According to the leading blog tracking and searching site, Technorati, as of Spring 2007, the firm had counted a total of about 80 million blogs, and was adding about 120,000 new blogs to its index each day. To get some sense of how quickly the number of blogs have increased over the past few years, consider that Technorati had counted a total of 32 million blogs in 2006, and just 9 million the year before that. And while Technorati reports a recent slowing

FIGURE 1.2

In the first quarter of 2007, Technorati was tracking 80 million blogs

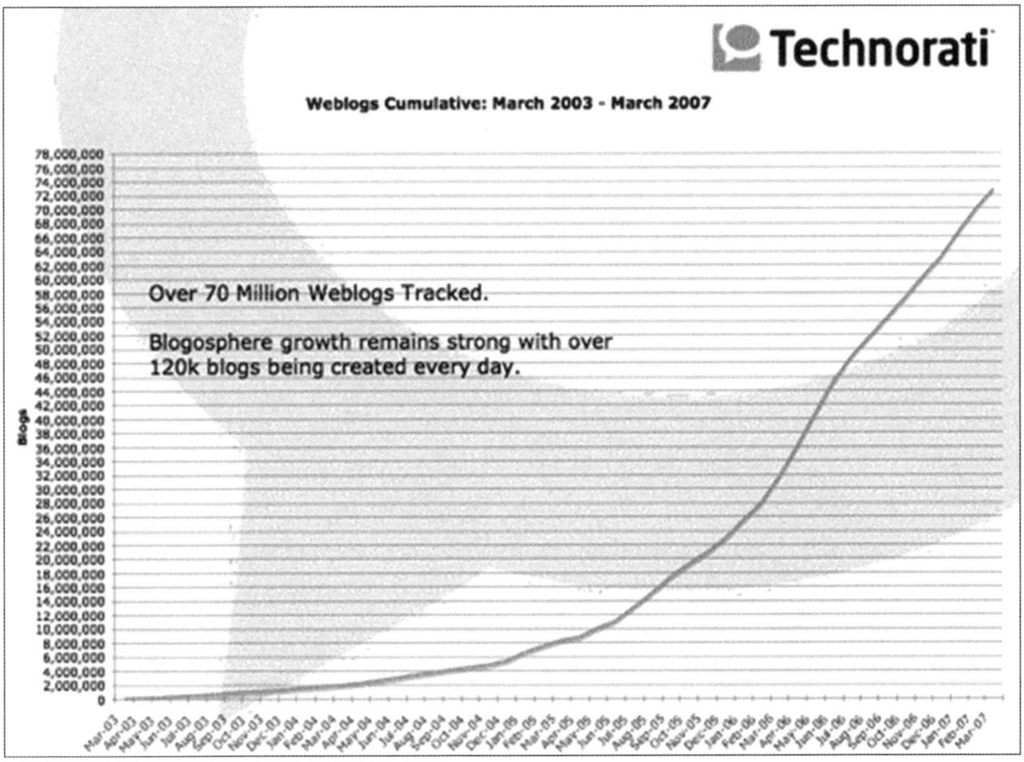

of the growth rate, the actual number of blogs continues to rapidly increase. The 2007 number represents more than 700 percent growth over two years.

Technorati also tracks the frequency of individual blog posts on the blogosphere. Its Spring 2007 study reported about 1.5 million postings per day, which corresponds to about 17 per second. Figure 1.3 illustrates this data, along with days of peak blog postings, (which as illustrated, corresponds to key breaking news events.)

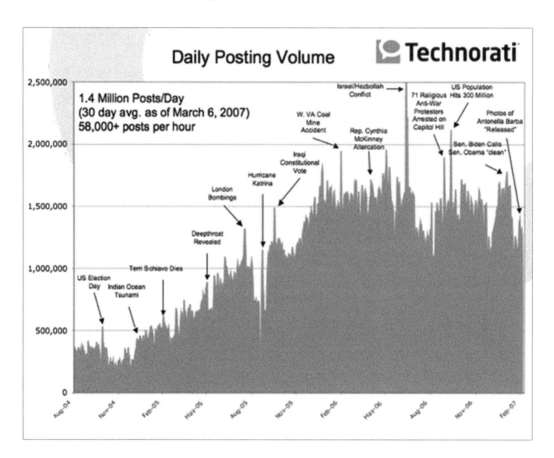

FIGURE 1.3

The number of blog posts on Technorati

One way to get a sense of the rise in the overall profile of bloggers as a growing influence as a media source as well, can be seen by looking at another Technorati chart, which examines the popularity of mainstream media compared with blog sites. In Technorati's April 2007 report, there were 22 blogs among its top 100 most popular sites. In its previous Q3 2006 report, there were only 12 blogs in the Top 100 most popular sites.

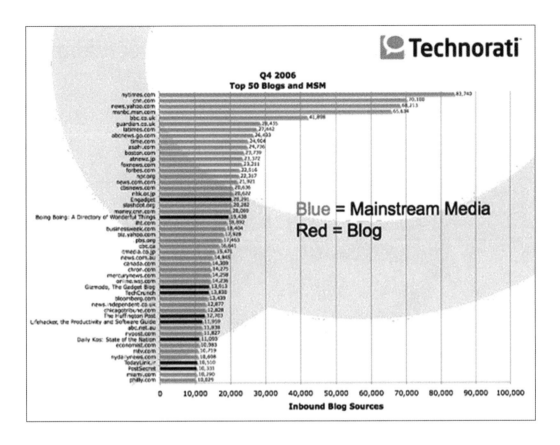

FIGURE 1.4

Technorati's *State of
the Live Web Report,*
April 2007

*Of the most popular 100
media sites, 22 were blogs
(this excerpt shows the top
50 sites; nine of which are
blogs)*

Clearly this rise in the number of blogs is one way to calculate this new medium's impact. However, it's not only the sheer number of blogs that is making these new forms of media and conversation more influential, but also their emergence as a more relied-upon news and information source.

While Technorati provides lots of other charts and breakdowns of trends in the blogosphere, one other point that I think is important to examine is its breakdown of blog postings by language. According to Technorati's data from the fourth quarter of 2006, the language with the highest percentage of blog postings was not English, but Japanese, which made up a total of 37 percent of the posts. Next was English at 36 percent, down from 39 percent from Technorati's Q3 2006 report, which was followed by Chinese at 8 percent. Technorati CEO David Sifrey noted in his own blog at the time the report was released that the "newcomer" to the top 10 languages was Farsi, reflecting the growth of blogging in the Middle East, particularly in Iran. (More about non-English language blogs in Chapter 9).

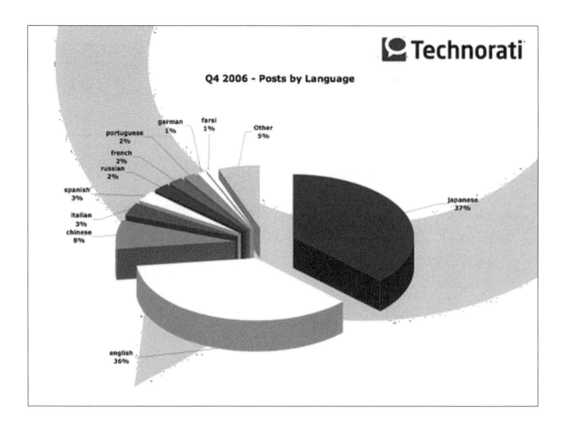

FIGURE 1.5

Blog Postings, 2004

According to Technorati, the highest percentage of blog postings in the fourth quarter of 2006 were in Japanese, followed by English.

Beyond the Blog: Other Forms of Consumer-Generated Content (CGC)

Blogs get the most hype and attention, and it's true that these new forms of communication and publishing have had an enormous influence on a wide range of social institutions, from business to politics to journalism to education. But they are not the *only* form of social media. In addition to blogs, Technorati tracks several *other* forms of consumer-generated content as well. As of May 2007, Sifrey wrote in his blog that when you include not only blogs, but also user-generated video, photos, podcasts and other content, Technorati was tracking a total of *250 million items*.

This book does put most of its emphasis on blogs, vs. other forms of social media, and does this for a few reasons:

- Blogs have been the fastest growing and most dynamic part of the consumer-generated media sphere.

- Bloggers have become closely connected with the mainstream media's news cycle: as a source of leads and grassroots opinion for mainstream journalists; as incisive critics and fact checkers of the mainstream media; and as new and alternative information sources for news readers.

- Because of the links created between blogs, and their highly networked nature, bloggers' messages become highly amplified throughout the Internet.

- Nearly all blogs syndicate their postings by generating news feeds (RSS). This makes blogs powerful publishing platforms, as posts are picked up by various news and conversation aggregating sites.

- Search engine users commonly turn up blog postings, both on regular web search engines (like Google), as well as specialized blog search engines (like Technorati).

- Often a blogger represents the opinions of an influential person in a niche area of some kind, thereby attracting an audience of informed and enthusiastic readers. When this occurs, the blog and the conversations occurring on that blog can become an influential source in that industry or sphere.

The Problems with Social Media

Although it is vital that researchers understand and attend to what bloggers and others are saying and doing on the Internet, all of this can be an extremely confusing area and hard to get a handle on. There are several factors that make finding relevant discussions online and making sense of it all so difficult:

- **Information overload.** Information overload is not a new problem by any means (read Alvin Toffler's *Future Shock*, Random House, 1970) but with over 100 million new blog posts per day, the problem continues to get worse. And that's not even counting all the podcasts and online videos being uploaded. How can you find the relevant, substantive, and trustworthy conversations?

- **Digital tool/site overload.** This is a new and rather odd problem. To overcome information overload, an increasing number of blog search engines, content aggregators, "meme" surfacers, news readers, and all types of free and fee-based information aggregation solutions and tools are continually being introduced. These are designed to help Internet users filter and sort all the news, commentary, and communication that flies through the Internet every second. While many of these are useful, and covered later in this book, it's becoming just as difficult to keep up with these solutions as it is to solve the original problem of sorting through all the information!

- **Spam, splogs, and "pay per post" bloggers.** As people have figured out how to make money from blogging, there has been an increase in fake, deceptive, and shady blogs and blogging. This doesn't help with the problem of information overload and establishing the credibility of what you find.

- **Web 2.0 hype.** How do you really know what you "absolutely must" be doing and paying attention to on the Internet, versus how much of this is simply media, information technology, and software vendor hype? Whereas the Internet, blogs, and other forms of social media represent a critical new force for marketers and business research, they are not a replacement for all the other kinds of research you're doing, or a wholesale substitute for doing more traditional market research.

One other concern about gathering market intelligence via social media is particularly important and deserves some special treatment. That is, how can informal listening replace the traditional methodologies of market research: the survey, poll, and focus group? Doesn't just listening to people chat online and post various content fail to meet the tried, true, and scientifically derived methodologies used for so many decades in the market research profession? What about steps like defining one's universe, performing random selection, ensuring that a sample is representative, preventing self-selection bias, and all the other safeguards that help ensure that the results of a market research effort can be counted on as reliable and valid?

These are valid concerns, so let's discuss them.

Listening to Social Media vs. Traditional Market Research

Traditionally, when a company wanted to gather information about its customers' preferences, or get up-to-date information on the overall market environment, it would embark on some type of market research project. It might use a quantitative approach to gather data, and create some kind of survey. Another tried and true approach is qualitative, where a facilitator is employed to conduct a focus group and query a small number of targeted customers directly for their views and opinions.

While there have always been poorly designed and conceived research projects (e.g., badly worded surveys or focus group questions, or polls that suffer from a self-selection bias such as those conducted by television call-in polls and magazine reader surveys), the fact is, when designed appropriately and scientifically, these methods for learning about customers and market have worked pretty well for much of the 20th century. Good market researchers pay close attention to following the necessary methodological rigor required to achieve scientifically accurate results. That means defining their universe clearly, choosing a valid method for obtaining a random sampling of respondents, ensuring that the sample selected is projectible to be representative of the defined universe, sorting and analyzing the data accurately, calculating the resulting statistical and non-statistical margins of error, and so on. All this is done to help ensure that the results are as accurate and reliable as possible.

In addition to these primary research strategies, another traditional approach in market research is to use secondary sources and leverage the work of other researchers. This could mean purchasing published data from a syndicated market research firm such as Simmons Market Research or NPD. Firms like these collect and filter primary data from customers by use of supermarket scanners, through extensive surveys, and other methods. Another option is to purchase an already published or off-the-shelf market study from a market research publisher. These publishers, such as Euromonitor or Forrester Research, may conduct their own primary surveys, but usually employ secondary research techniques, such as aggregating trade articles, compiling government sources, culling existing surveys, and conducting interviews with industry experts to write a research report on an industry, market, or company.

The world today is very different than it was in the 1950s when these market research methods were developed. It's a lot different today than it was even in 1999! These tried and true methods for gathering data on current and potential consumers, while still sound when done scientifically, just don't work as well as they used to for revealing useful information, and can't always be counted on as the best approach.

There are a couple of reasons why this is the case. The decline in the effectiveness of surveys and polls for marketing purposes is well known. For a variety of reasons, people don't respond as well to mail, phone, or in-person surveys as they used to. There are more concerns over personal data privacy; people are overloaded with too much information, and everyone is just too busy to take the time to respond to a business survey. Furthermore, in an age where it seems everything is polarized, many people simply don't trust surveys anymore, no matter how scientifically they were conducted. (And that's especially true when the survey results contradict their pre-existing views!)

While published studies and reports have their place, they no longer necessarily represent the best approach for learning about current and future customers. Again, there are several reasons why this is true:

1. Surveys and off-the-shelf published reports, even those that are created with a fast publishing schedule reflect conditions that *were*, and not what *is now*. Published studies generally reflect the mindset, attitude, and behaviors of at least several months ago, and more typically, a year or more ago. Given the rate of change of society and business today, particularly anything related to technology, that kind of information is considered old and outdated.

2. Surveys, off-the-shelf reports, and even traditional focus groups are generally limited in what kind of opinion and commentary they are able to solicit, because the answers will be based on the specific questions that were originally posed. In other words, marketers can only receive responses to those questions that the researcher has *assumed* are the most important ones to ask. Listening to consumer conversations on the Internet permits marketers to hear unsolicited opinions and views that bubble up more naturally and without the researchers' prodding or initial assumptions.

3. If the marketer did his or her sampling scientifically, the answers obtained in a survey or focus group should be representative of the larger target market. That's important for extrapolating the answers to the larger universe, and determining the likely current needs and views of that larger population, but this technique does not bring to the surface another kind of customer from whom it is important for organizations to get opinions—the *influential* consumers who may

have a powerful voice in their community and are listened to by others in that market. Nor can surveys or focus groups surface any kind of buzz that may be surrounding a company, industry, product, or product feature. Again, paying attention to consumer conversations on the Internet can provide this kind of knowledge.

The key point I want to make here is not that traditional market research is no longer useful or that it should be discarded. Like any tool or method, it cannot do everything, and traditional market research approaches have some built-in drawbacks in their ability to provide a timely understanding of customers. Some of those drawbacks are becoming more apparent and severe. So it makes sense for firms to at least supplement these methods with approaches that don't suffer from the same limitations, by engaging in strategic listening to consumer conversations on the Internet.

You might wonder whether strategic listening is just adding confusion and bad data. Can listening to bloggers and conversations on the Internet be considered reliable and sound market intelligence? After all, market research has been predicated on the premise that in order to obtain useful and reliable results, the entire process must be performed in a careful and scientific manner; otherwise, you end up with bad and misleading information. So wouldn't reading blogs and making conclusions about your market be a risky or even dangerous process, as it follows no scientific methodology?

There are some who have expressed this position. For example, Bill Neal, co-owner and co-founder of Atlanta-based SDR Consulting, who is well-known and respected in the market research industry, has voiced concern over drawing larger conclusions from the kind of exceptional and unrepresentative samplings you might come across on the web.

I will discuss this concern in more detail in Chapter 4. However, my overall feeling is that the traditional methodologies for conducting market research and strategic listening can be considered complementary. If you want to discover the preferences and opinions of your typical customers, you do need to rely on traditional market research approaches like surveys and focus groups so that you can scientifically select representative samples, extrapolate, and make broad conclusions. But you still can use the art (not science) of informed and careful strategic listening to complement that knowledge, and glean insight on other important elements of your market, such as:

- what's on the minds of those on the fringe;

- what a selection of passionate users are worried about right now;

- what some of the most influential people in the market are saying.

And that's where this book comes in. My goal is to help you develop the softer art of finding relevant blog and social media conversations on the Internet. This means knowing how to cut through the noise and trivia so you can locate just what you need, avoid getting buried with excess data, and have the knowledge and tools to evaluate the credibility of what you find. Then you'll be in a position to understand the strategic implications of what you've collected.

Moving Forward

Once you have an understanding of the importance of listening to social media, you need to figure out how to *find* the important discussions and bloggers that are going to affect your organization. How do you sort out the meaningful comments from all the noise. And how do you organize and make sense out of all of this?

The first step is to get a better understanding of the different forms of social media, and the potential of each type to provide you with meaningful market intelligence. This is what I'll examine in the next chapter.

CHAPTER 2

The Forms of Social Media

THERE ARE MANY terms floating around to describe all the content and social media that ordinary people are creating on the Internet. There are blogs, of course, but you'll also hear about web forums, newsgroups, ListServs, USENET, YouTube, Facebook, podcasts, and so on. How you can effectively search and strategically listen to all the conversation and content on these various forms of social media is examined in Part 3 of the book. But before getting much further, let's take a brief tour of each form of social media, describe the major types, and examine their potential for doing market research, gathering marketing intelligence, and spotting emerging trends.

Blogs

Although it's true that blogs are just one type of social media, they remain particularly noteworthy for several reasons. One is the sheer number as mentioned earlier. Another is that you can use sophisticated blog search engines that will let you employ a wide range of precision searches and filters so you can perform effective blog searching and monitoring.

What is a Blog?
David Sifrey

It is also on blogs where you'll most likely encounter what I call "key conversations." These are discussions where not just anyone, but influential thought leaders and an audience of informed and passionate readers share their experiences and opinions and debate and analyze the topics at hand. And it's on blogs where you can find authentic and unsolicited customer preferences and problems, unmet consumer needs, and get people's unvarnished opinions of companies, products, and features, and so forth.

Blogs are also a particularly powerful form of consumer content because their discussions can seep into the trade press, and sometimes even the mainstream media. That is the "viral" aspect of blogs—the ease and speed in which blog posts zip around the Internet, and it is also what give them that additional level of influence. Blogs inherently are built to allow for easy linking, and "trackbacks" (links from other blogs that reference a particular posting) which potentially make what's said on a blog reverberate throughout the blogosophere, and sometimes beyond as well.

But blogs are not the only place on the Internet where you can find authentic conversations, opinions and content from ordinary people. Here are other important forms:

Forums and Groups

Well before blogs emerged in the mid 1990s, there were (and still are today) a variety of types of places online that Internet users could have virtual discussions. These include bulletin boards, forums, USENET groups, and email-based discussion groups (such as ListServs). Here individuals can participate in tens or perhaps hundreds of thousands of groups of interest to a particular and often passionate user community, on topics ranging from aeronautics technology to zoology.

Somewhat oddly, although these discussion groups represent a gold mine of valuable consumer opinion and discussion, they tend to be overlooked these days by both amateur and professional researchers. One reason is that the search engines that index these discussions are not as well known as Google or Technorati. Another is that these older Internet discussion groups and forums have become associated with undesirable types of online communications: spam, irrelevant remarks, trolls, flame wars, and other unproductive discussions. Finally, perhaps these forms of Internet user conversations have been around so long (online USENET discussion groups and bulletin boards even preceded the creation of the World Wide Web) that they now seem too old fashioned to be of much value in the world of Web 2.0 and the blog.

Those concerns and objections are understandable, and have some truth to them. The search engines for forums and groups are not well known and you may find a lot of noise, spam, and irrelevant comments, depending on the particular group. In many ways, these discussion formats do seem kind of ancient these days.

However, at the same time, many of those concerns can be addressed and ameliorated so that you can include these kinds of formats in your social media research toolkit. This is explained in some detail in Part 3 of this book.

You also should be aware that there are different types of online discussion forums. They can be grouped into four categories:

- **Web-based forums**

    Forums are discussion boards that accompany a particular website. However, this category also includes certain stand-alone discussion forums on the web, where there is no associated website.

    While what you'll find on forums are too broad to categorize, I can say that they often include lots of enthusiastic, hobbyist, or passionate users. These kinds of groups can be excellent for learning about matters such as what customers like or don't like about their current products, or in their dealings with a particular company. For example, as a Prius owner and an occasional visitor to one of Yahoo!'s Prius Groups (there are actually several), I can speak from personal experience of the enthusiastic nature of the very passionate owners of these vehicles. Prius owners, on the whole, are an extremely satisfied and happy lot, but by reviewing the group's discussion, you can also find any gripes, as well as discover the drivers' own ways of getting around problems and get more out of the vehicle. Figure 2.1, for instance, is a thread about how drivers are sharing information on improving their mileage on the Prius while driving on Interstate highways

FIGURE 2.1

A discussion group for Prius users

Expand Messages	Author	Sort by Date
Re: Actual MPG on Interstate? In my opinion, MPG on Interstate is mostly determined by speed (ie. air friction), terrain, road condition etc. and driving habit does not impact much when the...	pri_them2 ☺ ✉ ✦	May 2, 2007 10:47 pm
Re: Actual MPG on Interstate? ... X 55 mpg at 72 mph? Unless you have 30 mph tailwind, I don't believe this is possible. MNBill ...	Bill Bartlett bill58103 ☺ ✉ ✦	Apr 29, 2007 6:12 pm
Re: Actual MPG on Interstate? ... Downhill terrain could help? Poster didn't say *all* of his driving is at 72mph, either. Instead of instantly disbelieving him, let's offer the benefit of...	Linda doingourpart ☺ ✉ ✦	Apr 29, 2007 6:19 pm
Re: Actual MPG on Interstate? ... 06], I cruise> in the right lane at 70-75. I arrive more relaxed and only add 30-45> minutes to the trip. As a plus, I get mid to high 50's in the Prius ...	mallonwc ☺ ✉ ✦	Apr 29, 2007 11:24 pm
Re: Actual MPG on Interstate? ... 06], I cruise> in the right lane at 70-75. I arrive more relaxed and only add 30-45> minutes to the trip. As a plus, I get mid to high 50's in the Prius ...	prius1111 ☺ ✉ ✦	Apr 30, 2007 6:08 pm
Re: Actual MPG on Interstate? ... X OK, do you want to ask him or should I? MNBill _____ _____ Explore the seven wonders of the world ...	Bill Bartlett bill58103 ☺ ✉ ✦	Apr 29, 2007 10:10 pm
Re: Actual MPG on Interstate?	Bill Bartlett	Apr 29, 2007

So one area where these discussion forums may prove to be particularly fruitful is when you want to hear from the enthusiasts and outspoken users of a particular firm, product-type or brand.

- **Community-based discussion groups**

  Google, Yahoo!, and MSN all allow their registered users to create groups to engage in an online discussion on any topic of the group creator's choosing. Many of these groups are tiny with just a handful of members, and are hardly active, but others have thousands of members and are extremely active with multiple postings daily.

- **USENET**

  USENET is the name of the original Internet-based online discussion groups. There are today many millions of USENET discussion threads and thousands of different groups, and you can tap into an archive extending all the way back to 1981!

  In the old days, you would have needed to download a special "USENET reader" on your PC to be able to subscribe, read, and contribute to these discussions, but today you can read and contribute to them on Google, which purchased the USENET collection (from a now defunct firm called Deja News) back in 2001.

  Because members of these groups are often enthusiasts passionately devoted to the topic of the group, USENET groups can serve as a kind of early warning system of issues, problems, and possible trends that are just beginning to emerge, perhaps even before the bloggers have picked up on it. A classic example of this occurred on a forum for bikers, where one of the members showed how easy it was to pick the Kryptonite bicycle lock with a simple ballpoint pen. But that posting didn't get much attention at all, until a blog picked up that discussion. Then the story began spreading quickly online, and eventually percolated up to the mainstream media.

- **Mailing List discussions**

  These have also been around a long time, and are the popular discussion groups where members' exchange comments and share ideas and opinions via email. The biggest and most well known of the mailing list discussion group formats is known as ListServ.

WHAT ABOUT "COMPLAINT SITES"?

Another place on the Internet where you can find unvarnished discussion about such as PlanetFeedback and Complaints.com companies and their products or services are on the handful of "consumer complaint" sites. These have been around for several years, and each one offers a different set of features and services. But all of these sites serve as an online forum where customers—lots of dissatisfied ones of course—can gripe, complain, and try to seek some redress in a public format.

These sites would naturally be of value for finding out what people don't like, and what is making them angry about the companies and products they have had dealings with. So these might be used for general company research, product research, and to get a sense of what's currently on consumers' minds.

Of course, because anyone can have a bad experience with any company and will have at least a couple of disgruntled customers, you have to be careful in drawing broader conclusions in what you discover. The key is to look for patterns and confirming information, even between sites, and note where a particular product or company's name comes up over and over. Don't forget that big name firms have more dissatisfied customers simply because they have more customers.

Audio and Video Sharing Sites

These days millions of people are creating audio podcasts and video clips and uploading them to sites like YouTube and other audio and video sharing sites for the world to see and hear. How much attention should you pay to these increasingly popular types of social media?

There's no doubt that some percentage of these consumer audio and video broadcasts could be useful for discerning important market related and trend information. However, purely from a market intelligence perspective, I don't yet recommend spending all that much time searching and monitoring them. There are two reasons why: one is technical, and the other content related.

The technical issue is the barrier that still exists and makes it so difficult to effectively and precisely search the contents of spoken words or images.

Traditional search engines are text-based. A user enters written text, and the search engine compares those words to its own text-based index of web pages, blogs, and so forth to find and then display matching results.

Searching on spoken words is quite a bit more difficult. Over the last few years, though, there have been some encouraging signs that progress is being made in this area to make searching partially possible. For instance some firms have figured out how to convert spoken language to text, and then generate written transcripts of the spoken text on the fly, and make those transcripts searchable. Other firms have tried different solutions. In Part 3, I examine two multimedia search sites that have done a particularly good job in trying to overcome this technical problem, and offer some search tips.

FIGURE 2.2

Tags

The tags assigned to a consumer video like this one of the singing elderly gentleman at Whole Foods makes these easier to search and find.

However, these approaches are still quite imperfect, as they rely on computer translation of spoken text, and so can easily miss words and make errors. And those difficulties exist for indexing audio. But the technical barriers for searching for images in a video are even more daunting. For example, how would one search for videos on the Internet that say, include images of people waiting at an airline terminal? Again, there are some ideas in the works, but they remain mainly in the lab and experimental.

There are some workarounds and alternatives for finding relevant audio and video sites that have had positive results though. One approach leverages the increasing popularity of "tags," descriptive information that users add to describe the content of an audio, video, or other piece of content uploaded to the Internet. For example, Figure 2.2 is a video from YouTube of a scene at Whole Foods, which includes tags. The good thing is that you can run a search on YouTube with a search on just the tags, and by doing so you may find the video you want, though again, you are not searching on the words (or images), but how the piece of content was described.

On the downside, tag searching is quite imperfect. For example, say you wanted to find videos where a specific product name was uttered. Unless the video clip was primarily about that product, it was unlikely to be tagged with that product name, and you will probably not locate it. Most content creators and users don't even bother adding tags.

These are the technical problems but I'm optimistic that a good deal of progress is going to be made in this area fairly quickly and that searching of speech on audio and video will become more possible.

The other problem relates to the substance and usefulness of multimedia user content, and may be more difficult to resolve. Its value falls short in two areas. First, when compared with the more conversational forms of communication on blogs and forums, podcasts and videos are primarily "one way" communication tools. Second, a high percentage of the user-generated videos are so silly and juvenile, that they are simply less valuable for finding insightful conversations and true market intelligence

Again, there are important exceptions. Some videos that are posted are compelling enough to cause others to react by posting their own videos in response, and in a sense there is a kind of conversation that's been created, and that conversation is conducted via video, and not written words. And, some smaller percentage of consumer videos are not trivial at all, but contain important information for marketers.

For instance, there may be circumstances where a consumer's podcast or video can offer some interesting grassroots perspective and provide some business insights. Or in some cases you may really need to view a video image to truly understand an issue or topic. For example, say you need to find a video that demonstrates how someone is using a snow blower, or what kind of experience they are having at a store or restaurant.

Also, if you are studying social media itself, then the content of the videos may be less important than simply being able to analyze how people are using these sites or finding out what kinds of videos are getting the most attention.

Another way that both consumer audio and video can become a more useful resource is when a particular podcast or video clip generates a lot of comments and further conversation. Not only does this indicate that the broadcast has perhaps hit some kind of cultural nerve, but it also means that you'll now have some text-based conversation surrounding the topic of the podcast or video.

Finally, one other problem is that compared with text, it's just more difficult to work with audio and video. When you are reading blogs, forums, and the like, you can print them out, and then edit, highlight, circle, pass that edited file to colleagues, and so forth. With an audio or video file, you can upload it to your own blog or in-house wiki, and use it to spur a conversation, but it is just not as easy to annotate.

With all that said, I want to emphasize that I'm not saying that podcasts and video clips have no value for market research and trend spotting at all. It's just that I suggest that overall when you are dipping into this fast moving, complex new medium, your time will likely be better spent with the text-based discussions as you'll find on blogs, forums and social networking sites.

Social Networking Sites

Finally, another form of social media where millions of people have discussions and share content are the social networking sites. The purpose of these, and other smaller online social networks, is primarily social. That means facilitating communication between existing friends on the network, helping members find new online friends, sharing information about oneself, posting pictures, and allowing other kinds of lighter exchanges of a social nature.

The best known of the large consumer social networking sites are Facebook, MySpace, and Ning. MySpace was initially targeted to teenagers and young people, and while it is still predominantly populated by younger people, there are adults too that participate. Facebook was first made available exclusively to college campuses, but in 2006, it made its network available to the general population and as of this writing was the fastest-growing social networking site. Today anyone can join Facebook, and find and connect with existing or new "friends" as contacts are called, and join a regional, or company or school based network, or one of thousands of niche topical discussion groups. (Note that Facebook's regional, educational, and workplace networks are "closed" communities. Only the members of that network can connect with and see other members' profiles and communications.)

As for their value for market and trend research, it depends on the particular network, but in general if you can tap into conversations occurring on relevant discussion groups that operate over a social networking site, the approach and value would be similar to searching conversations on Web forums and other types of Internet based discussion groups. The tools for doing searching and monitoring on these social networking sites are somewhat more limited though—these practical considerations, and research strategies are covered later in this book in Chapter 11.

MYSPACE VS. FACEBOOK

How does MySpace differ from Facebook? Both are popular social networking sites, but appear to attract different types of members. The well-known social networking expert danah boyd found certain class distinctions and demographic differences between users of MySpace compared with users of Facebook. Facebook, said boyd, has been attracting more middle- and upper-class and college-educated users, whereas there are more working-class users of MySpace.

CHAPTER 3

The Art of Tracking Trends

AS I WILL discuss later, there are lots of sites and tools on the web that purport to help people find the latest online buzz and find clues to identifying trends. However, although they are fun to use and can offer some thought provoking morsels on what terms people are searching on, discussing, and linking to, their value for identifying meaningful trends is limited.

Why? One reason is that these tools are primarily "counting" mechanisms—that is, a quantitative methodology that focuses on the question, "how many?" That is, how many times have people mentioned a particular word or phrase? How many links have been made to a particular news story? How many bloggers are linking to other bloggers? How many votes are there on popular news, blog, and video posts?

This kind of quantitative approach is not the best tool to discern something as messy as identifying emerging trends. Figuring that out takes a more subtle analysis than a counting mechanism. It requires deeper immersion, a knowledge of broader context, an understanding of the subtleties of what one is looking at, and hard analysis. I'll examine how to actually engage in this more subtle trend spotting process in Chapter 14. But here let's just spend some time discussing the basics of trends and trend tracking.

Why Track Trends?

Tracking trends is about being prepared for the future. Ironically, the phrase itself has something of a retro, anachronistic sound. Perhaps this is because "futuristic" sounding activities like trend-tracking bring to mind now-dated cultural icons that represented the future in the 1960s and early 1970s: for instance, Future Shock, the Picture Phone, World's Fairs, and George Jetson. It also doesn't help that over the years, in the corporate setting, trend-tracking activities have been given dusty and dull titles like "environmental scanning" or "current awareness," which conjure up images of pale faced clerks hunched over messy piles of newspapers, clipping out articles.

The fact is, being aware of significant changes that will have an impact on your industry, company, products, customers, and potential customers helps any organization do a better job of anticipating where the market is going. And the earlier you can spot the emergence of a trend the more control and options you have in dealing with it on your own terms.

What is a Trend?

What makes one thing a trend and another just a fad? Both terms are used to describe a new phenomenon, but a trend has characteristics that make it distinctly different. A trend builds over time, has staying power, and is long lasting. Trends also typically emerge out of some deep underlying cause. Fads, by contrast, are fast-moving phenomena. They seem to appear out of nowhere, and are gone as quickly as they arrived. Fads reflect the mood of the moment rather than a steadily growing, deeper, long-lasting movement.

Here are some examples of possible trends versus fads:

TREND	POSSIBLE UNDERLYING CAUSE
Increase in purchasing of second or even third homes, including homes abroad	Baby boomers' disposable income/retirement plans; ability to work and communicate remotely
Growth of demand for locally grown foods in supermarkets	Baby boomers' concerns over health; general increased awareness of global environmental issues
Increased sales of hybrid vehicles	Increasing gasoline costs; concerns over greenhouse gases and environmental issues
Decline of use of public libraries for research purposes	Digital generation's emphasis on relying on peers and social media from home for advice and information
Increase in outside contractors and retired people as consultants for businesses	Brain drain from corporations as baby boomers retire; need for baby boomers to supplement income and desire to remain in work force
Increase in cancellations of cable television subscriptions	Younger people's preferences for online media; cultural expectation that all media should be free on the web; decline in high quality programming
Increased sales of sun-protective clothing	Growth of popular awareness of impact of sun on skin

All trends represent meaningful changes—meaningful in that they are going to be around for a long time, emerge from larger contexts and causes, and will likely have an impact and play out in various segments of culture and society. Perhaps the classic and most significant trend that illustrates a generational trend's power on the wider culture was the rise of women in the workplace in the 1970s.

What, in contrast, are examples of fads? They might include:

- Paris Hilton
- Sneakers with roller balls
- Celebrity diets
- "Bling"
- Indoor Zen water sculptures
- Icicle-style Christmas lights

These kinds of words, product, and phenomena pop up quickly and are "hot" for a while but don't really have major impact on people's lives. Then they just disappear. A classic meaningless fad: the Hula Hoop.

Although the source of each individual trend varies, there are a couple of basic drivers typically found behind true trends:

- **Generations**

   Strong trends are often driven by the force of a generation. Of particular note, of course, are the baby boomers. The boomers have had, and continue to have, an enormous impact on the U.S. wherever they are in their lifecycle. That's due primarily to that generation's sheer size, but their influence is also reflective of its members' preference for change and reinvention.

- **Fringe Thinkers**

   Fringe thinkers are another driver of trends. These are people outside of the mainstream who have opinions or behaviors that would be considered "on the edge." Oren Harari says that fringe thinkers "tend to be marginalized, ignored, and make people uncomfortable. " However, he says, these are the people to whom firms that want to understand trends should pay the most attention.

   As an example, Harari recounted how the big record labels had plenty of clues starting in the late 1990s that "something" was going on with digital music. At first it was really just a small band of what some might see as "crazies" trading music over modems, but that activity began growing exponentially. The recording firms ignored them at first, but eventually responded with panic and lawsuits. Harari says that if these firms had taken the fast growth in that activity seriously, the recording industry would have seen the growth and emergence of downloading and file sharing of music, and perhaps could have responded in a way that enhanced their business (as did forward-looking Apple, with its iTunes).

Traditional Methods for Finding Trends

Although this book, is focused on the latest and most volatile sources for identifying trends—blogs and other forms of social media—to really understand trend tracking you should be aware of the traditional sources and principles for locating emerging trends that preceded the online world.

First, let's talk about those pre-Internet sources. Many, if not most, still remain valuable for identifying trends. The primary source that serious trend trackers have traditionally turned to has been the media, which itself would include:

- Newspapers, including political, local, alternative, and international newspapers;

- Magazines, including popular publications, trade journals, niche journals, fringe publications and sometimes scholarly journals

- Radio and television broadcasts

Other sources that have long been used for identifying trends have included:

- Conferences and exhibitions. Possible new industry or market trends might be gleaned not only by attending the official presentations, but by reviewing the new products displayed at the exhibit hall, and perhaps most importantly, catching the buzz in the hallways to pick up tidbits of news and gossip from personal conversations from the attendees and vendors.

- Speeches
- University journals and research lab publications
- Surveys and polls

- Travel to other countries to observe differences and look for
  surprises
- Personal conversations, overheard in a public place or with
  friends and family

Spotting True Trends

Today those traditional sources are still used, but a lot of trend tracking is being done on the Internet. In either case, the really critical question remains the same: just which conversations, observations, insights, activities, statements, and the like are really worth paying attention to? Consultant Peter Francese says that businesses want to discover "large, underlying trends that will seep out and influence a larger population."

But how to detect which conversations reflect those big trends is the big question, and I hope you weren't expecting an easy answer. As Oren Harari told me, "If there was a simple formula, I would have patented it long ago."

Although there's no magic bullet, there are some approaches and tips that will enhance your capability in discerning the jewels from the junk. Knowing a real trend when you see it is certainly more art and intuition than it is science, but that doesn't mean that you can't learn how to develop that art and how to pay attention to your intuition. There's also the matter of experience. The more time you spend reading and looking for trends, the more your ability to do so will be honed.

It might be helpful to first discuss what is generally NOT worth your time or attention when scanning information for trends. In my view, for the express purpose of discerning trends, you should not spend much time with:

- **Surveys and polls**

  Many polls and surveys are not scientifically conducted, and even those that are may give you only a snapshot of a previous moment in time, and will be bounded by the assumptions, that are reflected in the questions of the survey provider. When done correctly and thoughtfully surveys and polls can be good information, but they are not a prime source for detecting clues to emerging trends.

- **Expert opinion and pronouncements**

  The problem with expert opinion is that many people become experts by being specialists in their field. That's fine of course, but they may be too narrowly focused and wedded to one way of looking at the world. Again, expert opinion can be a valuable source for certain types of research, but is less valuable for locating trends.

- **Flash-in-the-pan phenomenon**
  Following up on the previous discussion that distinguished trends from fads, if there is suddenly a great surge in conversation about some breaking news event or hot new development (as will often be reflected in the buzz trackers and examined in Chapter 13), these are not likely to have staying power, and are not worth spending lots of time on.

- **Irrelevant Information**
  If something is clearly irrelevant to your research scope, then it is not worth your time. Be sure, though, that what seems on the surface to be irrelevant at the moment, might not have some impact at a future point.

- **Celebrity, trivia, entertainment chatter**
  Unless you are looking at a related meta issue (e.g. how will celebrity culture impact the future of new media, for example), it's best to steer clear of all the Internet-based discussion on celebrities that takes up so much of the blogosphere.

Once you know what to steer clear of, how do you know what to pay attention to? Again, there is no way to provide a single formula, but I can provide you with some guidelines and thoughts that have worked well for me.

I'd say that you should pay attention to those bloggers and conversations that:

- Expand your understanding of some subject or phenomena;

- Suggest answers to questions you have had on a subject or phenomena;

- Articulate for you something that you have suspected or been thinking about.

In Chapter 14, I'll provide some practical strategies and tips that you can apply to social media so you can actually surface and identify conversations and consumer content that are most likely to indicate a true emerging trend.

Chapter 4

How Credible Is Social Media?

YOU MAY be able to figure out how to find and aggregate discussions from bloggers and other voices on the Internet, but how do you know whether what you turn up is credible and trustworthy? How do you know if a remark is honest or the person knows what he or she is talking about? And how can you tell if someone's opinions are *meaningful*, in that others are paying attention to them, and that his or her comments are representative of other people? This chapter will help you do this difficult and often frustrating job of determining credibility in the blogosphere and other places on the Net where you find consumer comment and opinion.

This chapter provides the larger context for how to think about the various aspects of social media credibility, while Chapter 15 in Part 3 offers practical evaluation strategies to you can take active steps to assess the credibility of blogs and other social media you encounter on the Internet.

When it comes to determining the credibility of a piece of information or a particular information source, researchers, grad students, journalists, historians, librarians and others with information-intensive work and expertise have long followed a fairly standard checklist, whether explicitly articulated or not. These tried and true methods would include trying to determine things like the following about a particular information source:

- What is the information source's mission/purpose?

- What people are associated with that source and what are their affiliations and interests?

- Where else is the source cited, and by whom?

- What is the background and credentials of the writer(s)?

- Does the source/writer present information in a professional, clear, and organized manner?

These kinds of general source evaluation questions usually still work when applied to blogs and other conversational media. But because the nature of these sources is so different than the traditional types, evaluation strategies need to be refined and honed to better fit the kind of anecdotal, digital, conversational information sources we are focusing on in this book.

Trying to figure out the mission and official credentials of bloggers, for instance, is not as important as figuring out their influence on others, or just their plain old honesty. And because the culture of blogging permits, and actually encourages a more emotional, and even angry mode of communication at times, it's not useful to say that a person who presents his or her argument in a cool, logical way should always be viewed more credible than someone who sounds like they're ranting. Sometimes the ranters are right.

Chapter 15 provides practical tips on how to better evaluate social media sources, but before getting into these details, let's step back a bit in this chapter and recount just how—and how quickly—blogs have come to play a significant role as a commonly relied upon information source. After all, until the mid 1990s or so, although the concerns over the credibility of sources were usually applied to what we'd read in newspapers and magazines, hear on the radio, or watch on television. With the advent of the Internet, and particularly the growth of blogs, our collective notion of what should be considered a potentially credible source of information, and even who we call an expert has changed and expanded dramatically.

Blogs and Journalism

Since the late 1990s, there's been an ongoing (some would say, *ad nauseum*) discussion in and around journalistic circles on whether bloggers should "count" as journalists. The answer to that question naturally depends on one's definition of a journalist. Some have and continue to define journalism by specific skills, training and experience; others simply by the act of communicating to an audience. Others have defined journalism by "intent" examining *why* a person is communicating and what he or she wants to achieve.

Note: *While the whole "is blogging really journalism?" issue is beyond the scope of this book, to read more about it, see **Digital Dilemmas: Ethical Issues for Online Media Professionals,** [Blackwell, 2003], a book I co-authored with Chris Shumway).*

This debate peaked around 2003 and while it is still certainly a legitimate question (and it can be very important for practical matters—e.g. the answer will determine who qualifies for a press pass, and more importantly, who qualifies for legal and constitutional protections afforded only to journalists), as the strict boundaries between bloggers and traditional journalists have become blurrier, the debate has simmered down some.

For the business researcher, the theoretical question about whether bloggers deserve to wear the mantle of journalist is not really too important. There's *no* question that blogs and bloggers are now part of the larger news/information creation and dissemination cycle; and in many ways have significantly and permanently altered it. They've accomplished this, and continue to carve out new ground in the information and media sphere in many ways, including:

- being first to break a new story;

- keeping issues alive that are ignored or dropped by mainstream print journalism;

- making traditional journalists accountable for inaccuracies and questionable reporting;

- providing alternative and fringe viewpoints not represented in the mainstream press; and

- serving as a source of leads for traditional and mainstream reporters.

Blogs have become such a significant part of the media, in fact, that at a January 2005 Harvard conference on journalism, bloggers and credibility (cyber.law.harvard.edu/webcred/) media scholar and NYU journalism professor Jay Rosen stated that: "Bloggers are developing the platform that journalists will one day occupy." In other words, as journalism moves quickly online, the bloggers have arrived there first. Furthermore, the news media is not just heading online, but by many measures, online news has already overtaken print. At the same conference, Rosen said:

> When I went to my first blogger conference in 2003, I discovered that by 2002 **the majority of the readership of *The New York Times* were readers of its online edition**—and this is still true to this day. But a majority of the workers of *The New York Times* feel they are working for a traditional newspaper that has an online edition, but it is actually the other way around. That is the gap that American journalism is living in today.

This "gap" was noted by Rosen ba-ck in 2003, in referencing his discovery from 2002! That gap is still there and it is growing.

Bloggers have opened up literally millions of new "channels" of information. But whereas this has made so much more information available to all of us, it's also made it more difficult to figure out what and who to believe and trust. At that same conference, Harvard Law School professor Jonathan Zittrain summed up the paradoxical problem of getting at the truth when we have too many information sources. He brought up the saying that a person with one watch thinks he knows the time, but the person with two watches is less certain—and now, "We have a world with thousands of watches. And some watches are pegged to other watches."

Echoing this point, Rosen noted, "It used to be that the job of journalism was to publish information to 'reduce uncertainty.' The new model is to put out information which increases uncertainty—and, it's not till then that the process of reducing uncertainty begins." (By "then" Rosen was referring to the debate, discussion, arguments, that typically follow an initial bloggers' posting)

No matter how we view bloggers, though, today we can't rely on the traditional gatekeepers and filters of book or journal editors, producers, and fact checkers to do this scrutiny for us. We have to do much of that filtering and weeding ourselves. Now, in order to separate all the new and useful information from all the additional noise, we have to be more informed, be more skeptical, read more carefully, and understand how different types of information and media forms are created and disseminated.

One reason why some bloggers have been able to become a trusted source for some people is that running a blog implies some level of commitment by its creator. There is the time and effort needed to write the entries, respond to comments, and typically to create some personal context and framework for the blog that defines and guides its mission over time.

However, certain other forms of consumer-generated content have not yet really established themselves in this manner even as well as blogs have. Here I'm including comments (left on blogs or discussion forums,) or videos uploaded on sites like YouTube for instance. When these are generated on-the-fly or spontaneously, the creators don't have the time or accountability to build up a reputation as trustworthy or suffer any negative consequences from providing inaccurate or misleading information. These forms of social media can be valuable. Indeed, the premise of this book is that you should not be ignoring them. But strictly from a credibility standpoint, they represent even shakier ground than blogs.

What is Credibility?

We all feel we have a fairly good, if perhaps not precise, understanding of what we mean when we use the word "credible." And when that term is applied to an information source, which could be a piece of media text or an actual person, it means we can rely on the source to provide us with accurate information, that the source does not hide relevant interests, and is not unduly influenced by significant biases. (For many, though, a credible source is one that conforms to one's pre-existing views or at least that shares similar values.) Ultimately, a credible source is one that we can put our trust in.

And so we will all say that we believe this newspaper but that not one, and that columnist or source but not that one, and that expert or authority, but not this one. But can we apply the way we assess credibility to bloggers and other ordinary conversations on the web? I'd say that there are certain fundamental principles and characteristics of a credible source that does transcend its form. These include:

- Passes along, reports, or states accurate information and takes some minimum level of care and competence to avoid passing along bad information.

- Is honest and does not knowingly deceive the reader.

- Does not have a hidden agenda that will distort its message.

- Builds up a reputation over time and can be counted on.

But there are additional factors we need to consider when evaluating bloggers and consumer conversations on the web. For example, because bloggers represent a source of *anecdotal* information, these sources need to be assessed as you would evaluate any other anecdotal source.

An equally important consideration in determining the credibility of blog conversations is to consider the *context* of the type of research you are doing: i.e., are you primarily trying to discover:

- Complaints, compliments, experiences of product use, and consumers' dealings with a company? If so, then you will be particularly concerned with ascertaining the *factual accuracy of the assertions* made by bloggers, whether there are any hidden agendas and uncontrolled bias, and if those persons' experience are *representative* of a larger group.

- Who the leaders are in an industry or market niche whose opinions others listen to and follow? If so, then you may be most concerned with ascertaining the *authority and influence* of a particular blogger, creator of online video, or other online voice.

- Whether some unknown blogger's observations, opinions, and analysis about your market and industry are worth paying attention to and taken seriously? If so, then you may be particularly concerned with determining the bloggers' *level of knowledge and expertise.*

The Question of Objectivity

What about objectivity? Most readers and researchers will likely profess that they want their sources to be objective.

On the matter of objectivity, in the blog world, things are quite a bit different. Unlike traditional journalism, most bloggers are not objective, nor do they consider objectivity to be any kind of worthy goal. In fact, blogger culture generally feels that since there's no such thing as pure objectivity; anyone that pretends to be objective is a sham. In many bloggers' view, those who view themselves as "objective" sources might be seen as less trustworthy than the blogger who just gives his or her opinions flat out and says what he or she believes, no holds barred. You should not even look for objectivity in the blog world, and probably not even fairness.

That said, and without getting into the much larger discussion of yet another thorny journalistic issue on the whole notion of objectivity, although you might find this perspective unsettling, it has its merits. It has served discussions on the blogosophere quite well, and provided a good complement to the more constrained methods of the traditional news media.

The pitfall that you do need to be aware of here is the (rare) blogger who may be pretending to believe one thing while actually supporting another with a hidden agenda. So while you aren't going to be looking for objectivity in bloggers, you do want to believe that the blogger that you are reading is honestly portraying his or her opinions and identity.

Let's move to the discussion in this section from objectivity to honesty. The first question, is dishonesty a problem in the blog world?

It's impossible to know for sure, but my best answer to this is that while there are trouble spots, it is not a big concern, at least not yet. At the same time, though, there are a few new types of incentives that are increasing the rewards for some blogging to be dishonest and fraudulent.

One is companies that create fake blogs or seed blog conversation so as to create buzz or to try to steer and manipulate the conversation to benefit their firms and products.

A second is the emergence of spurious, meaningless, and fake blogs, called "splogs." Splogs are created solely for the purpose of leveraging contextual keyword advertisements from Google and other contextual ad programs that automatically appear on a website. By creating a splog, a blog owner gets a little income each time someone clicks on one of those contextual ads.

And the third is when bloggers are hired by companies to blog about their products in order to create buzz and generate a word-of-mouth marketing campaign.

I think the first concern—firms that create phony blogs or try to manipulate blog conversations—is only a minor concern for researchers. And splogs are more of an annoyance that feeds the problem of information overload rather than an issue of blogger credibility, because if you come across one, it's pretty obvious that it's a spam blog with no real substance.

But it is the paid blogging phenomena that is the most worrisome. In Chapter 15 I take some time to discuss this matter, and provide a few practical tips on what you can do to spot and avoid them.

The Question of Representativeness

Let's say you're tracking what people online are saying about certain products, services, or consumer behaviors, and you've come across some bloggers that you have determined are honestly making important points. That's all well and good, but do these people represent anyone other then themselves? So, for example, if you come across lots of discussion among a handful of bloggers who are very enthusiastic about buying and eating food that's grown locally, how do you know if you can legitimately extrapolate those conversations to be representative of any kind of larger population?

Ensuring the representativeness of a focus group or survey takers to one's larger target universe is, of course, a bedrock of reliable market research. So how can you put any kind of stock into comments on blogs that you have just randomly encountered?

At least one well-known figure in market research has publicly expressed concerns on just this matter. In a much linked to and discussed online conversation with Toby Bloomberg of Bloomberg Marketing, on her Diva Marketing blog, in June 2006 Bill Neal, a senior partner at the strategic marketing firm SDR Consulting in Atlanta, (Neal is known to some as the "Godfather of Marketing Research,") raised several objections to the use of blog and consumer conversations for market research. His primary concern was its value as any kind of scientific or reliable measure of the market as a whole. Here is an excerpt of his remarks:

> " . . . In many ways it [CGM] combines the worst elements of non-scientific research—self selection and advocacy—both positive and negative. That is, those out there in the Internet world who are generating their own media are self-motivated to do so and are not representative of any defined population of buyers. And, given the fact that they have taken a public position on a particular product or service, it means that they more often than not have exceptional or non-typical attitudes about those products and services. . . .
>
> "The information they [consumers] generate may be true, or not true—there is no way to discern which. Therefore, the information generated by those folks is neither credible nor reliable."

Source: *http://www. mpdailyfix.com/2006/06/ is_there_something_ rotten_in_c.html*

I spoke with Neal in a follow up about a year after he made these remarks, and he told me, "I still stick to those concerns but some clarification is in order. I have no problem and feel it is appropriate for people to monitor all this consumer discussion, because there are people that are highly engaged that help identify trends, and can alert us to new things coming down the pike. The hang up that I have, and what firms like Nielsen BuzzMetrics is trying to do, is to extend the volume and intensity of their projection to a general population. And that is not scientific and projectible as a research methodology."

My own take on the issue of blogs and representative sampling is that I fully agree that reading blogs and consumer conversations certainly does not qualify as a scientific method of doing market research. And if you're a financial service firm, and you've discovered a bunch of people online saying, for example, that they are fed up with getting unsolicited credit card offers in the mail, this doesn't mean that these views are representative of all consumers, and you wouldn't roll out a new marketing strategy based on that and nothing else.

However that does not mean that what you discovered is not valuable in its own right and not worth paying attention to. The key point is that when you are engaged in strategic listening, *you are not trying to do traditional market research*. Rather, you are trying to act more like an ethnographer to carefully observe and to discern the subtleties of what you are hearing online to get a feel for what people are saying, feeling and thinking, unsolicited. You're trying to pick up on what is getting people excited; what the fringe thinkers are saying; who is influencing others; and how all this could impact your current or future business. Doing strategic listening online is not a substitute for traditional market research. Marketers still need to engage in the tried and true activities to get reliable and projectible data. But the Internet now offers an opportunity to complement traditional research with this completely different but also valuable input, and it should not be ignored.

Peter Francese, who in the past had also expressed concerns about using blogs as a substitute for good market research, acknowledged that there are certain types of market related research where representativeness is not important. He says that discussions on the Internet can be valuable for companies as a way to be alerted to complaints and comments about their products. To give an example, Francese says suppose a firm manufactures a device and discovers via a blog discussion that the product is causing certain problems for physically handicapped people. The company did not know this because it didn't test its product on people with that disability, but now the flaw would be revealed, and the firm could take some action to remedy it. For this kind of use, Francese says, "The relevance of representativeness goes out the window."

NOTE

I followed up with Nielsen BuzzMetrics to get its response to Neal's concern. In an email message, the company's VP of Marketing Max Kalehoff replied that "the measurement and analysis of CGM is not intended to specifically parallel traditional conventions of representative sampling common in traditional panel measurement methodologies . . . while average, "representative" measurements are important, CGM data offer unique and complementary advantages:

- First, people who create CGM are, by definition, self-selecting "speakers." They are not the "middle-of-the-bell-curve," but do typically represent the most engaged consumers who self-organize by affinity, on particular topics. That's a profound and important way of understanding consumers, social groups and their behaviors. It's all about consumer-centric market segmentation, versus organizing consumers according to how marketers "think" they should be organized.

- Second, CGM creators typically are leading indicators and provide tremendous insights about brands. Related to segmentation, the ability to target according to brand involvement or influence is a profound concept.

- Third, CGM measurements are different than traditional representative sampling techniques because observations are made as reality happens, versus trying to re-create reality in a scientific laboratory. While CGM measurements are limited to studying what can observe in the natural world, the insights typically reflect what people actually care about, versus what they were prompted to care about.

Authority and Influence

Another way of assessing a blog's value relates to whether a particular blogger's views have a high degree of credibility among others. In other words, is the blogger influential?

As marketers are well aware, finding influential consumers or authorities in any market niche is important, both on and off the web, simply because of the power those persons may have to affect others' decisions. In the blogosphere, it's particularly important because so often the key conversations about a company, industry, product, or topic, occur around an influential person's blog .

But just what do we mean by influence? And how might influence differ from other terms that are bandied about in the blogosphere so often, like "authority" and "popularity"? Finding a dictionary definition is a good way to begin a discussion about a word, (but not to end it), so let's take a look at some definitions of these terms from one well used source, Merriam Webster Online:

> **Influence:** Etymology: from Medieval Latin influentia, from Latin influent-, influens, present participle of influere to flow in, from in- + fluere to flow
>
> Def 3 a : *the act or power of producing an effect without apparent exertion of force or direct exercise of command*

> **Authority:** Etymology: Middle English auctorite, from Anglo-French auctorité, from Latin auctoritat-, auctoritas opinion, decision, power, from auctor.
>
> Def 2: 2 a: *power to influence or command thought, opinion, or behavior*

You can see that there are a couple of interesting distinctions between authority and influence. Authority is linked, both by origin and use, to a more *direct* ability to act to exert power whereas influence is something that can happen or flow *indirectly*, or without overt action.

And let's take a look too at Mirriam Webster's definition of another word that is used often on the web, either explicitly (when counting links or clicks) or implicitly to distinguish bloggers and other textual or human sources of information: "popular."

Popular: Etymology: Latin *popularis*, from *populus*, the people, a people. Def 4: 4 : *commonly liked or approved <a very popular girl>*

Unlike authority and influence, which relate to a type of power that one has, directly or indirectly over others, being popular relates to a flow that moves the other way, as a larger group (the people) bestows approval on another.

But popularity on the Internet, so often measured by incoming links, has become conflated with authority and influence. As blogger Steve Rubel has written: "Links—be they Google or Technorati—have turned the entire concept of authority into something rather trivial—popularity. Does this mean Britney Spears is an authority just because she's popular?"

Note that just because there are these distinctions, it does not mean that a popular blog can't also be influential or authoritative. Often there will be a correlation. It's just that one can be popular without being influential or an authority.

Let's provide a little more context on these terms. Jon Kleinberg is a professor at the Department of Computer Science at Cornell University in Ithaca. In 1997 he wrote paper titled *Authoritative Sources in a Hyperlinked Environment*, (http://www.cs.cornell.edu/home/kleinber/auth.pdf) which looked at what he called "hubs and authorities" (hubs are sites with lots of outlinks and authorities are sites with lots of inlinks] where he examined the entire notion of what is and what should best be called authoritative on the web.

In a telephone interview, Professor Kleinberg offered some additional perspective on these terms. Authority, he said, is found to be a balance between popularity and quality, meaning, if something is of high quality but nobody knows about it, then it really can't be an authority; and if something is very popular, but not of high quality, it can't really be called authoritative. To be authoritative, Kleinberg says, you have to be endorsed by others that are also authoritative. It's a circular process, he explained, that has its roots in how academics determine the authority of their colleagues via citation analysis. When authorities cite professors' works, it bestows a level of authority upon the person whose work is being cited.

Being influential, Kleinberg says, is a bit different in that it implies more of a dynamic, and connotes the ability to cause things to happen. (For readers

One commenter to Rubel's question replied: YES: "I would say . . . Britney Spears [has] the power to influence others . . . (although the concept can be quite frightening . . .) due not because of knowledge, but commanding manners . . . Personally, I think the line between popularity and authority might (at this point in human history) be blurred.

that want to delve into the classic academic treatment of the social nature of influence, I recommend *Diffusion of Innovations*, a classic work in sociology, by Everett M. Rogers, Free Press, 5th ed., 2003.)

Paying attention to the dynamic of "causing things to happen" as a measure of influence is important because the standard metric on the web and in the blogosphere for identifying prominent bloggers has generally been to simply count incoming links. However this does not really identify the impact of that blogger on his or her readers. As blogger Matt Galloway put it, "Influence is really about watching the reaction of the listener—not measuring the speaker."

The Problems with Popularity

There are other inherent problems when a searcher relies on the approach of simply counting links to rank bloggers. Perhaps the biggest one is that if all incoming links are counted equally, then it is not possible to distinguish the *context* of the incoming links. In other words, does an incoming link from a highly linked-to blog represent a source that is truly knowledgeable on the topic that the researcher is interested in, or is it just a blog that has lots of unrelated links? Flemming Madsen, the founder of the U.K.–based social media analysis firm Onalytica, put the problem nicely like this:

Source: *Who are the most influential authorities on Business Blogging?* Onalytica, 2006

If you search Technorati for "bird flu" and only want to see posts with high authority you get a page full of links to large news media. Google News came up on top when I did it.

Nobody believes that Google News is an authority on "bird flu". They are a news aggregator.

The reason why they appear as the number 1 result is because they have an enormous number of inbound link sources.

But are those who link to Google News linking to it in the context of "bird flu?" Some may be, but I think it's safe to assume that people link to Google News from all sorts of contexts.

As a consequence of mixing up non-contextual popularity with authority on issues, the major news media appear to be the biggest authorities on anything.

In fact, because Engadget, a hugely popular blog about "gadgets" has so many inbound link sources it appeared twice on the first page of the search results for "bird flu" in Technorati (filtered for maximum authority). I'm sure it will come as a surprise to even the writers of Engadget that they are one of the world's foremost authorities on bird flu.

So it's a big problem to assume that just the blog with the most incoming links (from web pages or from other bloggers) is going to be authoritative or influential, since you don't know the nature of the sites or blogs that those links are derived from.

In Part 3 I'll discuss a few strategies you can use to try to improve your blog searches so that you are able to get a more filtered result of bloggers who come from the topical communities that are relevant and important to you.

There are a couple of other problems with counting links as a key way to assign credibility to blogs. One is that people may link to blogs for a wide range of reasons. Sometimes they may do so to make an academic-like citation or referral, but other times they are just pointing out a piece of information, or to refute and disagree with a blogger. And, because bloggers are aware that when they link to a popular site, there may be a link back to them, which can boost their own rankings, there are also situations where bloggers link to highly ranked blogs just for the purpose of trying to give their own blog's ranking a boost.

The Value Chain: From Popularity to Authority to Influence?

Let's take a look at the whole chain that is built on the web then, where popularity gets called "authority" (notably on the blog tracking site Technorati); and how authority relates to influence and expertise.

The first question is to take a close look as to whether lots of links-in to a blog *always* mean popularity? That's usually true, but keep in mind there is a whole industry of search engine optimizers and others with an interest in getting links to a site solely as a way to boost one's ranking on search engines.

Does popularity mean authority? Sometimes it does, but a blog could be popular because it has lots of gossip, emotion, and is a site that people "love to hate," so it may not be authoritative beyond just being popular.

Authority implies influence only if the audience or listeners actually changes their behavior and actions based on what that authority figure says or advises.

And of course influence is not the same as expertise. One can cause a change or have an impact on another person's behavior based on propaganda, emotional appeals, or ways other than having knowledge or skills.

Therefore, this chain of associations that leads from incoming links to influence is as solid as the strength of each connection between the chain's links, and there are a lot of "ifs" along that chain.

In Chapter 15 I'll provide some sources and strategies for locating popular—and perhaps influential—bloggers. I'll also provide additional strategies on how to surface those that are more likely to be truly influential as well, and offer research strategies that go beyond just counting incoming links.

Knowledge and Expertise

When you want to find a true expert in a field, listening to conversations of unknown bloggers and consumers is probably not the best strategy. Instead you should do more conventional research. Search a database of professional and trade journals, find book authors, conference speakers, professors, and persons cited in news articles. Blogs and consumer conversations are typically best used not to surface expertise, but as outlined in this book, for grassroots opinions, personal experiences, and a possible window into social trends.

Sometimes, though, when you are reading a blogger's account of some matter—comments on trends in the PC industry, innovations in customer service, how to attract birds to a backyard or whatever—you'll want to get a sense of if the person is truly knowledgeable about what they are blogging about.

Before the Net it was fairly easy to determine if some person you had not heard of, should be considered to be an expert. Typically, experts were identified by their official credentials (e.g., a PhD) or by an accomplishment recognized by their peers (e.g., authoring a book, having articles published in industry journals, or speaking at industry conferences). While these are still indicators of expertise, the Internet has allowed millions of people who do not have official credentials, but who do have real knowledge on a subject to demonstrate their expertise in a public forum.

So today in order to determine the knowledge and expertise of a particular person on the Internet, you can no longer rely just on official credentials, but will need to look more carefully at how the person *demonstrates* his or her command of a subject.

CHAPTER 5

The Ethics of Strategic Listening

THE ACTIVITY of listening, monitoring, and engaging bloggers and other people online is fraught with potential ethical minefields. It can be easy, either knowingly or unknowingly, to transgress your own ethical standards or those of your organization.

Below are the kinds of ethical issues you may run up against. I'd like to offer some advice on how to navigate these pitfalls in a way that ensures your own personal integrity, and your organization's as well, and discuss why following these guidelines also will serve your self interest.

I've broken these down the ethical pitfalls of strategic listening into the following categories:

- Privacy Violations

- Identity Deception

- Phony Authenticity

- Manufacturing Buzz

Privacy Violations

Although by now most people know that what they say on the Internet is going to be potentially available to anyone anytime, because members of discussion forums and chat rooms may have varying understanding and expectations on how their words could be used, these still occupy a somewhat "quasi-public/private" space. For this reason, I recommend following these guidelines to avoid impinging on others' privacy:

1. Don't reprint anyone's name in full in any kind of public document without that person's permission. You might even consider following this rule when distributing material to a wider audience within your own organization.

2. If you plan to use anyone's words in advertising, other kinds of promotions, or reports, you should try to obtain permission first, even if you are not planning on identifying the person. The ethic on the Internet has been that "you own your own words."

3. You should also be careful about drawing broad conclusions about specific individuals based on their online speech, activities, sites visited, and other behavior while online. What people do, say, and seek online represents only a narrow aspect of who they are as a person, and without the larger context of knowing people in the fuller aspects of their lives, it is easy to make wrong, and sometimes dangerous assumptions about others (e.g., this person is a show-off; this person has a certain sexual orientation; this person may be a political radical).

As John Battelle has written, we are increasingly being defined by our digital "clickstream"—what we click on and participate in online. But therein lies the danger, as legal scholar and author Jeffrey Rosen warns, in his book, *The Unwanted Gaze* (Random House, 2000).

At the beginning of the twenty-first century, new technologies of communication have increased the danger that intimate personal information originally disclosed to our friends and colleagues may be exposed to—and misinterpreted by—a less understanding audience. For as thinking and writing increasingly take place in cyberspace, the part of our life that can be monitored and searched has vastly expanded. E-mail, even after it is ostensibly deleted, becomes a permanent record that can be resurrected by employers or prosecutors at any point in the future. On the Internet, every Website we visit, every store we browse in, every magazine we skim, and the amount of time we spend skimming it, create electronic footprints that can be traced back to us, revealing detailed patterns about our tastes, preferences, and intimate thoughts.

Identity Deception

It should go without saying that pretending to be someone you are not to influence an online discussion presents real ethical problems. There have been notable cases where an employee of a firm, or someone with a vested interest in a firm, participated in a blog or online discussion forum about that firm, and pretended to be a neutral party as a way to steer and shape the conversation in a certain way. And when these are uncovered, the persons that engaged in deception suffer the consequences.

In one well publicized event, in July 2007 it was discovered that the CEO of Whole Foods, John P. MacKey, had, for several years and in over 1,000 separate postings, disguised his identity and used an alias on a Yahoo! investment board to talk up his firm, and to bad mouth competitor Wild Oats Market. This deception was revealed when Whole Foods moved to acquire the Wild Oats Market chain in 2007 and the information surfaced in a long footnote in a report by the FTC regarding an anti-trust investigation (Whole Foods was eventually successful in its acquisition).

In that case, the CEO just ended looking silly, though there was some initial concern that it could have hurt the chances of Whole Foods to complete its acquisition. In another case, also well publicized, the deception went as far as creating a fake blog and damaged the reputation of the PR firm behind the ruse. That blog, called Wal-Marketing Across America, was purportedly being written by a couple of "regular" folks who wrote about their excursions and experiences while driving to various Wal-Marts around the country, and shared sentimental stories of the firm's workers. In late 2006 that blog was exposed as being a creation by Wal-Mart's PR firm, Edelman.

Edelman's reputation plummeted. Until that point, in fact, the firm had a very good standing in the blog world for its innovations in how blogging could be used effectively in marketing, but its practice on the Wal-Marteting blog was soundly thrashed in the business press and online.

This has been the case over and over, whenever a firm is discovered to be doing anything online that is in the slightest way deceptive and dishonest. Bloggers are exceptionally talented at outing fakers and deceivers, so not only do you act unethically when you set out to mask your identity online or pretend to be someone you're not, but you also put your entire reputation on the line.

Phony Authenticity

Along with a move towards transparency, there's also a trend among businesses, particularly online businesses, towards authenticity, or perhaps just cultivating the characteristic of authenticity. Rather than presenting oneself as a giant, faceless, uncaring, bureaucratic, phony public relations-driven corporation, companies are learning (and being advised) that they will be more successful if they can drop the corporate-speak and PR phoniness and begin to treat and talk to others as regular people rather than seeing them as prey.

So why, you might wonder, are we still getting robotic monotone scripts from retailers, such as "Can I interest you in our Bacon Lover's Supreme Omelet"? as the first thing said to us when we pull up to a Dunkin' Donuts, or whatever, other retailer's latest upsell script might be?

For a rare few large firms (think Google, at least in its earliest days) and lots of small businesses you may know personally, authenticity comes naturally. These firms don't need advice on how to act like human beings toward their customers and other people. In other cases, firms have woken up to the fact that the business-as-usual corporate approach is not an effective way to relate to others, and have dropped or worked to modify it and genuinely tried to become more authentic. But as you might guess, many companies don't "get it" at all, and so now, rather paradoxically, *are pretending to be authentic.* That is, they go through what they think are the proper motions, and make a few superficial changes so they appear to be natural, authentic, and human. But they do this only because they see it as "the new way" to win over customers, and still don't understand or believe the deeper message about the importance of authenticity in all relationships.

And while being a phony is not really unethical, it is still a form of deception. More to the point, you only hurt yourself if you think that authenticity is something you can pay lip service to, but not embed deeply into your organization and business relationships.

Manufacturing Buzz

I've already discussed how important positive word-of-mouth is to a company's success, and why it's vital that firms pay attention to what's being said about them and their products, and for getting a sense of how they are perceived in the market.

Historically, word-of-mouth was something that emerged organically from customers' experiences with a firm or its products. Customers tried out a product or service, had a great (or awful) experience with it, mentioned it to a friend or family member, and then these relationship-based conversations would either help spur sales, or if negative, cause a decline. Although there have been attempts by firms to consciously create a positive buzz (e.g., holding a Tupperware party), in general the way a firm would get positive word-of-mouth would be based primarily on its performance, assisted (or hurt) by accompanying marketing and public relations activities.

Although this book focuses on new market research opportunities and not marketing strategies the two activities are pretty well intertwined. Naturally, the whole point of collecting information is to do something smart based on what you learn: e.g., introduce a new feature, launch a new product, enter a new market, rethink your customer service, or do something else. But one action that marketers may well be tempted to engage in—recruit bloggers and other individuals online to begin spreading positive word-of-mouth about one's product or firm—is another areas of ethical concern.

Over the last 10 years or so, as awareness of the power of word-of-mouth grew, and companies realized the technique's power and ability to spread online, firms began developing and launching viral or guerilla marketing campaigns to consciously manufacture buzz. Sometimes firms would start a word-of-mouth marketing campaign and recruit individuals to talk up the firm's product in bars or at parties, in order to create that much-sought-after buzz, which could then propagate itself, either offline or online.

Prominent firms that have nurtured buzz marketing "agents" to spread the word have included Dell, Hershey, Intuit, and Kraft. Perhaps the most prominent of these was Procter & Gamble, with an initiative called *VocalPoint*. That program recruited hundreds of thousands of mothers, chosen to participate because they already had large social networks. The mothers were then hired to talk about P&G brands to their friends. A related program by P&G, called *Tremor* was designed specifically to solicit highly connected teens to use their social connections to talk about P&G's clients' products. Tremor's clients reportedly include Dreamworks, Coca-Cola, and Toyota. Another prominent player in this "buzz creation" space is a Boston-based firm called BzzAgent. Its clients are reported to include Kellogg, Ralph Lauren, and Anheiser-Busch.

Research on these kinds of programs has shown that launching a buzz marketing campaign *does* appear to directly increase sales, and so companies continue to be extremely interested in doing more of this kind of activity.

Although much of this attempt to create buzz occurs offline, because conversation moves so quickly and easily on the Internet, there has been increasing interest among firms in making this happen effectively on the Internet. And given young persons' interest in participating in and linking to "friends" on social networking sites like MySpace and Facebook, it is even more tempting for those who want to create some buzz about their new product think about how and where to seed these networks to generate that positive buzz.

As a result, some firms are either hiring out, or attempting on their own to recruit others to chat about their product on the web. Some have gone a step further, and hired firms like PayPerPost, whose clients pay a fee to bloggers to regularly write about their products and services, again in the hopes of getting others online to talk about them.

So what's ethically wrong about getting bloggers to talk about your product? There are several concerns. Perhaps the most important regards the matter of disclosure. From an ethical standpoint, it's clear that if people hired to create buzz don't disclose to the other party (i.e., readers of their blogs) that they are being compensated or induced to do this by the manufacturer, they are being dishonest. The blog readers will be deceived if they believe that any recommendations or positive discussion about the products from that blogger are based purely on the merits of the product, and not from a prior business arrangement.

Some of the larger and better known buzz-agent firms require their agents to disclose their affiliation. One of the most prominent BzzAgent, did not have such a requirement until December 2005 when it began mandating affiliated bloggers disclose their relationship with the firm. BzzAgent explained that its policy change stemmed from its discovery that disclosure increases trust and improves the effectiveness of word-of-mouth marketing. However, some of these changes also were likely spurred by a complaint filed with the FTC by the consumer advocacy group Commercial Alert about these firms' practices. The FTC, while declining to investigate buzz marketing firms, issued a statement in December 2006 that stated that companies that engage in word-of-mouth marketing where people are compensated to promote products to others, must disclose those relationships.

There is even a trade organization of marketers who regularly engage in word-of-mouth marketing called the Word of Mouth Marketing Association or WOMMA, based in Boston, Massachusetts. WOMMA has created an explicit code of ethics that states that full disclosure is required when firms engage in word-of-mouth marketing. (See the link in Appendix B for WOMMA and its code of ethics.)

At a bare ethical minimum—and more recently from a legal standpoint as well—firms that consciously decide to work with bloggers or others on the Internet to create buzz need to fully disclose, or have their "agents" disclose, that they are talking about the product because of a relationship to the company.

Even if there is complete honesty and disclosure, there are other relevant ethical issues that marketers should consider before embarking on the path of consciously manufacturing buzz:

- Most of us already suffer from too much information, too much confusing information, and a blurring of the line between information and promotion and advertising. Do you really want to add to this confusion?

- Consider if you really want to contribute to the blurring of the line between the honest exchange of feelings and thoughts that characterizes friendship and using that friendship or personal acquaintance in a more mercenary business fashion. Most of us value our friends and families, and don't want to see precious relationships and conversations become just another commodity up for sale along with toothpaste and tires.

- Some people who offer themselves up as buzz agents seem to be doing so out of a desperate need to be listened to, and to feel a bit of empowerment in their own lives. While one could argue that offering those people this opportunity is a good thing, you might also wonder if it is just exploitative.

As with the other ethical areas discussed above, there are also relevant reasons of self-interest. Even with full disclosure, by working to consciously manufacture buzz you give legitimacy to such an approach, and tacitly support the premise that conversations on the Internet may be authentic or manufactured. This creates more suspicion and mistrust among users in determining which online conversations are authentic and which are mere shills. In a sense, you contribute to a "poisoning of the community well" that all Internet users, including yourself, have come to rely upon

Also, from a more practical standpoint, consider if creating a buzz around your product is really what is needed to make your organization succeed. After all, no amount of buzz is going to improve your reputation or make people buy a product that's a real dog. First things first. If you spend all your time trying to create buzz when you should be spending your time making a high-quality product, offering quality customer service, getting your finances in shape, and working on other business fundamentals, you're just fooling yourself. Jeff Jarvis, the well-known blogger and media analyst, in a reaction to the efforts by some in marketing and pr to try to figure out how to get positive discussion from bloggers put it this way:

> You cannot buy our word of mouth. It's ours. You cannot buy buzz. You have to earn it. The only way to get either is to create a good product or service and to treat your customers with respect by listening to and being open and honest with them. . . . That's it. No trade associations needed. No conventions. No codes of ethics that people sign and then find loopholes through. No Star Chambers for errant marketers. Just tell the truth. It really is that simple.

Source: *http://www.buzzmachine.com/2006/11/09/word-of-my-mouth/*

The Flip Side of Strategic Listening Ethics

Although all of the above ethical guidelines towards strategic listening are framed as "don'ts"; don't invade people's privacy; don't judge people based on their online behavior, don't be phony, don't deceive, and don't try to manufacture fake buzz; there is a flip side to all of this, and that guideline can be framed as a "do." Not only is it an ethical activity, but it is also a savvy and effective marketing technique.

Do reach out and respond—truthfully, genuinely, and helpfully—to those persons on the web that have had problems or issues with your firm or products, or have some issue they need to voice to the appropriate person. Many people are desperate to be heard, and if you can reach out, listen to them, and respond in a truly (not phony!) way that shows you care, and will genuinely try to help and do something about it, you will have helped soothe an unhappy customer, and perhaps created a more loyal one. You also will have received valuable feedback for your firm so that you can make any necessary changes that you see legitimately need attention.

PART 2

CONTRACTING OUT THE JOB

Look Dave, I can see you're really upset about this. I honestly think you ought to sit down calmly, take a stress pill, and think things over."

—HAL, the ultimate in "sentiment detection", discerning anxiety in the voice of his human crewmate, Dave

2001: A Space Odyssey

I hope Part 1 of this book has helped convince you of the importance of attending to conversations and content occurring that's happening on blogs and other types of social media. But that just raises the obvious questions—what can you do about it? How can you best begin to efficiently engage in strategic listening to tap into all this available market intelligence?

You have two options: you can learn to do this job yourself or you can contract out the work to a third party vendor. Although I will outline reasons later on as to why I believe that in the majority of situations, it is best to perform strategic listening yourself, there are certain circumstances where a case can be made for hiring a vendor to do the job for you.

This section of the book will help you determine if you should contract out the job to a third party, describe how the various social media monitoring firms differ, discuss the validity of some of their claims of their ability to automatically analyze social media and human sentiment, and finally, offer some tips on how to choose the right vendor for your needs if you do choose this route.

CHAPTER 6

The Blog-Monitoring Industry

ALTHOUGH when it comes to strategic listening I think that when possible it's best to do it yourself, there's also no question that a roomful of PCs crunching away on millions of bits of data and consumer conversations will do an immeasurably faster and more efficient job than you can ever do in scouring and aggregating the sheer amount of discussion that's occurring every second on the Internet. As IDC analyst and information linguistic expert Susan Feldman says, "With the sea of information available, manual tracking can't cover more than a teaspoon of the relevant information."

Moreover, blog-monitoring vendors do offer certain capabilities and features that you can't do at all (at least yet) or as easily on Technorati or other sites where you can search and filter social media yourself. For instance, vendors can do a more efficient job in:

- Filtering out duplicate entries and spam

- Helping determine if particular blog postings of the name of a popular company or brand (e.g., Coke, Google, Apple, etc.) are relevant to the actual company or brand or just an aside and superfluous.

- Tracking the reach and voice of individual bloggers

- Tracking and analyzing comments left on blogs (it is difficult to track comments by using blog search engines or RSS)

- Providing clues for identifying the most influential bloggers

- Employing software that can segment bloggers and consumers by certain demographic attributes

- Employing software that can do sophisticated word parsing and linguistic analyses

- Surfacing conversation and patterns that are occurring "around" your topic of interest, but that you had not determined or known to be relevant ahead of time

- Applying "sentiment analysis" technology to identify which discussions' tones are positive and which are negative. (More about this in Chapter 7)
- Providing detailed customized reports with lots of charts and graphs
- Providing personalized attention, consulting, and marketing and branding strategy and advice

The question is, do you really need all of these additional features and capabilities? Marketing expert Andy Beal suggests that you may need them if you have a "significant, ongoing issue" that you need to be tracking continually. For instance, if you are in a regulated industry and there are continual changes, you may benefit from the sophisticated ongoing tracking capabilities that you can get from a blog-monitoring vendor. Another reason you might decide to contract out this work is if you need to do as comprehensive a job as possible, and continually stay informed each time a blogger or consumer mentions a company, product, or issue.

Then there's the question of cost. Most of these vendor-based solutions are not cheap and typically run five or even six figures and up per year. But if you happen to be a Fortune 1000 firm, and you already have allocated millions of dollars per year in your marketing budget, then subscribing to a blog-monitoring vendor may not represent a significant new expenditure. And if you want to be sure you're covering all your bases, then taking this route and looking at it as extra insurance might not be a bad idea.

If you do contract out though, I'd still strongly advise that you supplement it with some of your own research and monitoring. Doing this will give you direct exposure to the online conversations of your current or potential customers, so you can at least get a flavor of what's being discussed. Doing this will also put you in a more knowledgeable position about what people are saying online, so that when you do talk to a blog-monitoring vendor and are reviewing their offerings and reports, the information you review will be more meaningful. Also, if you do hire a blog-monitoring vendor, you will be in a better position to flag something you come across in one of its reports that just doesn't look right to you based on your own time scouring the blogs.

Because blog-monitoring vendors vary a good deal in their content or sources, features, and overall approach, you'll want to know how to distinguish the different types. I'll discuss this in some detail later in this chapter.

The Rise and Development of the Blog-Monitoring Industry

As you might imagine, what I'm calling the blog-monitoring industry, is a new field. For context, I'll offer a mini history of this new niche industry's birth and growth.

Blog-monitoring firms are a modern outgrowth of a field that has been around for a long time, the press clipping industry. By the mid to late 1990s, as digital news and information began moving to the Internet, the word "alerts" became the new default term to describe services that offered frequent and regular updates from articles published in the media that matched the subscriber's keyword profile. The term was being used by newly emerging automatic news discovery services, which included both free and fee-based offerings. The way these news services worked was that Internet users could create keyword profiles to describe what kind of news they wanted to be alerted to, and the service would scan dozens or hundreds of individual news databases or individual sources on the Internet. Whenever a keyword match was made, the user would be sent an alert with a headline and an abstract of the full text to the new items via their email.

*For a detailed, though now largely out-of-date examination of the news alert industry and the choices for users, see my **Choosing and Using a News Alert Service,** from **Information Today**, published 2004.*

By the early 2000s, news alerts were also being offered directly by Google and Yahoo! for their own news collection, and this method for staying informed of late-breaking news and information had become quite popular among the general population of Internet users.

Blogs and Company Reputation and Image

By around 2003, the importance of the newest and most uncontrolled type of Internet based news source—the blog—was becoming apparent. Discussions on blogs began having an impact on a variety of social institutions: politics, the media, education, and, of course, business. And at least for some discussions that were occurring in the blogosphere, it became clear that just because a discussion started on a blog, it didn't end there. Bloggers' conversations would get linked to by other bloggers, who themselves would be linked to by other blogs, and some conversations would expand throughout the blog world. If a particular discussion generated enough attention and emotion among bloggers and blog readers, an editor at a more traditional media outlet, perhaps a trade journal, a specialized news service, or a wire service might notice it and write about it. If that happened, it would improve the chances that the matter being discussed would then bubble up to the mainstream media. How news and information was being created, filtered, and disseminated was, therefore, radically altered by discussions taking place in the blogosphere.

Soon businesses began discovering the impact that discussion on blogs, particularly negative discussions, could have on their firm. In what is likely the most publicized example of how powerful the sting can be of even one unhappy blogger, Dell Computer was forced to address what came to be known as the "Dell Hell" blog post. A popular and influential blogger, Jeff Jarvis of Buzzmachine.com, wrote a long and bitter post about his ongoing negative experiences with his Dell PC, and in his dealings with the whole company. The enormous amount of anti-Dell discussion and comments that the posting sparked on his blog was quickly picked up on other blogs, and eventually compelled CEO Michael Dell to respond publicly in the blogosphere itself to address the complaints.

FIGURE 6.1

The impact of blogger Jeff Jarvis' rant against Dell has become a legend in the blogosphere on the power that bloggers can have on businesses.

BuzzMachine

by Jeff Jarvis

« June 20, 2005 | Main
| June 22, 2005 »
June 21, 2005

Dell lies. Dell sucks

: I just got a new Dell laptop and paid a fortune for the four-year, in-home service.

The machine is a lemon and the service is a lie.

I'm having all kinds of trouble with the hardware: overheats, network doesn't work, maxes out on CPU usage. It's a lemon.

But what really irks me is that they say if they sent someone to my home -- which I paid for -- he wouldn't have the parts, so I might as well just send the machine in and lose it for 7-10 days -- plus the time going through this crap. So I have this new machine and paid for them to FUCKING FIX IT IN MY HOUSE and they don't and I lose it for two weeks.

DELL SUCKS. DELL LIES. Put that in your Google and smoke it, Dell.

LINK | Comments (253)

: HOME
: Email me
: About me

Archives:
06/05 ... 05/05 ... 04/05 ...
03/05 ... 02/05 ... 01/05 ...
12/04 ... 11/04 ... 10/04 ...
09/04 ... 08/04 ... 07/04 ...
06/04 ... 05/04 ... 04/04 ...
03/04 ... 02/04 ... 01/04 ...
12/03 ... 11/03 ... 10/03 ...
09/03 ... 08/03 ... 07/03 ...
06/03 ... 05/03 ... 04/03 ...
03/03 ... 02/03 ... 01/03 ...
12/02 ... 11/02 ... 10/02 ...
09/02 ... 08/02 ... 07/02 ...
06/02 ... 05/02 ... 04/02 ...
03/02/a ... 03/02/b ... 02/02
... 01/02 ... 12/01 ... 11/01 ...
10/01 ... 09/01 ... Current
Home

Source: *http:// members.forbes.com/ forbes/2005/1114/128.html*

It quickly became clear to business that bloggers had the potential to badly damage a company's image and reputation. In November 2005, *Fortune* magazine ran a cover story titled "Attack of the Blogs," accompanied by an illustration of a fist emerging from a PC, and socking an executive.

Certainly by 2005, the importance of paying attention to bloggers became much clearer to businesses, particularly for those who worked in public relations, brand management, and anyone else whose job was to pay attention to corporate image and reputation.

It's worth talking a little more about the relatively new discipline of reputation management. Over the past several years, corporations have taken note of how the financial health of companies suffers when their image and reputation takes a hit, evidenced by cases like Enron, WorldCom, Adelphia, and Martha Stewart Living Omnimedia, among others, and so a firm's reputation itself has evolved as a particularly valuable organizational asset to guard. As a result, some firms have even created a Chief Reputation Officer position to direct that function. The need to attend to conversations on blogs gave this reputation management function an even higher profile.

So a new problem and need was being articulated by businesses. How do we keep track of what is being said about us—and about our competitors—by bloggers on the Internet, so we can watch out for our reputation, and take action, preferably proactively but at least defensively, to repair any possible damage we see occurring. As the market abhors an unfilled need, companies emerged and began introducing solutions to fill that gap, and a new industry was formed.

The highly respected business online news vendor Factiva (created as a joint venture between Reuters and Dow Jones) introduced an "Insight for Reputation" online monitoring product that would include conversations on blogs along with its standard collection of online newspaper and journals it was already monitoring for its clients. Other firms that had offered electronic PR clipping services also began adding blogs to their source list. And some of the Internet-based "news alert" vendors also expanded or added blog coverage.

As the nascent blog-alert/monitoring industry developed and expanded, some vendors began distinguishing their news and blog-monitoring capabilities by promoting the use of special software. That software, these vendors claimed, would not only aggregate blog postings and alert its clients to relevant mentions of their topics of interest, but also inform them of the larger *meanings* of certain conversations. These vendors promised that they could tell their clients whether the emotion, tone, or "sentiment" of key discussions was positive, negative, or neutral. This sentiment detection software, which is considered a type of natural language processing (NLP) is discussed in Chapter 7.

This emerging blog-monitoring field continued to change and evolve. In January 2006, Intelliseek, which had been the largest and most prominent firm in this space, was acquired by a competitor, BuzzMetrics, a Nielsen company. Nielsen is the giant global media and information firm whose properties include ACNielsen and Nielsen Media Research. The new merged firm was given a new name: Nielsen BuzzMetrics (www.nielsenbuzzmetrics.com), and was headquartered in New York City. The move by Nielsen to incorporate blog and online media monitoring was seen as a strong confirmation by analysts that the blog-monitoring industry had come of age.

Beginning in 2006 various blog-monitoring firms promoted other ways that their software could discern even more meaning and value from bloggers' and other online consumers conversations. For instance, Umbria, a Colorado-based blog monitoring firm, received a great deal of press for its claim that its online conversation-monitoring software not only aggregates blog postings and detects positive or negative sentiments, but can even determine the demographic and market segmentation of the bloggers themselves.

Interview with
Pete Blackshaw
CEO, Buzzmetrics

FIGURE 6.2

Results of Umbria's tracking of blogs to measure Microsoft's marketing effectiveness for its Windows Mobile OS vs. competition, from January 1, 2006–July 2, 2006. Reprinted with permission.

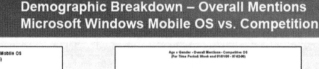

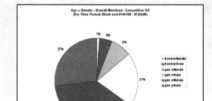

Key Findings

- Microsoft skews toward an older audience (greater representation from Generation X and Boomers) relative to the audience for Competitor OSs indicating that the young Generation Y segment has greater propensity to mention Competitor OSs.
- Microsoft also skews toward an overwhelmingly male audience (74% males versus 53% males for Competitive OS speakers).
- Generation X males make up the largest demographic audience speaking about Microsoft Windows Mobile OS (41% of speakers), compared to Generation Y females which are the largest demographic audience speaking about Competitive OSs (39% of speakers).
- Microsoft Windows Mobile OS and Competitive OS have a similar share of Generation Y males speaking about them (23% for Microsoft Windows Mobile OS versus 27% for Competitive OS).
- Judgmentally, younger, Generation Y bloggers tend more toward early adoption of new brands and products. Overall, the Microsoft and Windows brands are aging and may have greater appeal to older Generation X and Boomer segments who are most familiar with the brand.

For example, Figure 6.2 shows some excerpts of findings in a report that Umbria provided to Microsoft that used its software to create these kind of demographic breakdowns for Microsoft. Microsoft engaged Umbria to find out what bloggers were saying about its operating system.

From a market researcher's perspective, this kind of demographic segmentation capability could make blog monitoring even more valuable. But does the technology really work? To learn more, I spoke with Umbria's CEO Janet Eden-Harris, to get detailed explanations on how her software works to make these demographic determinations. She explained on the phone and later in an email note, "It's an algorithmic-based program that is trained to look for word patterns and contextual matters to identify age, gender and "tribe" [subgroup characteristics], and the software is constantly learning. We can train the software by taking, say, 100,000 posts from a blog that has meta-data, so we already know the age and gender breakdown of the group. We take a 10 percent sampling of this and run an algorithm to find the dispersions. By comparing how the software performs to what we know is already true, we can test and tweak the software."

Eden-Harris told me a little more about that "Tribe" concept, where the software is supposed to identify a group of bloggers based on a common subject (e.g., they all talk about snowboarding) and then analyze the rest of the conversations this virtual tribe of people are having. She says that the software clusters those conversations to create a richer profile of what other things many of these people have in common. They might, perhaps, talk more than most about eating organic foods, or liking heavy metal bands, or owning a dog.

Stepping back a bit, while blog-monitoring remains a new and still evolving niche discipline, firms that engage in this activity were semi-officially given the mantle of a real industry when in the fall of 2006, a leading technology analyst firm, Forrester Research, published a research report, titled *The Forrester Wave: Brand Monitoring*. That report analyzed the competitive landscape of a handful of key blog-monitoring companies together as one organized discipline. (The Forrester report focused on these companies' ability to assist its clients in monitoring news and discussion specifically on brands, but these firms' also perform blog monitoring for its clients for lots of other reasons as well.)

By mid-2007 at least a few dozen firms were offering some variation of the conversations this virtual tribe of people are having. She says that the software clusters those conversations to create a richer profile of what other things many of these people have in common. They might, perhaps, talk more than most about eating organic foods, or liking heavy metal bands, or owning a dog.

Stepping back a bit, while blog-monitoring remains a new and still evolving niche discipline, firms that engage in this activity were semi-officially given the mantle of a real industry when in the fall of 2006, a leading technology analyst firm, Forrester Research, published a research report, titled *The Forrester Wave: Brand Monitoring*. That report analyzed the competitive landscape of a handful of key blog-monitoring companies together as one organized discipline. (The Forrester report focused on these companies' ability to assist its clients in monitoring news and discussion specifically on brands, but these firms' also perform blog monitoring for its clients for lots of other reasons as well.)

By mid-2007 at least a few dozen firms were offering some variation of news alerts, pr clipping, and blog-monitoring services. A listing and short description of the most prominent of these firms is included later in this chapter.

Comparing Blog Monitoring Vendors

Although each has its own approach, methodology, and algorithm, all the blog monitoring vendors do generally follow the same approach:

1. **Collection of Data**

   The vendor employs a crawler to go out onto the Internet to find and index blog postings and any other social and traditional media sites it collects and monitors.

2. **Processing and Filtering**

   The vendors' PCs are used to aggregate, sort, filter, and analyze all the collected text. This step would also include the elimination of duplicate data, and the classifying, and "tagging" of the collected data with words and/or into categories so the client can retrieve it more efficiently.

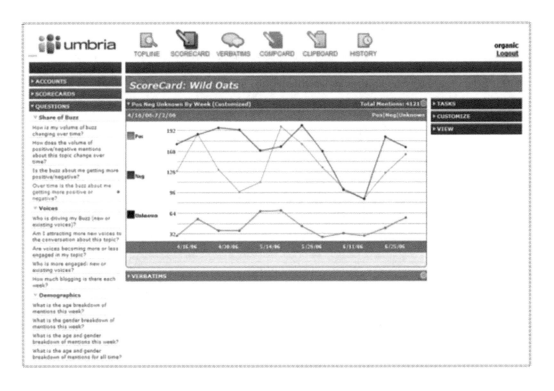

4. Analyzing Data

Here the aggregated data is further sorted in a manner to assist the client. If the vendor uses a natural language processing program to detect sentiment and analyze meanings from the text, that analysis would be applied as well.

5. Communicating Results

Finally the aggregated and analyzed information needs to be communicated in some manner to the client. Typically this means some type of viewable dashboard, as well as reports, usually in the form of a document, with lots of charts and graphs. Sometimes the data is communicated via alerting methods too such as email or RSS.

Another way that blog-monitoring vendors are alike is that they are all quite expensive. Typically a year's subscription might start in the low five digits but can easily be six digits+ for the more robust and customized systems.

However there are also some significant differences among the vendors.

FIGURE 6.3

Blog-monitoring firms typically present findings in charts and graphs. Reprinted with permission.

Among the most important ways in which the firms differ are:

1. Types of sources tracked or monitored

2. Level of customization possible by client

3. Ability of client to create advanced keyword searches

4. Ability to surface patterns not related to the client's keywords

5. Use of sentiment detection technology

6. Ability to identify demographic and other consumer segments

7. Training and technical support

8. Extent of customer service

9. Features on dashboard

10. Types of reports generated and customizability of reports

11. Final cost

What You Get When You Work with a Blog Monitoring Vendor

If you decide to subscribe to a blog-monitoring firm's offerings, the process and deliverables will of course vary based on the particular vendor, the product set you choose, and your own needs. But to get a sense of how the process could typically work, Umbria's Janet Eden-Harris explained what one of her "typical" clients might encounter when approaching her firm.

She said that a typical client might come from the product management part of the organization. It's in that function, she says, where there is a need to manage the existing product line, come up with ideas for new ones, and determine promotion and pricing. This division also usually has a sales force to train and the P&L revenue responsibility for the products, as well.

Eden-Harris says that her firm approaches a client engagement more like a research brief than a consultative engagement. Umbria, she says, meets with a prospective client to identify their needs and what they're trying to understand about their consumers. She said Umbria then uses its technology to find relevant conversations, analyze those conversations for sentiment, age, gender, new voices, theme clustering, and so forth and provide the data to the client in the form of a presentation and report that details the findings based on conversations over a three-month period.

That report typically contains implications and possibly recommendations for action for major findings. She says Umbria works with most clients on a subscription basis, so findings are updated every three months or more often for clients with a more urgent issue they're following, and can track results quarter over quarter. Umbria can also overlay key triggering events such as marketing campaigns and PR issues that may spike conversations in the blogosphere.

For a deliverable, Umbria's client obtains a survey that includes about three months of collected and sorted data. That data is typically broken down by a weekly basis, and trend data is displayed across the timeframe. Among the elements included in the survey are the number of voices speaking, new voices being added, with additional information on whether the new voices represent a new theme or just the same people talking over time.

She says that the firm will also make recommendations on new product ideas, and how the client might approach its competitive position. For instance, she said that Hallmark, one of its clients, did not realize that GenY female clients used its product as much as they do and that a segment of their younger female customers were cynical about commercial holidays—Valentine's Day in particular. This led the firm to consider developing a new line of more sarcastic online greeting cards.

Another client, Wild Oats (see Figure 6.3) was interested in Umbria's findings that the GenY segment was passionate about buying organic products, and that they were much less price sensitive than their baby boomer counterparts. In addition, Umbria determined that GenY bought organics because they believed the products were higher quality and were good for the environment whereas GenX bought them because they wanted to do the right thing for their families. And baby boomers—who were also active bloggers about organics—bought them for the health benefits. Umbria also found that people loved going into the stores because of the free food samples.

Choosing a Vendor

There are significant differences among the blog and media monitoring firms, so to make a smart choice in selecting a blog-monitoring vendor, try to get answers to as many of these questions as you can, or at least use these as a guide in distinguishing the content and features between the vendors.

Sources

Questions about the product

Q What kinds of sources do you monitor? For example, in addition to blogs do you also monitor:

- Online discussion groups? Which ones: newsgroups, Web forums, social networking sites, other?

- Consumer complaint forums?

- Corporate sites that include discussions?

- Podcasts?

- Video sharing sites?

- Mainstream media sources online (e.g., nytimes, wsjonline, business journals etc)

- Other?

Q For each of the sources you do monitor, do you try to be comprehensive and track all discussions, or is your approach selective, where you take just a sample? If selective, what percentage do you track? How do you determine which ones to sample?

Q If you track multimedia sources like podcasts and video sites, what sources do you use? How do you index the substance of the audio and video content? Do you index the tags and commentary around the media?

Q Are you able to track conversations in languages other than English? Which ones? Do you provide the information you've collected in the native language or are there translation options?

Q How timely is your product: what is the lag time between when a discussion is posted and its availability to me? Is there a way that I can be alerted to important postings instantly?

Q How do you get rid of spam and duplicate entries?

Q Do you try to identify the most "influential" posters and bloggers? If so, how? And how do you define "influential"?

Q What other special features do you offer to help me make sense of the blogosphere? For example, do you locate new voices on a topic? How quickly a conversation is spreading to others online?

Q Does your system require training? If so, do you provide it? Is the cost included?

Q How much personal assistance will you provide our organization in creating our keywords and search terms for our profile?

Q Do your reports include sentiment/tone analysis?

- If so, explain how it works

- What level of accuracy do you claim?

- How much human input and review is provided to check and review the software

Q Do you offer any kind of demographic analysis of the bloggers and speakers you've tracked?

Q What exactly *is* the deliverable? What format is it in? How often is it updated? How customizable is what I will get? What is the level of detail that I can drill down to?

Q What kind of human customer service do you offer? How is it accessed? What days and hours is a live person available?

Questions about the company and its offerings

Q What are the qualifications and backgrounds of your analysts? What are their backgrounds in marketing or market research?

Q Does your firm focus on particular industries or vertical markets?

Q Can I view a sample report?

Q Do you offer a free trial?

Q Do you have the names of any clients I can speak with as references?

Q What is the estimated cost for my organization?

Q Do you offer any satisfaction guarantees?

Vendor Directory

As of late 2007, the following firms and their offerings were considered the

- **BrandPulse:** A customized client dashboard
- **BrandPulse Self-Service:** Light, self-service version of the BrandPulse dashboard
- **BrandPulse Insight:** Analyst reports focused on specific issues, key insights, trends, and early-warning

Nielsen's clients include several Fortune 1000 firms, including Canon, Ford Motor Company, General Motors, HBO, Kraft, Microsoft, Nokia, Procter & Gamble, Sony, Target, and Toyota.

Biz360: Market360

Biz360 was traditionally focused on providing electronic press clipping services. As part of its offering it integrates what it calls a "media signal" feature that measures the *reach* of a particular firm's message. It also promotes a proprietary form of sentiment detection that the firm calls "Point-of-View Sentiment Technology," a natural language processing (NLP) software that the firm claims learns its client's rating preferences for positive, negative ,and neutral content and automatically applies sentiment ratings across millions of articles.

Converseon: Conversation Miner

Launched in 2001, Converseon was created as a communications agency to leverage the new media and technology to help businesses understand consumer conversation on the Internet. In addition to monitoring the media, the firm provides new media strategies and search marketing advice to its customers. Its clients include Dow, Hitachi, PayPal, and Coldwell Banker.

Factiva: Factiva Insight Reputation Intelligence

Factiva was founded in 1999 as a joint venture between Dow Jones & Company and the Reuters Group, and was fully acquired by Dow Jones in December 2006. Factiva's strength is its ability to integrate its massive database of authoritative business news sources, along with blogs, to surface both news and conversations for its clients.

FAST: MarkeTrac

FAST or Fast Search & Transfer is a developer of enterprise search and real-time alerting technologies. Its product, MarkeTrac, gathers and processes content from the web, documents, syndicated news feeds, third party research, blogs, audio, video, RSS feeds, databases, and enterprise applications. FAST MarkeTrac applies sentiment analysis for its clients.

Monitor 110

Launched in 2007 with a lot of hype and some acclaim from the industry press, Monitor 110's tracking services is geared specifically for stock traders, hedge fund traders, and the institutional investor community. Its potential for providing the same kind of tracking functions for other business vertical markets has been discussed.

MotiveQuest: InstantBuzz; BuzzSurvey; MotiveTrak

MotiveQuest focuses specifically on analyzing online conversations, and it puts a lot of emphasis on certain vertical markets: automobiles, computers, electronics, cellular, health, and entertainment. It also stresses its strategic consulting. The *Forrester Wave Report* cited MotiveQuest's technology platform as one of its particular strengths. The firm offers three levels of online conversation tracking: InstantBuzz covers the shortest timeframe; BuzzSurvey is for conversations over a longer period; and MotiveTrak provides ongoing reports. The founder of MotiveQuest, David Rabjohns, stresses his decades of work in marketing at firms like IBM, Pepsico, Saatchi & Saatchi, and Leo Burnett.

TNS/MICymfony: Orchestra

TNS Media Intelligence, which acquired the news and blog-monitoring firm Cymfony in February 2007, provides strategic advertising information. Cymfony had been around since 1996 and was an early provider of conversation tracking services, with clients that included U.S. intelligence agencies. The firm's current clients include Accenture, JiffyLube, and VeriSign.

Umbria: Product Tracker, Brand Tracker, Trend Tracker, Marketing Tracker, Umbria Connect

Umbria's claim to fame is its ability to perform the demographic segmentation, discussed above, as well as its special focus and expertise on monitoring blogs specifically for market research purposes. The firm also likes to point decades of work in marketing at firms like IBM, Pepsico, Saatchi & Saatchi, and Leo Burnett.

TNS/MICymfony: Orchestra

TNS Media Intelligence, which acquired the news and blog-monitoring firm Cymfony in February 2007, provides strategic advertising information. Cymfony had been around since 1996 and was an early provider of conversation tracking services, with clients that included U.S. intelligence agencies. The firm's current clients include Accenture, JiffyLube, and VeriSign.

Umbria: Product Tracker, Brand Tracker, Trend Tracker, Marketing Tracker, Umbria Connect

Umbria's claim to fame is its ability to perform the demographic segmentation, discussed above, as well as its special focus and expertise on monitoring blogs specifically for market research purposes. The firm also likes to point out its strengths in spam filtering, voice analysis, the ability to analyze what topics are most important to consumers and most frequently discussed, and its sentiment detection. Umbria's Tribe Analysis tool is promoted as a way that clients can surface common interests and opinions of bloggers and others who participate in online conversations that share a demographic profile or have other commonalties.

PR Newswire uses Umbria's technology for the blog tracking service it markets to its own clients, called MediaSense Blog Measurement. That service measures blog conversation around press releases.

CHAPTER 7

Sentiment Detection: How Accurate?

THE TERMS that vendors use most often to describe the capability to detect whether a particular online conversation is primarily positive or negative is "sentiment," as in, "sentiment analysis" "sentiment detection" and "sentiment mining." What those terms refer to is a type of natural language processing software that the vendors employ that is supposed to be able to analyze the specific words from a particular piece of text, and detect whether the author's discussion overall can be said as having a positive, negative, or neutral tone.

Let's learn a bit about what's behind sentiment detection: how it works, and some of the real challenges faced by the technology and users of the technology.

As discussed in the previous chapter, many of the large vendors that offer a blog-monitoring solution are promising that they can not only inform you what bloggers and others are saying online, but that their software can even tell you whether particular discussions can be categorized as positive or negative.

A Form of AI

Sentiment detection falls under a category of artificial intelligence (AI) called natural language processing (NLP). While specific applications of NLP vary, the primary goal of NLP software is to determine and understand not just what people say or write, but what they actually mean. Users of natural language processing search engines, for example, are supposed to be able to enter their search query in ordinary language (e.g., "Is it too hot in July to travel to Mexico City?"), rather than in a typical search engine query with key words (e.g., July "Mexico city" travel hot).

On the simplest level, sentiment detection software is supposed to be able to determine that a blogger who wrote, "I love my Blackjack PDA" is expressing a *positive* statement; and another that posts, "I'm sick and tired of getting credit card solicitations from Chase Bank" is a *negative* sentiment.

The reality, of course, is that interpreting sentiment in language is rarely that easy. Whereas some words and phrases can be neatly categorized as positive or negative, language use is of course often ambiguous, and meanings will differ greatly based on context. NLP software is notorious for getting tripped up with language that employs sarcasm, irony, the use of more than one negative in a sentence, and other tricky sentence structures.

There are other concerns with sentiment detection technology. Marketing consultant Andy Beal, of Marketing Pilgrim, which specializes in online marketing and advertising, pointed out to me that even if sentiment detection software proves to be accurate in analyzing a particular discussion, it could still be misleading for the larger context. As an example he says that the software may accurately capture and report a positive tone in a complimentary discussion about a particular company, but if the comments that follow that discussion are all negative, it really changes the sentiment of that particular post, and this can easily be missed by the software. Or, if a company had a problem but fixed it, people may say something positive about the firm, which can also be confusing for an automated system to correctly assign a sentiment. Any time there is text that contains a mixture of words with both positive and negative connotations, a sentiment detection program can easily be thrown off.

And NLP can be subject to lots of errors even when applied to text from a straightforward source of information like newspapers, press releases, wire service stories, and other standard documents. Blogs and social media sites pose an even more difficult challenge. That's because discussions found on social media sites are so loose and filled with bad grammar, abbreviations, slang, and other non-standard language.

How Sentiment Analysis is Employed

In a simple application of sentiment detection for monitoring blogs, a vendor might employ it to scour blog postings and other defined conversations on the Internet to search for specific words that have been predetermined to have positive or negative sentiment, (e.g., *sucks* = negative sentiment; *rocks* = positive statement). The software would also look at the frequency and placement of those words or phrases, and then analyze the overall tone of the text to help clients figure out if the comments should be categorized as positive, negative, or neutral.

The blog-monitoring vendors themselves do a pretty good job in describing what sentiment detection is. For example, on its web page, Nielsen Buzz-Metrics provides a good example of the particular words and phrases that its sentiment detection software identifies for assigning sentiment, as shown in Figure 7.1.

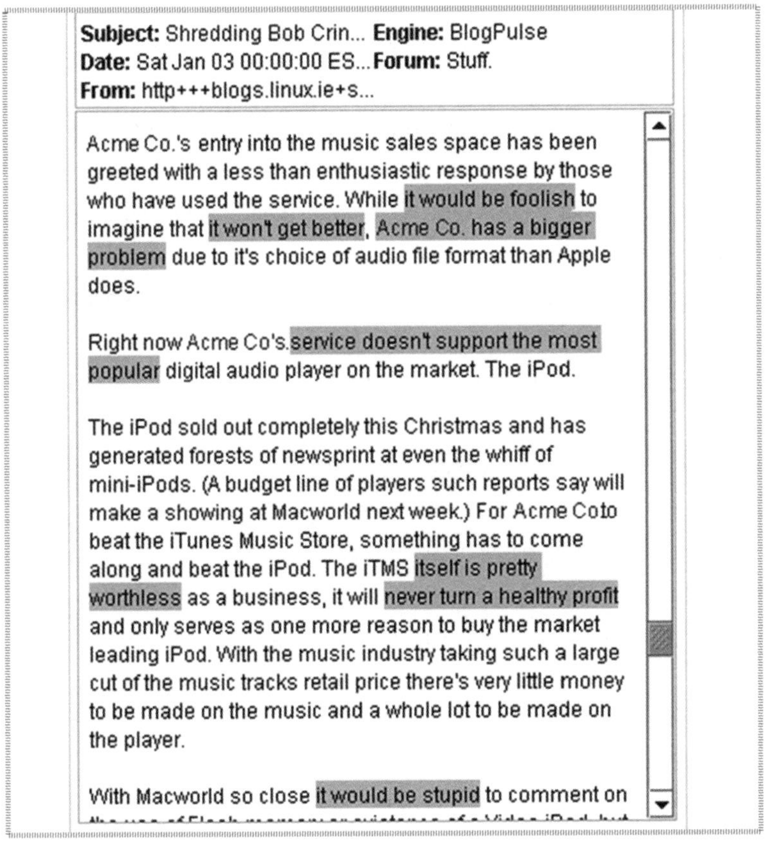

Subject: Shredding Bob Crin... **Engine:** BlogPulse
Date: Sat Jan 03 00:00:00 ES... **Forum:** Stuff.
From: http+++blogs.linux.ie+s...

Acme Co.'s entry into the music sales space has been greeted with a less than enthusiastic response by those who have used the service. While it would be foolish to imagine that it won't get better, Acme Co. has a bigger problem due to it's choice of audio file format than Apple does.

Right now Acme Co's.service doesn't support the most popular digital audio player on the market. The iPod.

The iPod sold out completely this Christmas and has generated forests of newsprint at even the whiff of mini-iPods. (A budget line of players such reports say will make a showing at Macworld next week.) For Acme Co to beat the iTunes Music Store, something has to come along and beat the iPod. The iTMS itself is pretty worthless as a business, it will never turn a healthy profit and only serves as one more reason to buy the market leading iPod. With the music industry taking such a large cut of the music tracks retail price there's very little money to be made on the music and a whole lot to be made on the player.

With Macworld so close it would be stupid to comment on

FIGURE 7.1

An example from BuzzMetrics identifying words that convey sentiment.

At first glance sentiment detection might seems fairly straightforward—just find the words in a piece of text that are positive or negative, and then aggregate and count them up to make some kind of quantitative assessment of the author's feeling about the subject. However, it's rare—particularly in the blogosphere—that figuring out the meaning behind what someone is saying is going to be so simple.

The blog-monitoring vendors claim that their sentiment detection technology is accurate, and you'll hear claims of accuracy that typically are in the 70 to 80 percent range, which actually isn't that bad. Ted Kremer, the chief technology officer at Umbria explained to me that even among humans, people don't always agree on the sentiment of a particular word or phrase.

Based on Umbria's own research, he says that agreement in a group can be as low as 66 percent, particularly if there is any specialized jargon or if words were used in a non-typical manner.

There are many who are skeptical of the entire concept of automated sentiment detection. David Sifrey, the founder and CEO of Technorati told me that the whole technology is "black magic, hocus pocus and snake oil." A softer but still real criticism comes from PR firm Edelman's popular blogger Steve Rubel, who says that sentiment "is still a guess for almost everyone—even Google doesn't do this."

It's important to keep in mind that NLP is a young and still developing science. Commercial applications of NLP have only recently become widely available for more popular uses, and research to develop and improve NLP capabilities is still actively underway at university research laboratories around the country and around the globe.

To find out more about NLP and its capabilities and limitations, I spoke with Lillian Lee, an associate professor at Cornell University's department of computer science in Ithaca, New York, and a well-known expert researcher in the NLP field. In an email message, Lee provided an example of how the context of a particular discussion is so important in how NLP interprets the sentiment behind a phrase. Here is the example she sent to me:

Lee's example is derived from a 2002 paper she wrote with a former grad student, Bo Pang, who later worked for Yahoo! Research.

Here are three sentences:

- This laptop is a great deal.
- A great deal of media attention surrounded the release of the new laptop model.
- If you think this laptop is a great deal, I've got a nice bridge you might be interested in.

Lee contrasted the sentences words and meanings like this:

"All three sentences contain the same phrase 'a great deal,' but the opinions expressed are, respectively, positive, neutral, and negative. The first two sentences use the same phrase to mean different things. The last sentence involves sarcasm, which, along with related rhetorical devices, is an intrinsic feature of texts from unrestricted domains such as blogs and newsgroup postings— 'language in the wild,' if you will. It's not the case that just looking for 'obvious sentiment indicators' can always allow for correct classification."

Lee gave me another example of how certain texts can poses problems for NLP.

"This film should be brilliant. It sounds like a great plot, the actors are first grade and the supporting cast is good as well, and Stallone is attempting to deliver a good performance. However, it can't hold up."

She described the problem for NLP software algorithms like this:

"Notice that there are many positive words in this passage. So, simply counting up the number of positive vs. negative words, as many sentiment-analysis algorithms do, would lead to the conclusion that the passage is positive overall, which is exactly wrong. What this example illustrates is that to really 'do sentiment right,' one needs to engage in rather sophisticated language analysis, and indeed come up with algorithms that can understand the 'flow of argument' in a passage, message, or document."•

Another Approach

Assigning sentiment to specific words or phrases is not the only way that NLP software can detect the emotional tone of a text or conversation.

Another approach is to rely on machine learning. With this approach, computers are fed a body of related text (called a "corpus") where selected words and phrases and jargon have been called out and tagged by humans who identify the meaning and sentiment of those words and phrases that are specific to the particular subject domain of the text. In general, machine learning works best when the text is derived from a *limited* domain or subject area; this makes it easier to understand which words and phrases have a specific meaning or sentiment within a very specific context. For example, if you had a body of text that was all about real estate markets, the software could be taught to make a negative connotation to text that contains the words "bubble" or "cooling" and a positive one when encountering the word "appreciating."

The bottom line? While sentiment detection can and does work under the right circumstances, it can also be easily thrown off and make inaccurate assessments. Clearly, we're still quite a long way off from having computer technology that has the ability to detect human emotion as imagined back in 1968 by the creators of *2001* where the cybernetic crew member HAL could not only communicate by speaking, but detect emotional stress from its onboard human companions.

Sentiment Detection is Still Useful

Despite its real flaws, most analysts acknowledge that sentiment detection technology, when used appropriately, understood, and kept in the proper context, can still provide useful information. The hard part is that as a user, it's not really transparent nor obvious as to how the technology works, or whether or not a particular report you receive is likely to be accurate. One businessperson I spoke with who used Umbria's sentiment detection technology to gauge the needs of telecommunication users in the U.S. for a potential product expansion told me, "It's hard to tell if the technologies are very accurate . . . my understanding is that they [Umbria] have developed something that works." The primary benefit, he said, has been to "validate our own intuition."

And that's fine of course, but it is something of a problem for the blog-monitoring firms—how can they prove the credibility of sentiment detection and language analyses? Because blog monitoring and sentiment detection is a young and emerging business, the vendors in this arena are working hard to position themselves and distinguish their offerings from their competitors by pointing to some differentiating feature or claimed superior technology.

A FREE QUICK-AND-DIRTY SENTIMENT ANALYSIS SITE

Would you like to get a quick feel for how sentiment detection software works? You can do this by linking to the site OpinMind. Just enter a word or phrase (or click on "advanced search" for more options) and you can get a quick look at how OpinMind's software analyzes the sentiment of bloggers on whatever term you entered.

This site, which seems to draw primarily from MySpace blogs, provides a good example of both the promise and the perils of basic sentiment detection software. The image below illustrates how it works when it is working well. The search was on the word: Ikea. You can see how employing the words "love" and "fantastic" resulted in a blogger's discussion about Ikea being categorized as positive; and the words "boring," "hate," and "sucks" resulted in a negative sentiment.

But we also found several areas where the software was tripped up. For instance, we did other searches, on the word, hillary, and another on verizon. In the hillary search, the statement "comparing hillary clinton to an evil movie character is wrong and stupid" was characterized as negative; and on the verizon search, a blogger that wrote "i like verizon's people, coverage, and data speed but I cannot abide by these changes" was characterized as positive.

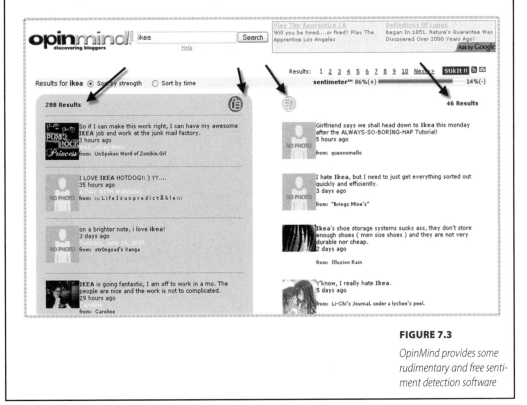

FIGURE 7.3

OpinMind provides some rudimentary and free sentiment detection software

QUESTIONS TO ASK ABOUT SENTIMENT DETECTION

When it comes to trusting that a piece of software will truly be accurate in assessing bloggers' sentiment, you're pretty much in the dark. After all, when a vendor informs you via a nice, neat chart that it has deemed one conversation positive and another negative, how do you know what those analyses were really based on or derived from? Asking the following questions to a vendor ahead of time can provide you with the key information you need to be a more informed user of this still emerging technology:

- What kinds of sites does your sentiment detection software work on—media sites, blogs, newsgroups, other?

- Can you explain the method your software uses to detect sentiment, i.e., a simple counting of words, language parsing, machine learning, or a combination of these?

  ▶**TIP** Ask for a detailed explanation. Look for vendors that combine multiple approaches.

- Is your NLP software proprietary or from a third-party vendor?

  ▶**TIP** If from a third party, do some research to find out more about that vendor and its software.

- How long has your software been out of beta? How many actual clients do you have? Do you have any references I can speak with?

- What level of accuracy do you claim for your sentiment detection? What is that number based on?

  ▶**TIP** Ask for copies of documents or studies to back up the vendor's claims.

- Can you provide your technology's accuracy scores at various levels of recall?

  ▶**TIP** Accuracy declines as recall increases—find out what level of recall is associated with a vendor's accuracy claims.

- Do you rate sentiment based on an individual entity level, the full document level, or both?

- Do you rely on any human input or review in your process?

  ▶ **TIP** The more that humans are involved in the process, the more likely you are to get accurate results.

- Can you provide some sample client reports to illustrate how the sentiment detection process works?

Future Trends and the Big Picture

Natural language processing is a young field and the technology has a long way to go before it can be relied upon more consistently as an automated method for understanding the meaning of human speech. One area that is particularly challenging, and where a great deal of effort is underway, is in trying to create software that can get a sense of the larger meaning of conversations in audio podcasts and in videos. So far, the main approach has been to rely on the tags created by users to describe their content. But Kremer, the chief technology officer at Umbria, told me that tags are often misleading and not always helpful. He says that it is more fruitful to try to locate the conversations that are occurring *around* a podcast or video, and analyze these to better surface the content and meaning of the podcast or video.

And in any discussion of the future of automated language analysis technologies, there is a word that looms large and strikes no small amount of fear into the hearts of the current crop of blog sentiment detection vendors. The word, or company to be more precise, is Google. While there's no direct evidence that Google has plans to enter the sentiment analysis arena, industry observers believe Google could do so easily, if and when it wanted to. With its resources, brainpower, market reach, and computing power, it would be perfectly positioned to make an explosive impact. Oh, and if Google wanted to introduce its service for free, and support the whole endeavor via contextual ads, well it could do that too.

CHAPTER 8

Alternative Blog-Monitoring Solutions

THE VENDORS mentioned in the previous two chapters can be grouped together loosely as part of the emerging blog/social media monitoring industry. But there are also a couple of other approaches that certain vendors are taking that offer a different method for making sense of online consumer chatter. One of these approaches is to try to identify the most *influential* blog conversations; and another offers a "private label" solution to *facilitating* online consumer conversation. This chapter takes a look at both of these alternative approaches.

Influence Surfacers

A firm called BuzzLogic has a variation on the theme of using sentiment detection technology as a key way to make sense and find the most significant blog conversations. BuzzLogic, founded in 2004 by Jeffrey Glover and Mitch Ratcliffe, takes the approach that measuring sentiment is too hard to perform reliably and therefore presents trust problems for the client.

However, the principals of this firm believe that calculating a particular blog's "influence" is a more doable proposition. So it has put its efforts toward creating software that can identify and surface which bloggers—and individual blog posts—are the most influential ones occurring around a specified online conversation. BuzzLogic also created its service as a more affordable alternative to the high price tags of firms like BuzzMetrics and Umbria where subscription fees can easily run to six digits. BuzzLogic, in contrast, is priced in the mid four digits per year, making it more easily justified for the medium- or even the smal-sized firm, non-profit, or other institution that does not have a huge marketing or PR budget.

The way BuzzLogic works is that it sends out a spider to crawl and index words on about 100 million pages on the web that were pre-determined as most likely to be fruitful as a source of online conversations. That includes blogs as well as open forums and specified corporate sites where there is a level of interactivity and conversation. BuzzLogic also indexes online main-stream media sources (e.g., *The New York Times* online, *WSJ Online*, trade jour-nals online, and so forth). The firm created an algorithm to locate the most influential sources within a particular conversation.

The $64,000 question, of course, is what constitutes "influential"? We all think we know what the word means and who we think counts as hav-ing influence in our lives and in our industry, but how do you reduce that pretty soft concept into a precise algorithmic criteria, find examples, and then quantify it?

I discussed this issue of defining and measuring influence, particularly in contrast to terms like "authority" and "popularity" at some length earlier in this book, but here let's look more at BuzzLogic's approach.

According to a company spokesperson, BuzzLogic's definition of influence is that an "influencer" is "a post or publisher generating a significant volume of *relevant* inbound links and comments about a particular topic or conversa-tion, within a specific timeframe." For BuzzLogic, then, influence relates not just to the number of incoming links to a source or blog, (which might be

FIGURE 8.1

A search on "Barak Obama" surfaces the most influential blog conversations around that person, as defined by BuzzLogic.

defined as only a measure of popularity) but to *relevant* incoming links.

So that raises the question: what defines "relevant"? According to the firm, relevance is determined by examining several factors around a particular online conversation: who is talking/who is listening; who refers to whom; who connects to whom; the popularity of a site; and the frequency of postings. On its site, BuzzLogic states that it determines influence this way:

> BuzzLogic's algorithms take more than a dozen factors into consideration when determining influence. A key piece is the ability to determine both the influence of the people discussing a certain topic, and the composition of the audience linking in to (or "listening") to that conversation. This means both the relevance and overall popularity of an individual post, along with the relevance and popularity of all in-linking posts, are dynamically measured. . . . The algorithms also factor in time, to demonstrate growing or diminishing credibility.

As discussed earlier in the book, taking into account the relevance and context of who is doing the linking to a blog, rather than just counting the total number of links, does help get around the problem that a blog will be surfaced as authoritative simply because so many other sites and blogs link to it, regardless of what those sites and blog are about. So in theory, BuzzLogic's approach makes good sense.

The proof, of course, is in the testing of the product, and I did get a chance to spend time trying a Beta version out myself in a review for my monthly journal, *The Information Advisor.* My personal impression was that while BuzzLogic is an intuitive, clear, and well designed product, I was not fully convinced that its algorithm consistently retrieved the influential bloggers around the topics that I tested the service on. Key bloggers that I knew of in certain fields were often not uncovered at all. Perhaps BuzzLogic would prove to be more reliable for other types of topics and searches, but perhaps not. It was hard to tell.

And therein is the problem. It's the same kind of problem I believe exists with sentiment analysis software: when we take a soft, messy and analog human experience—emotion or influence—and try to use a software program to reduce that subtle, sometimes subconscious determination into bits, something is inevitably going to be missed and lost in the translation, but it will be hard to detect when and how.

Note that BuzzLogic is not the only vendor that tries to help clients iden-tify influential bloggers and blog posts. Onalytica is a U.K.–based firm that takes a similar approach by working privately with clients using its own algo-rithm to help them find influential bloggers on specified topics.

Private Label Solutions

Another approach that's been taken by a couple of other firms is to create a *customized* community of selected consumers, where they converse online, but that discussion is walled off from the rest of the Internet and available only to clients. Two of the major vendors of these private label solutions are: Hosted Online Communities by Communispace and Hosted Conversations, which is a joint venture between PR firm Edelman and RSS feed aggregator NewsGator.

Hosted Online Communities is designed to help clients obtain relevant consumer conversations on the Internet, but unlike the solutions from the blog-monitoring firms, these online conversations don't take place on blogs, newsgroups, discussion boards or other public web spaces, but in a special walled off "online community." That community is expressly custom created by the vendor for each client, and the participants in that community are recruited and invited to participate by the vendor.

One of the leaders in this field is a firm called Communispace, of Water-town, Massachusetts, headed by CEO Diane Hessan. Hessan explained to me how her firm sets up these online spaces, and why she believes they can be a more valuable alternative to listening to conversations on the open web.

Hessan says that the first step in her firm's process is to spend a signifi-cant amount of time with the client to discover precisely the kind of person the client is trying to appeal to, and needs to hear from. For instance, a manufacturer of tennis equipment that wants to introduce a new racquet for women just starting the sport might tell Communispace that it wants the firm to locate females in a certain age group that recently joined a tennis club, and have only started playing the sport in the last year. Or perhaps an organic supermarket chain thinking of creating a new store concept might ask Communispace to locate target consumers who are primary grocery shoppers and who care about health and wellness.

Once Communispace knows what kind of person its client wants to reach, it relies on its "member recruiting" experts to know just how and where to find prospective community members, as well as what kind of incentive they need. Here's how she describes the process: "We will work with the client on a detailed spec, and then members are typically recruited online. They receive an authentic email that lays out the excitement and benefits associated with being part of the community, and they fill out a screener if they are interested. In a typical situation, our goal is to find about 400 people that meet the specs. Sometimes we want a mix: perhaps the client wants one-third people who are passionate about their brand, others who don't care, and some in the middle. If the client gets very specific we'll recruit to that spec—we have expert recruiters."

Hessan says that sometimes clients want to pilot a community for six months, but that most continue for a much longer period.

What do the participants actually do in their online community? Pretty much whatever Communispace's client asks them to do. For example, the client may give "assignments" to the group (e.g., this week go to the produce section of your favorite organic supermarket, then come back and talk to the group about your impressions of the quality of the fruits and vegetables); or the client may have the members keep a diary of their assigned activities. Communispace's customers can engage the group too. For instance, the client may ask the members direct questions to stimulate a discussion about a particular topic or ask the members to fill out a survey or download relevant videos, or mystery shop. Or the client can brainstorm product ideas or possible new features with the group, or just hang back a bit and listen in to the discussions taking place. The list of innovative ways to use a community is a long one, Hessan says, and that often the most valuable insights come from conversations generated by the members, rather than those on the client's mind.

Communispace usually assists in moderation of the group, and provide guidance to the client on what conversations seem to be significant and worth paying attention to. Hessan says, "We may analyze the conversation and say 'you know there is a lot of energy around this issue of X' and we suggest you dig around this more deeply."

And what do the participants get out of this? Surprisingly, not all that much! Hessan said that typically the compensation consists of a $10 online gift certificate or a few free product samples from the client. Although some participants do drop out over time, a significant number of participants continue to contribute regularly over a long period of time.

Given the low level of compensation, you might wonder why there is such an active level of participation. At least, I did.

Apparently there are a few reasons. One is that people just want to feel they can be of help if they've been asked to do so. But even more important, I think, is that so many people just want to have a voice, or at least feel that they do. A lot of people, it appears, are dying to be heard, and being invited to an online community gives those people an opportunity to voice opinions and are at least pretty well assured that *someone* is listening and paying very close attention.

So what are the pros and cons of tapping into a more controlled conversation like this vs. listening to blog and online discussions on the open Internet? Hessan says that a big advantages to her approach is that with a privately hosted online community, the client knows exactly who is saying what. You not only have precise and verified demographic and lifestyle information about each participant, but there's also no question or worry that someone is not who they say they are, as can and does happen on the open Internet. Furthermore, the client has received permission to use the conversation for its own purposes and with a private group, the client has an opportunity to get feedback on more confidential issues that they might not be ready to share with the general public. Lastly, the benefit of a smaller group is often that the members feel special, and thus are much more likely to participate openly.

The other big difference is that in a private online community, the client is not only listening, but just as with conducting a traditional focus group, the client has much more control in engaging and leading the conversation, getting a back and forth momentum, and building a dialogue. Another subtle but potentially valuable advantage is that this approach provides a direct path between the customer's expressed feedback and experiences back into the company.

So what's the downside? Well first of all it's not inexpensive. Hessan says that to set up the whole operation, a client will pay about $200,000 per year. Another potential downside to consider is whether creating a pre-configured community like this means that you're also creating a manufactured conversation and experience. For better or worse, discussion that takes place on blogs and the open Net are unsolicited, authentic, free flowing and bubble up from the genuine desires, passions, and interests of those that populate the Internet. Some of this real passion could be lost when trying to recreate and stimulate the growth of conversation in an online "lab."

Another private label solution, called Hosted Conversations, is a joint venture between the giant PR firm Edelman, which has become active in the consumer-generated media space, and NewsGator, a leading provider of RSS feeds. Hosted Conversations is what the firms term "brand sponsored topic-based communities" and is available only as a service to Edelman's own clients.

For Hosted Conversations, Edelman creates a customized "informational" website on whatever industry or topic is of interest to its client. It does this by pulling in selected RSS feeds from bloggers, news sites, videos, etc. from the open web. (NewsGator provides the backend technology to get the feeds.)

Once the site is created, Edelman promotes it to attract and bring in a community of users, and then creates discussion forums where the participants can converse on the topic covered by the site. The client firm can then place ads on the site and listen or participate in the online discussions. Because those conversations are on topics of interest to the client, they could provide market insights valuable for the client in planning new products, features, customer service, detecting trends and so forth.

Note that this service is only available to Edelman's existing clients, so it is of some limited value to the wider business community. I also think the concept raises some practical and even ethical concerns. One issue is the appropriateness of scraping bloggers' and other consumers' messages and content as a way to have them unknowingly earn money for private clients. Another is the legitimacy of creating an advertising site but calling it informational; and again, in a sense, forcing bloggers unwittingly to become a form of advertising.

I think that if you want to attract consumer conversations on your industry and market on your own like this, you can do so much more simply and upfront just by starting your own blog. There you can post your own, relevant thoughts and analyses, and start some interesting authentic conversations and share your ideas with your blog's visitors. If your blog is good with compelling content, you'll get an audience, get linked to by others, and as a result you'll learn what's on your customers minds and their feelings, without the rigmarole or the somewhat furtive Hosted Solutions approach.

Finally, while outside the scope of this book's focus on research and listening, it's worth noting that some firms are going beyond listening to consumers online and are engaging in a more interactive process with consumers that's sometimes called "co-creating." Co-creating is both a business philosophy and business strategy and means not only listening to online customers, but working together, in a kind of partnership to brainstorm, design, and create products together. Those co-creation activities could range from soliciting ideas for advertising campaigns to designing new features for a current product to brainstorming and testing out ideas and approaches for a complete new product launch.

FIGURE 8.2

Lego is an example of one firm that's engaging its customers—here, kids—in "co-creation" activities online

Several firms are actively engaged in co-creation activities. There are even websites that are expressly set up for co-creation activities. Figure 8.2, for instance, is Lego's "Mindstorms" site, which works with kids to help the firm design and construct toy robots for the company.

To learn more about co-creation, I recommend reading customer satis-faction guru Patricia Seybold's book on the topic: *Outside Innovation: How Your Customers Will Co-Design Your Company's Future* (Collins, 2006) as well as C.K. Prahalad and Venkat Ramaswamy's *The Future of Competition: Co-Creating Unique Value with Customers* (Harvard Business School Press, 2004)

PART 3

DO-IT-YOURSELF TOOLS AND TECHNIQUES

As information volume increases, our ability to find any particular item decreases. How will we Google our way through a trillion objects in motion? We're staring down the barrel of the biggest vocabulary control challenge imaginable, and we can't stop adding powder.

—Peter Morville, *Ambient Findability*

A good case could be made for the benefits of doing strategic listening activities yourself rather than hiring them out. As with most important business endeavors—particularly those that involve getting a sense of your customers and your market—there's no substitute for getting your hands dirty. By immersing yourself directly in the world of consumers and their concerns, you can glean the subtleties of what's on their minds, what's really bothering them, and what they want and like, in a much more visceral and meaningful way than if you hired a vendor to aggregate these conversations, and had them cleansed, filtered, and pre-packaged them for you into tidy charts and excerpts. There *is* value in having this work done for you by a third party; it will certainly save you time, and you'll get more data and lots of extra features and charts. It's just that something will be lost in this process (in addition to a big chunk of your cash!).

But of course there is one big problem in deciding to take on the job yourself of trying to make sense of the blogosphere. As you probably already know, blogs, forums, Twitter, YouTube, and all the other places where people chat and share information represent a true cacophony, and there are literally millions of conversations occurring at any minute on countless topics. And more than 99 percent of these conversations are just not going to be useful to you. They will include spam, splogs (spam blogs), trolls, trivia, idle chatter, and discussions on topics not of interest to you. Of course, there will be a small number of conversations that are insightful, reflect your customers' preferences and wants, or offer you real hints of important emerging social trends.

So what are your options if you want to do this strategic listening yourself? Are you relegated to trying to wade your way through hundreds of millions of blog posts, and forums in the hope that you'll come across the important ones? That would seem like quite the impossible task, not to mention a very unpleasant job!

Fortunately there are options that can help you quite a bit in this monumental job, and many of these solutions are free and available to anyone. The Internet has permitted thousands upon thousands of individuals to express their creativity and talents online and many have expressed their capabilities by creating all sorts of free digital tools and sites with the express purpose of helping other people sort through blogs and social media sites. In fact, there are so many of these neat and useful sites, tools, and widgets that it seems that we live not only in an era of information overload, but, as one wag called it "innovation overload!" That's a *good* thing, but the key is to know which of these Net-based innovations are most worth your time.

While these sites and tools don't exactly make the job of do-it-yourself blog researching a breeze, using them these can make your job more efficient, and actually make all this a doable task.

In the chapters that follow I will identify and describe what I have found to be the best of these sites and tools. By the best, I mean those Internet sources that a) are most likely to help you gathering and filtering the most relevant blog and other social media postings, and b) will assist you in avoiding becoming deluged with too much irrelevant information and noise. I've also tried to strike a balance between describing more timeless Internet research principles, along with descriptions of actual current sites and tools so you can see how these work in practice. As you know, search engines and sites are regularly redesigned and versions are continually updated so when you read this book some of the specific features I've shown you here could be recon-figured, or gone, and new ones are likely to have emerged in their place. However, once you have the context as to how these search engines, sites, and tools work, what they do, and how to get the most out of them, you'll be in good position to adjust your own search strategies accordingly. (And if you are using the digital version of this book, you can click on the links to get to these sites and search tools directly.)

This is the "how-to" section of this book which will give you detailed instructions for using features on Google and Technorati, surfacing market intelligence from other Internet sites, establish-ing email alerts and RSS feeds, tracking buzz, analyzing and assessing the credibility of what you find, and gleaning what the future may entail.

CHAPTER 9

Market Intelligence via Google

Google Web Search

By far the best known and most popular of the web search engines is Google. Over the years, Google has won the hearts and minds of Internet searchers, and for good reason. Its primary appeal is that it has been the search engine that consistently seems to do the best job in getting the most relevant web pages placed at the top of a user's returned results list. Google achieves this by applying its proprietary page-ranking algorithm called PageRank. PageRank ranks the relevance of web pages based on several factors, including the frequency and placement of matching keywords, but particularly by emphasizing the number of incoming links to a particular page. This method is used as a way to gauge the "popularity" of a particular web page, which serves as a rough but useful indicator of a kind of word-of-mouth recommendation from other web users. Google has also become a leader in web search because of its excellent advanced search options, its collection of integrated research-related features and sites, and its clean and uncluttered look.

Although Google does offer a separate blog and discussion group search engine (discussed later in this section), it is important to note that when you run an ordinary web search on Google, blog pages *are* also included because when you run Google's web search you are searching Google's index of all the HTML web pages it has recently crawled. Since blog pages are also written in HTML, Google's index includes blog pages in addition to the traditional more static web pages.

Since you can directly limit your search just to blogs by choosing Google's blog search option, you might wonder why you would want to search for blog conversations on Google's regular web search engine?

Even if you focus on Google's blog and groups search engine to find social media type conversations and content, there is also a good rationale for not neglecting Google's web search even when you're searching for blog discussions. Using Google's web search engine can be a good strategy if you need to cut down on blog post overload. That's because Google's web page-ranking algorithm operates so that *only the most popular web pages get a high ranking* in the list of matching pages that Google retrieves. And because blog pages are "competing" with all the other types of non-blog pages on Google's web search engine, this means that only the most popular blog posts are going to receive a high ranking on the list returned from a regular Google web search. In a sense, doing a search for blog postings on Google's regular web search sets up a more stringent Google authority filter, weeding out less well-known and less-linked-to blogs. This can be helpful when you want to only find the most well-known bloggers and blog postings.

See Figure 9.1 and Figure 9.2, which are examples of two searches on "jetblue" and stranded; one on Google Web Search, and the other on Google Blog Search.

As you can see, the search on Google's Blog search retrieves only blog posts, but just a couple of blog posts made the cut into Google's web search in Figure 9.1. So the bottom line is if you want to greatly filter out lesser-known blogs, using Google's standard web search engine can be a good option.

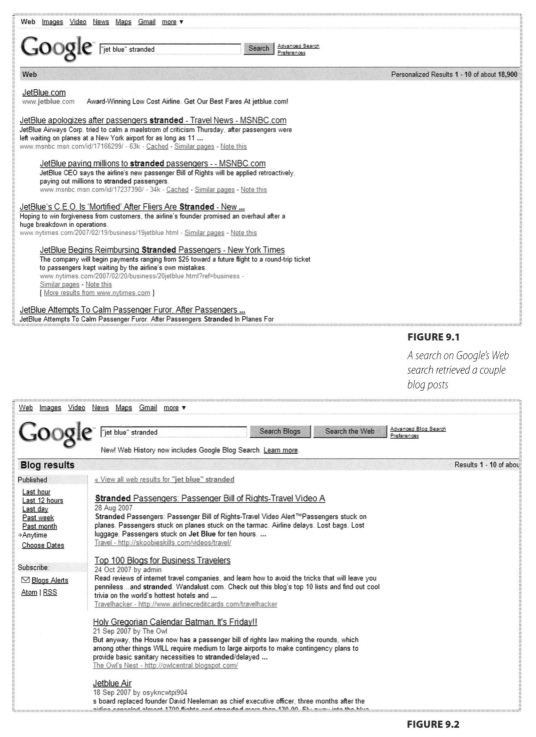

FIGURE 9.1

A search on Google's Web search retrieved a couple blog posts

FIGURE 9.2

A search on Google's Blog search retrieve only blog posts

EFFECTIVE SEARCH TECHNIQUES

It's not easy sorting and filtering all the sites and blogs you turn up in your searches, but there are some strategies to help make your searches more effective and productive. Perhaps the most important tip is to make your search statement as precise as possible. There are really two key aspects to creating a precise search. These are:

1. Understanding how to create a precision search statement;

2. Using the advanced search tools and limits offered by the search engine.

While the skill and art of creating a precise search statement is something that takes a bit of time and practice, it is not difficult to learn the basic principles. With some practice, you can quickly improve the quality of your search results. Here are the most important points.

1. Identify the best keywords

Think about whether the words you are entering into the search box (your "keywords") are the words most likely to be used by other people to describe the same thing. Remember, almost all search engines make literal matches of your words to the words in its index (of web pages, blogs, and forum discussions. If, for instance, you enter "green businesses" and someone else used the term "sustainable business" in her posting, then your search won't find that discussion. This means you need to think ahead of time of synonyms, technical terms, or buzzwords you should use.

Sometimes you won't discover what those preferred words are until after you perform a few experimental searches, read the results of what you turned up, and then note which words, phrases, and terms keep popping up. For instance, if you are trying to find discussions about some business activity in the province of Prince Edward Island Canada, you might do some initial searches, and then discover that often people refer to that province simply by its initials "PEI." Then you would revise your search and enter the term PEI, in order to retrieve discussions that use that popular abbreviation. You might also choose to run another search where you use the Boolean "OR" term (see below) to retrieve discussions that include EITHER the phrase "Prince Edward Island" or PEI, to cover both possibilities in one search.

There's more to this process of coming up with the best key words than just this, and you can take courses and read longer tutorials on the art and skill of keyword searching, but simply being aware of the importance of your key words and the need to be aware of finding and using the most common ones is a critical first step.

In general, certain types of words work better than others in a search. The most effective

EFFECTIVE SEARCH TECHNIQUES (CONT.)

words are *nouns*, particularly nouns that are unusual, such as a person's name, or a product name, rather than a broad term like "Europe" or "automobiles." Another effective type of search is to use noun phrases—two or more words used together as a string. Search engines typically support phrases with the use of quotation marks: e.g. you can enter a term like "pet food" to be sure that you only retrieve results that contain the phrase "pet food," rather than discussions that include the word "pet" someplace and the word "food" somewhere else in the discussion, but not related to each other.

Paying attention to the type of words you use, as well as using the terms that are most likely to retrieve results, can help ensure that your results are going to be more specific and relevant to your research.

2. Understand the Boolean Search

Another key to constructing a precision search statement is the use of "connector" terms: AND, OR, and NOT, (called "Boolean terms"). These provide specific instructions to the search engine on exactly what to retrieve, and what not to retrieve. You are probably already familiar with the basic functions of these terms, but if they are new to you, or you need a refresher, they work as follows:

Inputting the Boolean term AND between your words means that *both* terms *must* be included in an item in order to be retrieved. For example, the search statement: "cell phones" AND reception instructs the search engine to retrieve only those web pages that contain BOTH terms.

Important! These days, the vast majority of search engines "assume" that you want to have a Boolean AND between the words and phrases you enter into the search box, so it will assume an AND by default when you just input words and phrases. For most search engines, if you enter

"cell phones" reception

the search engine will automatically translate that search as a search for "Cell phones" AND reception.

Be aware that this is the kind of search you will likely be running when you enter multiple terms, which is a more restrictive and narrower search. (You can check the search site's "help," "search tips," or FAQ pages to confirm how the search engine works.)

Using the Boolean OR between your search words means that you want to create a broader and less restrictive search and you are informing the search engine that if a web page

EFFECTIVE SEARCH TECHNIQUES   (CONT.)

or forum discussion contains *either* term you enter that you want it to be retrieved. So, if you entered, for example "Cell phones" OR "Mobile phones" then you would get back results that included *at least* one (or perhaps both) of the two terms.

Finally, using the Boolean NOT between your search words means that you want to *exclude* a particular word or phrase. For example, the search, "Cell phones" NOT Razr, will retrieve results that must contain the phrase "cell phones" but must NOT contain the product name Razr.

Those are the basics on how Boolean operators work and how they can help you get more precisely what you want. But you need to remember that each search engine has its own rules and protocols on whether and how it permits you to use these Boolean search terms. For example, some may want you to use a plus sign rather than the word AND and a minus for NOT, so you should always look for a "help" or "search tips" type page that provides instructions on how the site supports Boolean search terms.

Finally, in addition to using Boolean terms, you can also use limits and filters to make your searches better. These are features that allow you to restrict which parts of a webpage, blog posting, or discussion forum your search words will be searched against. Although you will come across several different kinds of limits and filters on various search engines, below is a listing of what I believe are the most valuable ones for performing a more precise search.

FEATURE	VALUE
Limit search to words in **headline** or **title**	Helps ensure that your keywords are a primary focus of the discussion, and not a passing mention
Limit search to **author**	Can retrieve posts only from trusted or key people. Used on blog and forum search engines
Limit search by **date**	Can reduce older and therefore less useful discussions
Limit search by blog or forum **title**	Useful if you know ahead of time which specific blog or forum you want to search

▶ One of the advanced search features that you may come across that you should be more cautious in using is to limit a search by a broad subject category (e.g., "business," "entertainment," "culture"). The reason I don't usually trust this kind of filter is because you don't know how the creators of the search engine defined those categories. Besides, you usually can't predict where a relevant discussion might appear. A relevant discussion on a topic that could impact your firm may not necessarily appear in a "business" category, but in science, popular culture, health, or some other category.

Google Blog Search

Google also permits searchers to run a search of *only* blog postings, and no other web pages. To begin searching Google's blog search feature, you link to the main Google search page at *www.google.com*, and then click on the "More" tab, to bring up the "Blog Search" option.

In general, running a search on Google's blog search engine is pretty similar to conducting a Google Web Search. You input your key words or phrases into a search box, and then Google returns and ranks blog postings that included your words or phrases.

There are a couple of key differences, though. One is that Google blog search checks for new postings and content on a more timely basis than its web search engine does. Google blog search refreshes its index about every 30 minutes or less, rather than the once a day or every few days that Google's web crawler sometimes takes to update parts of its index. Another key difference is that when you view the results of your search, you can choose to see the blog posts ordered by date and time, with the newest postings at the top of the list.

Just as with a regular web search, you can also invoke Google's basic and advanced search features to make your search more precise. For instance, you can use quotation marks to indicate phrases; employ Boolean "or", or "not" commands (the Boolean AND is implied between words and phrases); and limit your search just to words found in the post title. And, as with a regular Google search, you can also restrict results by date and language.

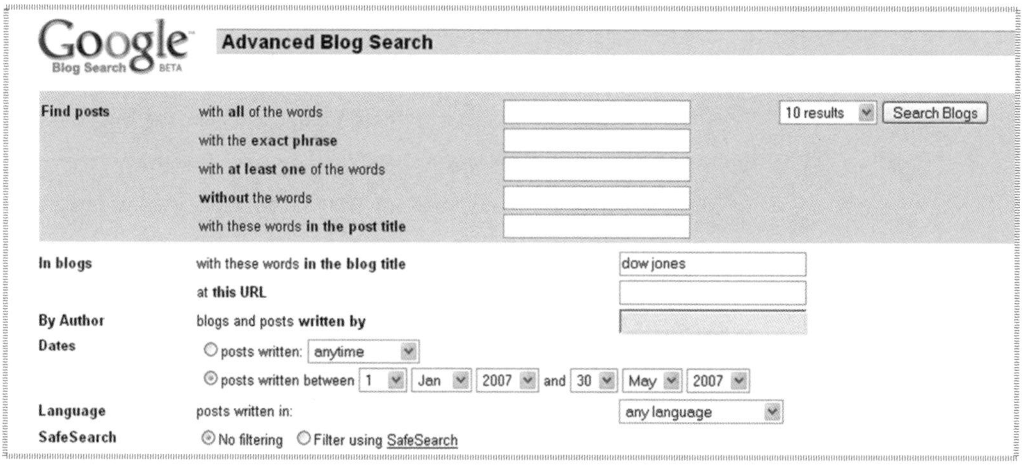

FIGURE 9.3

Google Blog Search Advanced Search Screen

There are a couple of other significant matters you should know about when running a Google Blog Search.

To create its index of blog postings, Google indexes the content of the syndicated news feeds (RSS) that most blogs publish today. Note the word *most*. Not all blogs generate a feed, and so you can't assume that you are searching the *entire* blogosphere when you do a search on Google blog search. Furthermore, because the feed itself may only provide a headline or short excerpt of the full posting, you may only be searching on the words contained in that shorter feed, not necessarily the words in the full text of the posting.

One downside to searching blogs on Google is that there is not much of an archive. The oldest blog posting extends back only to June 2005. This may not be a real problem though. Unlike searching journal or newspaper archives, it is uncommon for researchers to need to locate very old blog postings.

On the positive side, Google blog search offers some sophisticated search features, also available via its "Advanced Blog Search" on its main blog search page. Among the most important advanced search options are:

- The ability to limit keyword matches to word in the *blog's title,* via the "inblogtitle" feature;

- The ability to limit keyword matches to words in a specific *blog post's title* via the "inposttitle" feature. (For example, if you enter inposttitle: "Jet Blue" Google will retrieve only those blog posts that contain the phrase "Jet Blue" in the title of the post.)

- The ability to limit keyword matches to a blog post's *author's name* via the "inpostauthor" feature;

- The ability to limit keyword matches to words found in the *blog's URL* via the "blogurl" feature

Perhaps Google's greatest strength as a blog search engine is its use of a sophisticated algorithm for ranking blog postings. Like its web search engine, Google blog search also uses PageRank to calculate rankings, but integrates other factors such as references to a blog from a blogroll, timeliness, and, as a way to reduce the number of spam blogs, subscriptions to a blog's feed. Interestingly, Google also penalizes a blog's ranking if it discovers certain characteristics that indicate potential spam such as too many postings of the same size at the same intervals, lots of duplicate content, and content that includes words commonly associated with spam.

One other point that's important to remember about Google blog search is that Google owns Blogger, which is one of the leading blog creation hosting sites and so can easily leverage and index blogs on that platform.

In addition to its web and blog search functions, Google also offers a "Groups" search feature where users can search the text of the conversations of thousands of community oriented groups. These are covered separately in Chapter 11.

NON-ENGLISH BLOGS: THE BLOGOSPHERE IS FLAT, TOO

As mentioned earlier, the most commonly used language in the blogosphere in 2007 was not English, but Japanese. According to Technorati CEO David Sifrey, based on Technorati's regular survey of the blogosphere, as of April 2007, 37 percent of all blog posts were in Japanese. English came in second at 36 percent, and followed by Chinese at 8 percent. For the first time, Farsi, which is spoken in Iran, made Technorati's top 10 list, coming in at number ten at one percent.

The implications for business researchers are clear. If you are only accessing blogs in English, you're missing a huge part of the global conversation. This is especially important if you read or track key blogs to get a sense of the grassroots opinion of your firm or its products worldwide, to follow emerging global social trends, to gauge the satisfaction and needs of your customers, to find out more about your competitors, or for monitoring word-of-mouth.

Before getting into the details of how and where to search them, it's worth knowing how blogging in other countries differs from Western or North American countries. An analysis of the blogging environment in specific countries is beyond the scope of this book, but I can sketch out some of the broadest characteristics and distinguishing characteristics of blogs in a few non-Western countries.

Blogging in Japan

With a 100 percent literacy rate, and an ancient and highly respected tradition of communicating by text, it's not surprising that the blog, or as it is called in Japanese the "Borugu," (which translates as "online diary") is popular. It's also been suggested that because many Japanese are more restrained and shy in person, blogs may allow for a greater degree of self-expression than some might feel comfortable with in face-to-face communication.

There are a couple of interesting characteristics to Japanese blogging. Because of the prevalence of cell phones in Japan, many blogs are accompanied by more rich media than Western blogs and many of the messages sent to blogs may also seem less coherent,

NON-ENGLISH BLOGS: THE BLOGOSPHERE IS FLAT, TOO (CONT.)

more rambling with an instant diary-like, almost like a Twitter feel to the communication.

It's also worth noting that a high percentage of Japanese use social communities like Live-Door as the launching point for their blogs, and the Japanese still perform much of their online communications via a bulletin board system. The biggest online bulletin board in the world, 2channel, is located in Japan, and is considered an increasing source of influence in the culture overall.

Blogging in China

Although blogging in China is big and getting bigger—there's an estimated 20 million blogs in China, though only about 5 million of these are considered active—it should be noted that the place where the Chinese prefer to communicate is still the bulletin board services. There are a couple of reasons that have been suggested to explain this. One is that many Chinese prefer a more roundtable, collaborative type platform that seems oriented to encouraging dialogue, chatting for fun, and where everyone is on an equal playing field. Since blogs are created and run by a single individual, some are seen as overly authoritative. Another key reason for the popularity of bulletin boards is that it's easier to post anonymously on bulletin boards and one doesn't have to risk any consequences for what is said as one might have to when posting on one's own blog.

On that point of fear and online communication, blogging in China is directly impacted by the "great firewall of China." That means no access, restricted access, or unreliable access to many of the most popular sites on the Net, such as Flickr and Wikipedia, and a restricted version of Google. It can also mean poor or unreliable connectivity if domains outside of Mainland China are used for communication.

But in China most of these networked discussions may actually be happening outside of blogs. Michael Darragh is the digital strategist for China and Asia Pacific for Ogilvy PR Worldwide and is based in Shanghai. In an email interview, Darragh told me that in China, instant messaging is at least as popular as blogging, if not more so. Darragh said that the vast majority of IMs are performed over Tencent Holdings' extremely popular QQ service and MSN Messenger. Other home-grown portals in China include the omnipresent Chinese search engine Baidu and China's own version of del.icio.us, the social bookmarking site HaoHao, according to Darragh.

Another unique characteristic of blogging in China, says Darragh, is that nearly every celebrity has his or her own blog. In fact one of the most popular blogs in the world is by the Chinese actress Xu Xinglei.

NON-ENGLISH BLOGS: THE BLOGOSPHERE IS FLAT, TOO (CONT.)

As for the more ordinary online communicators, the typical blogger in China is a 30-year-old male. A common theme among business-oriented bloggers is using the blog to voice an anti-corporate, anti-multinational sentiment. The country that's most often the target of some of the anti-corporate sentiments is Japan, followed by the U.S. (I have posted some of Darragh's more extensive remarks about blogging in China on my blog, Intelligent Agent. See Appendix C for the permanent URL).

Blogging in Korea

As is widely known, all things digital and high tech are huge in Korea. According to Darragh, 85 percent of Koreans keep an online social profile! And it's in Korea where the concept of collaborative citizen journalism has been most successful, with the success of its online newspaper OhMyNews, a media site whose articles are contributed solely by ordinary citizens around the country.

There is a problem though in tracking and finding Korean blogs. Apparently the platforms that bloggers use in Korea do not support pinging, and without that method of making oneself known, sites like Technorati are unable to track the blog.

Here are a few options for finding and reading these non-English blogs and handling the language issue.

▶ **Hire an outside vendor**

There are public relations firms that promote the ability to manually track and translate non-English blogs, though these services can be very expensive. PR firms that offer this service for clients include Ogilvy PR and Edelman. In 2006 Edelman's "me2revolution" division set up a joint venture with Technorati to create a local Technorati version so users could search blogs directly by using German, Korean, Italian, French, and Chinese languages. (Some months later, Technorati ended up discontinuing its efforts to translate blogs in Korea and China.)

While there are blog-monitoring firms that perform manual research and translation of non-English blogs, the automated aspect of finding and aggregating non-English blogs that these firms rely on is still under development and presents some problems. Umbria's CEO Janet Eden-Harris told me that "the challenges aren't just technical. Because we use natural language processing to analyze text patterns to predict the sentiment, age, and gender of the speaker, as well as to identify likely spam and to do our theme clustering, we need to build and continue to enhance a significant lexicon—keywords, phrases, emoticons, and acronyms to help us with that analysis. That work needs to be done for every language."

NON-ENGLISH BLOGS: THE BLOGOSPHERE IS FLAT, TOO (CONT.)

I also asked Max Kalehoff, VP of Marketing at BuzzMetrics, the leading blog tracking firm about it's capability for monitoring non-English blogs. Kalehoff said, "Our business thus far has concentrated in the U.S. However, we've worked and had success in many of the major non-English Western languages over the past few years. It is important to note that Nielsen BuzzMetrics was recently fully acquired by the Nielsen Company, and has joined Nielsen NetRatings as an anchor service in the newly formed Nielsen Online. This development will accelerate the rollout of Nielsen BuzzMetrics services globally."

So there's work to be done, even by these fee-based, advanced technology blog monitoring firms.

There are a few firms based outside the U.S. that promote blog monitoring and consulting services and focus on blogging in non-English speaking countries. Among them are Attentio (Brussels), Scanblog (France), Integrasco (Norway), and CIC data (China).

▶ Search the Japanese "localized" version of Technorati

This option works if you or a colleague is fluent in Japanese. Although there will likely be more of these localized versions in development, currently Technorati offers just one "localized" version of its blog search site, called Technorati Japan (URL). What this means is that you can enter a search in the Japanese language, using Japanese characters of course, and receive results back in Japanese.

▶ Search English-language search engines/Sort and Filter by language

A few major blog search engines such as Google Blog Search, Technorati, and Bloglines index blogs in several languages and then permit searchers to restrict their search to a particular language or filter results by language. If you take this option and search using English words, while you can sort or filter by language, you can only find blogs that include the English text that matched the English language words you entered. This could still be a useful strategy when you are searching on English product names like iPhone or an individual's name, or in other cases where non-English speaking bloggers would use English words.

However, you will need to get the blog post translated, either by a human translator, or by one of the inaccurate, but occasionally helpful automated translation sites like Babelfish or Google Translate. The accuracy of automated translation ranges from marginally acceptable for personal and casual use to horrendous, but it's also true that sometimes you are lucky, and if you do achieve that marginally acceptable level and perhaps have a good old-fashioned language dictionary to help you out, you can get a rough feel for what the blog

NON-ENGLISH BLOGS: THE BLOGOSPHERE IS FLAT, TOO (CONT.)

post is about. If you find that you really need a good translation, you can always hire a human translator.

▶ Rely on "bridge bloggers"

There are organizations, sites, and individuals whose mission is to try to get more non-English voices, including bloggers, heard by people in the U.S. and throughout the Western world. They do so by finding and translating these non-English voices on the Internet. You can learn a great deal about the concerns, needs, problems, and a bit about these other cultures too by finding and reading the posting of bridge bloggers.

Probably the largest and most extensive source for finding bridge bloggers and reading selective blogs from all over the world would be the outstanding Global Voices site, a creation of Harvard's Berkman (no relation) Center for the Internet. The mission of Global Voices is to "aggregate, curate and amplify the global conversation online" and thereby to "shine light on places and people other media often ignore."

Georgia Popplewell, the managing editor of Global Voices who works out of Trinidad, told me in a telephone interview that Global Voices hires editors that are responsible for tracking blogs in a particular region and recruiting and managing a team of authors from that part of the world. Those authors work as human filters and are chosen based on the knowledge of the blogosphere they are covering. While it's up to each editor to decide what items to translate and post, Popplewell told me that in general, Global Voices tries to publish items that tell others about a country, explain the culture, and to try to amplify stories that are not being covered in the mainstream media. Global Voices employs language editors in Spanish, French, Russian, Bellorus, Japanese, Korean, and Persian, among others.

Global Voices has other related services and features for bringing the different parts of the blogging world together. The best way to get a sense of what it can offer is to link to its site and begin exploring it.

It's expected that there will be an increasing level of development of sites and solutions to make non-English blogs and other social media more accessible and understandable to English speakers. However, unless you or a colleague are fluent in another language there are no simple answers to reading non-English blogs and social media. It is not likely that there will be any kind of magic bullet that will provide seamless translations of non-English blogs or other websites for that matter, in the near future. Reliable language translation remains an area that technology has not yet conquered, and perhaps never completely will.

CHAPTER 10

Market Intelligence via Technorati

SINCE ITS LAUNCH in 2003, Technorati has become synonymous with blog searching. Although there are several other competing blog search engines (see the listing at the end of this section), and there has been a fair amount of criticism, particularly among bloggers, on its methods, accuracy, reliability, and its decision in 2007 to revise its home page and search features to focus on social media forms in addition to blogs, Technorati indexes the most blogs, and, in my view, offers the most useful blog search features and filters. Unfortunately, Technorati also has experienced more than its share of technical glitches, downtime , and error messages, reducing its reliability, and causing at least some blog searchers to use other sites such as Google Blog Search or one of the other competitors.

Still, there are several features and qualities that make have made Technorati stand out. First is its sheer size. As of April 2007, Technorati had indexed over 80 million blogs, and was indexing well over 1.6 million blog postings daily. Unlike Google Blog Search, Technorati does not just index bloggers' RSS feeds, but employs a crawler to index the full text of each blog posting.

However, it's not just its size that made Technorati the de facto standard for searching blog posts. It is all of its added features, capabilities, and extras. Those features are designed to make blog searching more precise, to retrieve more relevant and useful posts, and overall to make blog searching friendlier and more effective.

As mentioned, in the Spring of 2007, Technorati began increasing its coverage from primarily that of blogs to other consumer media forms as well. Specifically, it began prominently displaying photos, music, podcasts, and videos from YouTube and media from MySpace users. I will discuss searching these other specialized consumer media in Chapter 11.

Conducting a basic search on Technorati is simple. As with virtually all search engines, there is a basic search box where you can enter your keywords.

FIGURE 10.1

My home page for Technorati includes the search box, a link to my own blog, recent posts from my "favorite" blogs, and a list of the most popular searches and tags on Technorati

However, although it is simple just to enter your words in a search box, I advise you to get to know what is on Technorati's Advanced Search screen. These advanced search options are important to know in order to create an effective search, so let's spend a few minutes discussing them.

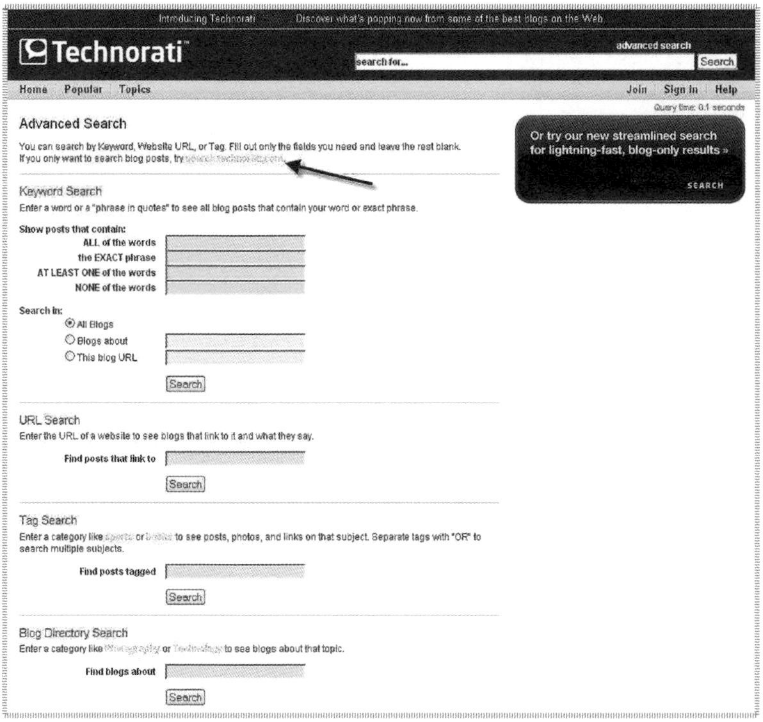

FIGURE 10.2

Technorati's Advanced Search permits more precise searching, as well as a search on a particular URL, Tag or its internal blog directory

Technorati's Advanced Search Options

Search Blogs Only

Note that right beneath "Advanced Search," Technorati informs its users that "If you only want to search blog posts, try search.technorati.com." This is a good option to consider if you want to search *only* blogs, and not all of the audio, video, and other forms of consumer content on Technorati. I actually prefer this blog-only search option, as Technorati's blog search interface is clean, fast, and permits searchers to filter and restrict the search right from the beginning by language, as well as by what Technorati calls "authority." Authority is Technorati's method for distinguishing prominence among bloggers, with authority based on the number of unique other bloggers that link to a particular blog.

I discussed some details and limitations of defining authority in this manner in Chapter 4.

Keyword Search

As with most search engines, just enter your keywords in Technorati's basic search box and you'll typically get back some useful results. The best searchers, though, know how to use a search engine's advanced search options and Technorati offers its users this option on its Advanced Search page.

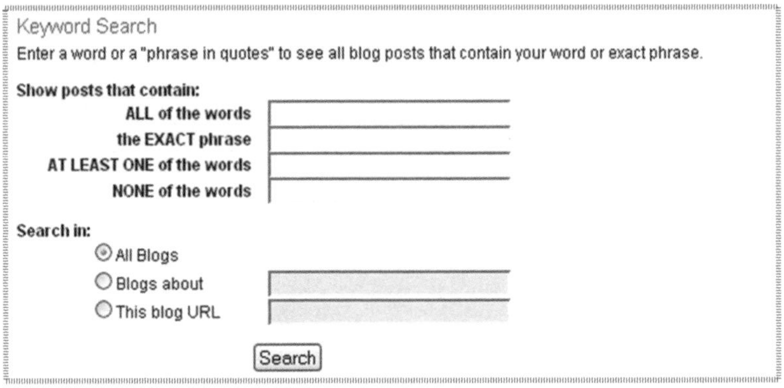

FIGURE 10.3

Technorati's Advanced Search page provides more precise search options

Keyword Search

Enter a word or a "phrase in quotes" to see all blog posts that contain your word or exact phrase.

Show posts that contain:
ALL of the words
the EXACT phrase
AT LEAST ONE of the words
NONE of the words

Search in:
⦿ All Blogs
○ Blogs about
○ This blog URL

[Search]

These options can help you create a more precise search. For example, perhaps you are trying to locate bloggers that are discussing the Blackberry PDA, but you are getting irrelevant results on the fruit. To avoid this problem, you could enter words like "pick plants fruit" in the "NONE" of the words box, and add words that are most commonly associated with your topic in the "AT LEAST ONE of the words" box.

Note that you can also conduct your search on Technorati in "all blogs," "blogs about," or "this blog URL." When you choose "all blogs," you are simply conducting your search on the text contained in ALL the blog posts that Technorati has indexed. If you choose "blogs about" than you are no longer searching the full text of all the blog postings, but are conducting a much narrower search to find blogs where the creators a) have registered their blog with Technorati, and b) written up tags that describe what their blog is about. So, while a search on "Blackberry" in "all blogs" would retrieve any and all blog discussions that contained the key word, a search in "blogs about" would only retrieve discussions of blogs where the blogger has said Blackberry is a key focus of his or her blog.

If you input your keywords into that box, your search will not be run on the postings on the tens of millions of blogs that Technorati indexes, but instead will run only on the few hundred blogs that contains that word in their descriptions. This kind of search offers quite a focused subset of the entire blogosphere. This is an excellent way to help ensure that your results are going to be drawn from a set of "pre-qualified" filtered bloggers who are only or primarily writing on your area of interest. By doing this you increase the odds that the results you get will be relevant to your needs. However, you will retrieve fewer results.

Right below this option is another advanced feature called "This Blog URL." Here you can enter the URL of a particular blog and limit your search to that single blog. This is a good option if you know of a certain blogger that you think is influential, and you're wondering what he or she has to say about a particular company, product, feature, or topic.

Another option on Technorati's advanced search page is "URL Search," which you can use to see which other blogs link to a specific blog. That can be helpful when you want to gauge the amount of discussion a particular blogger or blog post is generating.

Tag Search

If you choose the "Tag Search" option, Technorati does not try to match the words or phrase you enter to the full text of the words in its blog postings, but checks your words against the "tags" or short descriptions that many bloggers assign to their postings. Bloggers add these descriptive tags to their content so that their posts can be categorized by topic, and can more easily be shared and found by other Internet searchers.

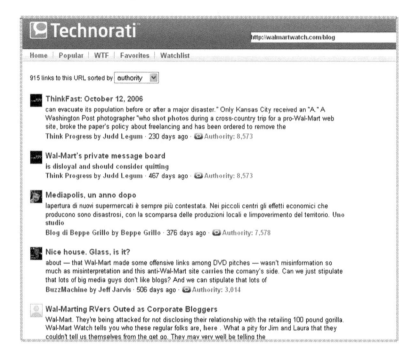

More on Tags

It's worth examining in detail the concept of tags and tagging, which is really one of the fundamental reasons why the whole two-way information sharing world of Web 2.0 works. Tags are words to describe what something is *about*. These informal tags created by ordinary users are called "folksonomies" as a way to distinguish them from the formal traditional "taxonomies," index terms traditionally assigned to books, articles, and other information sources by librarians and professional indexers. Unlike hierarchical taxonomies, which are created in a top down manner by subject and information authorities, folksonomies and tags are "flat" and non-hierarchical, and are generated "bottom up."

Tags make it easier for other people to locate relevant content. For instance, someone who wrote a long blog post about the 2007 jazz festival in Rochester, New York might include these tags with his posting: Jazz, Rochester, Music, "2007 Rochester Jazz Festival"

If you were trying to find blogs about this festival and keyed the words jazz and Rochester into a search box to find all blog postings that contained those words, you'd be buried under all the blog postings that happened to mention jazz or Rochester even if those words were just an aside as part of a blogger's discussion on a completely unrelated topic. But if a blog posting is specifically *tagged* Jazz, Rochester or better yet "2007 Rochester Jazz Festival" by the author, it means that the post is going to be *about* those topics, and so these words provide extremely useful guidance for searchers on the content and focus of that blog post.

Because tag searching is a precise way to conduct a search, this option is a good choice when you are researching common topics and want to greatly reduce the number of results. Figure 10.5, for instance, is the result of a search on Technorati for blog postings that are specifically tagged "jet blue" and "passenger bill of rights."

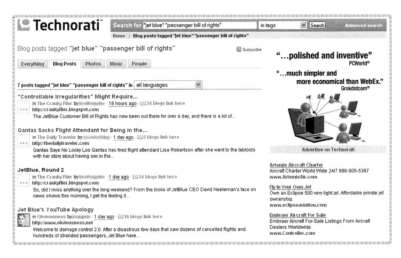

FIGURE 10.5

A tag search on Technorati helps retrieve more relevant results

Note how few blog postings were returned. However, all of them are specifically *about* the sought after topic.

There are also a few drawbacks to doing a tag search:

- It is estimated that only about a third of the blog posts on Technorati include tags. So by restricting your search only to words found in tags, you will automatically exclude most blog posts.

- Because tags are an "uncontrolled" vocabulary—that is, each person can decide for him or herself what words to choose—there is no consistency between the terms bloggers use to describe the same topic. For instance, to categorize a post about a report on the changing climate issued by the International Panel on Climate Change, one blogger might use the term "global warming" for his post on the report, whereas another might use the term "Climate Change." One might add "IPCC" as a term, and the other might spell out the organization's name, or perhaps not include it at all. Another blogger might just use the full title of the actual report as a tag. As you can see, while you can make some educated guesses about the most likely terms that a blogger would use in tagging his or her posts, unlike searching a traditional "controlled vocabulary" database such as in a library online system where only approved and agreed upon terms are assigned as index terms, it is impossible to be sure to find all relevant blog tags on a topic.

- Finally, another reason why you need to be careful about searching on tags is that even under the perfect circumstances—that is, when everyone is tagging his or her posts with the exact same terms—conducting a tag search is an inherently narrow search that can exclude finding blog posts that mentions the term in the full text but not in a tag. So again, tag searching is often the best strategy when you are searching on broad topics and your goal is to limit results. If you do tag searches for very obscure or narrow topics, you may find little or nothing returned.

Blog Directory Search

If you choose this option, Technorati will not search the individual blog postings themselves, but will find blogs in Technorati's directory, which is where the creators of the blogs describe what their blog is about. See Figure 10.6 for what is returned if you do a search on "climate change" in the blog directory.

FIGURE 10.6

Technorati's blog directory

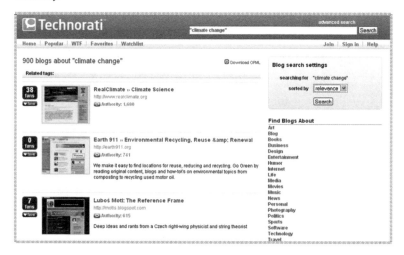

Like a tag search, this is another way you can make your blog searching more precise. In this case, rather than locating blog posts that have been tagged as being about your topic of interest, now you are finding specific blogs whose creators have described their own weblogs with the same words you used in your search.

Some Cautions

Although Technorati's blog directory search is a valuable feature, just as with tag search and its other specialized searches, there are some qualifications and cautions. Two key ones are:

Technorati's Blog Directory represents a tiny slice of the entire blogosphere. Not only does Technorati not index all blogs but its directory only includes those bloggers who have registered (or "claimed" in Technorati's lingo) their blog on Technorati and have taken the time to write up a description about what their blog is about.

You are relying on both the honesty and the ability of those bloggers who have registered their blogs in Technorati to be specific and accurate in describing their content.

Related tags

After you run a search, Technorati will suggest "related tags" that may be helpful to append to your search, so that you could narrow it and make it more precise. For example, when I did a search on the word "sustainability" Technorati told me that the following were related tags:

environment	global warming
energy	climate change
biofuels	green
bioenergy	politics
biomass	

Clicking on any of these tags automatically runs a new search with that term as a tag search; this will narrow your search and make it more precise. Note too that after a search is run, you have the option, via tabs, to see results not just in blogs, but in videos, photos, music, and even "events."

Refining and Other Advanced Technorati Features

There are several useful options available for further refining and getting the most out of your results from searching Technorati. First, you can filter the list of the returned blogs by what Technorati calls "authority"— the number of other bloggers that link to that blog. Technorati offers a useful "Favorites" feature, which I also cover separately in Chapter 14, along with the Authority filter as methods for determining the credibility of bloggers.

These are not the only useful features that Technorati makes available. Another one is the option to create an RSS feed from a keyword search. By doing this, you can continually remain updated on new blog postings that contain your keywords. I'll be discussing the value of RSS in chapter 12. Technorati also provides a "Watchlist," viewable right on the Technorati site itself that will keep you up to date on any new posts on your search, in near real-time.

A Few Worthy Competitors

I do want to reiterate that while I've chosen to focus on Technorati (and Google's Blog Search) as good examples of what you can turn up by using a blog search engine, these are certainly not the only good blog search engines out there. Other reputable and high quality blog search engines include Ask.com's Blog Search, FeedSter, IceRocket, and Sphere.

Each of these sites offers unique features and capabilities and are worth experimenting with. In fact, because each one covers a different segment of the blogosphere, and each has its own unique ranking method, it's good search practice to use more than one search engine, particularly if you want to be comprehensive, or you are searching on an obscure topic where it is difficult to find any results and you want to spread as wide a net, on the Net, as you can.

Meta Search Engines

Finally, I'd like to discuss one other type of search site where you can do efficient active searching of discussions on the web: meta search engines. A meta search engine lets you search several engines simultaneously so you can search more sites all at once. Some meta search engines will aggregate and combine the results from all of its search engines into one listing, while others show the results separately for each search engine.

- **Clusty.** While Clusty includes a variety of types of search engines, it does offer a "blog" category, which lets the user perform a meta search on a few key blog search engines: BlogPulse, BlogDigger, and FeedSter. Note also that Clusty is also a "clustering" search engine in that it examines the results of a search, and categorizes these into related topical areas, based on common words and phrases. You can see examples of both the meta search and the clustering features in Figure 10.7.

There are a few meta search engines that I feel are particularly useful for turning up blog and social media discussions: Clusty, Serph, and Zuula.

FIGURE 10.7

Clusty is not only a meta search engine, but also organizes ("clusters") related items together.

Note the "clusters" on the left hand panel in the image above. These groupings can give you a clue as to what kinds of words, terms, and issues are most often associated with the topic of your search. For instance, on this search for blog postings on the Rochester, New York based supermarket chain, Wegmans, you can see that a grouping of results was related to the topic "Pet, Recall." While grouping technologies like this are not perfect, I've been impressed by Clusty's capability.

- **Serph** allows users to search several conversational and social search engines and sites at the same time and includes blog search engines and news readers (Bloglines Feedster, Google Blog Search, Sphere and Technorati); news aggregators (including Digg, Topix.net, and News-Vine); social bookmarking sites (such as del.icio.us, and Magnolia); image sharing sites (Flickr); audio and video sharing sites (EveryZing, YouTube) and a couple of other search sites as well.

FIGURE 10.8

*Serph aggregates results
from several popular social
search engines and blog
aggregators*

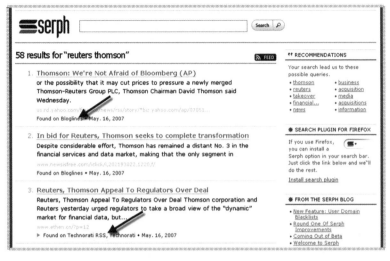

As is true with all meta search engines, there is some trade off in quantity and breadth of coverage versus precision when you conduct a search on Serph. In other words, while you can search more conversations all at once from multiple sources, you cannot as effectively employ precision search commands, limits, or filters as you can when you search any one of these sites directly. This is because meta search engines have to translate search statements to a kind of lowest common denominator standard that all the included search engines can process.

- **Zuula** can search several blog search engines at the same time. Zuula searches Google Blog Search, Technorati, IceRocket, Feedster, Blogpulse, and Sphere. (Users can choose to search various web, image, news, and job related search engines as well)

FIGURE 10.9

*The Zuula meta search
engine*

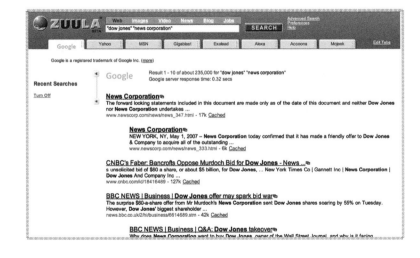

CHAPTER 11

Market Intelligence via Forums, Multimedia, Social Bookmarking, and Social Networking Sites

THERE ARE LOTS of places on the Internet, beyond the blog, where you can search collections of consumer conversation, content and other forms of social media to discover grassroots market intelligence. This chapter provides an overview of the best places to look: forums, multimedia sites, social bookmarking and social networking sites—and advises how to search them effectively.

Searching Forums and Discussion Groups

As mentioned in Chapter 2, because blogs—and more recently, user-created videos such as those on YouTube—have received so much attention, researchers tend to forget about the value of the older but still valuable discussion groups as a source of grassroots market intelligence.

While the kind of conversation and discussions you'll find on these forums and community sites are so broad that they are impossible to categorize, they are typically a fruitful place to locate enthusiast, hobbyist, or passionate users. Such groups can be excellent sources for discovering what active and outspoken customers like and don't like about current products, as well as their dealings with a particular company.

While there are several sites that offer forum and discussion board searching, I'll focus on three of the largest and fuller featured ones: BoardTracker, Google Groups, and Yahoo! Groups.

BoardTracker

BoardTracker is a site owned by Pidgin Technologies, an Israel-based firm. BoardTracker is not a particularly well-known site, but it's a good place to find online discussions because it focuses solely on indexing discussions from tens of thousands of web-based forums.

FIGURE 11.1

A search on BoardTracker for conversations on iTunes

FIGURE 11.1

A search on BoardTracker for conversations on iTunes

There are several nice aspects of BoardTracker. One is its advanced search and search limits. It also does a good job of retrieving relevant results. Other nice features are its ability to search on tags, view tag clouds, and create a customized "my threads," and its alerts feature where users can automatically be informed of new relevant discussions via RSS. BoardTracker also does quite a good job in indexing new posts, as it turns up threads from conversations that occur on the same day.

Google Groups

Google's "Groups" feature consists of a collection of two different types of Internet-based discussion groups. One is a collection of a significant number of all of the older discussions archived on USENET (going all the way back to 1981!). The other segment is an index to Google's own customized discussions, called Google Groups. Google Groups is where Google's registered users can create their own customized online group to discuss whatever topic they choose. You can search the Google Groups collection simply by first linking to Google's home page, and then clicking on "Groups."

There are several nice features to Google's Groups search. One is its clean and clearly labeled interface. Google has done a great deal of upfront work in organizing its groups' messages in a clear and organized manner to make them easier to find and sort.

Also, when you click on a message in Google Groups, you won't be directed to a web forum page, as these often display annoying flashing graphics, icons, and lots of irrelevant and distracting material. Instead you are simply linked to a clearly marked Google Groups discussion, where you can follow the various threads within the conversation in a more organized manner

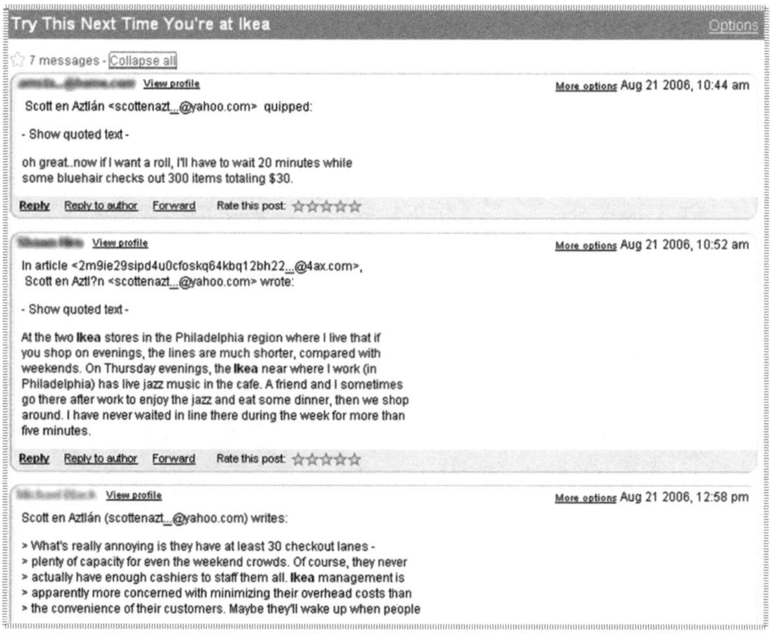

FIGURE 11.2

A search on Google Groups for discussions about Ikea

Another plus is that users can invoke Google's advanced search options, which helps make searches more precise, and apply a variety of other Google tools to make discussion searching more productive.

Yahoo! Groups

Like Google, Yahoo! enables its members to start their own discussion groups, and the site currently hosts nearly 8 million of them, organized into 28,000 categories. While the quality and activity of the groups naturally vary, Yahoo! seems to have done a particularly good job in cultivating a number of high quality discussion groups.

However, there is a catch in searching Yahoo! Groups. The site does not permit you to conduct a keyword search against the conversations in *all* of its groups simultaneously. Instead, you must first browse by category or search by keyword to *find* a specific group, and *then* conduct a keyword search of specific threads from just that particular group.

▶ **TIP:** *If you can find a relevant and active group, a keyword search limited to just that group is actually more likely to uncover substantive and contextually relevant results than if you searched all of the 7 million+ Yahoo! groups together.*

Evaluating Search Results

After you perform a forum or group search, you will want to know *which* of the discussion threads that the search engine has returned are most likely to be the important ones for you to click on and read. There is no way to be absolutely sure until you read the item itself. However, the initial results list will include some clues. If you pay attention to these clues, you can at least increase the odds that you'll click on and spend your time reading a discussion that's more likely to be meaningful for you. Here is what to look for:

- **Number of conversation replies in a discussion thread.** A couple of forum discussion search engines—BoardTracker for example—will display how many responses a particular discussion thread has received. One that has lots of replies (say 10 or more) typically indicates that the topic has struck some kind of nerve, gotten people excited, or has hit a hot button that is worth paying attention to.

- **Your keywords.** Many forum search engines will return a list where your keywords are bolded and highlighted in the section in the discussion where they were located. Be sure to glance at these to see if your keywords were really used in a manner related to your topic of interest, and if the surrounding conversation addresses the matters of greatest importance to you.

Where do email based discussion groups, like the ListServs fit into this? Unfortunately, there is no one single place where you can search the full text of an archive or recent postings from a set of these groups. That's too bad because the conversations that occur on mailing list groups are typically more substantive and have less spam and trolls then web forums and USENET groups. What you can do, though, is locate a specific mailing list discussion group that is relevant to your area of research, and then see if the group provides its own searchable archive, so you can conduct a search that is limited just to recent discussions on that list. Two sites that permit you to search for relevant mailing list groups are Tile.net and Topica.com.

Searching Podcasts and Video Sites

In Chapter 2, I discussed some of the problems inherent in using podcasts and videos for market and trend research, and discussed the tricky technical hurdle of trying to index spoken words. However, there are a couple of multimedia search engines that have at least gotten part way up the hill in figuring out how to incorporate a speech to text technology, and thereby provide some level of search capacity.

The two sites are Blinkx and EveryZing. Both index audio podcasts as well as videos, and permit users to limit a search to retrieve either one or both formats.

EveryZing

EveryZing, which was launched originally in 2006 as PodZinger, allows users to search hundreds of thousands of podcasts and videos. Many are culled from established and mainstream media and broadcasts and are not the amateur consumer-generated ones that are the focus of this book, but it also searches some of these, including videos posted on YouTube.

FIGURE 11.3

EveryZing permits users to specify and play the specific portion of an audio or video that contains the relevant keywords, which are highlighted in the text

EveryZing employs a speech-to-text technology that uses what are called "probabilistic hidden Markov models," or HMM. The method was developed by BBN Technologies, a firm known for its work in the development of the precursor of the Internet, ARPANET. According to EveryZing spokesperson, Barbara Loonam, the firm's technology works by first separating speech from non-speech (such as music or laughter), and time-stamping each word. This time stamp permits a "jump-to" capability that allows a user to start playing at a specific point in the audio or video file

That "jump to" feature is one of the distinctive things about EveryZing. You can not only search the words in the spoken text, but can then play the audio or video precisely at the point in the media's stream where your keywords were located. That's a pretty nice trick.

I'd say that EveryZing's overall speech to text accuracy, when I tried it, while far from perfect, was sufficient to locate audio and video sources that included the keywords I entered, and then allowed me to link to the specific excerpts that contained those words. Unfortunately, though, EveryZing is only able to apply its "jump to" technology to the content submitted by its regular broadcast partners, and not to its collection of YouTube consumer-generated videos.

Blinkx

Blinkx, a privately held firm founded in 2004 and located in San Francisco and London, has also made headway in indexing words inside of audio and video broadcasts. Most of Blinkx's videos are supplied by well-known traditional content providers, including Reuters, BBC News, MSNBC, CBC, *The New York Times*, and The History Channel, as well as business information publishers

FIGURE 11.4

Blinkx audio video search includes user generated videos

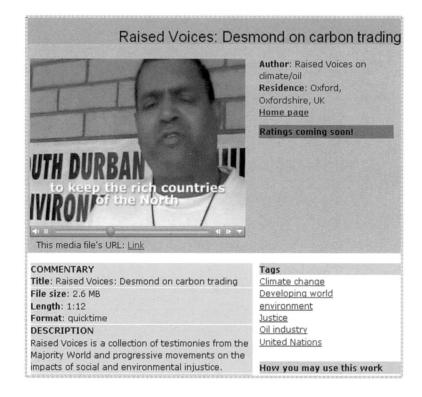

like Forbes, Bloomberg, and Businessweek.com. However, Blinkx also indexes consumer videos from YouTube, Google Video, MySpace and other repositories of amateur podcasts, and its advanced search page allows users to limit a video search to "user-generated" ones if desired. Its speech-to-text technology is derived from Autonomy Corporation, where Blinkx's CEO formerly worked as the CTO. An actual transcript of the spoken text is generated.

Blinkx is well designed, with a slick home page interface that displays a "wall" of recently indexed videos. I found that its search function works well, and liked that it permits Boolean-like searches. There's also a neat preview function, which works seamlessly to provide a quick sense of the initial content of a particular video before clicking on it to view the entire length. However, unlike EveryZing, Blinkx does not have the capability to jump directly to an excerpt of the podcast where your keywords are located.

Social Bookmarking

Another way to locate relevant and important bloggers, blog posts, and other social media content is by engaging in something called "social bookmarking." You can use social bookmarking to find websites, including blogs, that are saved and referenced by others on the Internet.

In many ways, social bookmarking sites represent a more powerful way to locate high-quality sites than using a search engine or subscribing to a news feed. That's because social bookmarks reflect choices of people on the Internet who consciously make a decision to point out and save a site or page for others to view. And because the contributor must go through the additional effort of describing and categorizing these selections with descriptive tags, these saved sites are more likely to be noteworthy.

Social bookmarks are an extension of the common web bookmarks ("favorites") that have been around for a long time, and with which most of us are quite familiar. But social bookmarking is the Networked/Web 2.0 approach to the bookmark. With social bookmarks, you don't just save your favorite web pages on your own PC for your own future use. Instead your bookmarks are uploaded to a public bookmarking site, and those pages can be made available for browsing and viewing (if you so choose) by other people. And, just as other users can find any sites or pages you've uploaded, you can find other people's bookmarks as well.

The premise behind social bookmarking is that it is likely that there are other people who are researching and monitoring the same topics that you are. So, rather than having to start from scratch to find the best resources, if you can find other people who have already found valuable pages, postings, and so forth, you can piggyback on their efforts and discover what they've located.

Social bookmarking goes beyond looking for blog and consumer media discussion and can be applied to all types of research. If you were trying to find good sources on trends in outsourcing in Brazil, you could search on those or related words on a social bookmarking site, and find Internet-based resources that others have described, (or *tagged*) with those words, and check out the sources yourself. Because people generally take the time to upload and tag only what they feel are valuable and noteworthy sources, you are, in a sense, getting access to other people's minds as a giant filter applied to the web. You'll have a thousand research assistants at your fingertips.

And that's not all. Not only do you get access to these web-based bookmarks, you can also surface contact information for those other people who have saved and tagged those pages. Those people may be looking for information on the same topic as you. And that opens up potentially interesting opportunities for making contact with those individuals, which may turn into a fruitful relationship for both parties.

How does social bookmarking work?

The whole process of plugging into one of these public bookmark sites is extremely simple. There are dozens of social bookmarking sites and they generally work like this:

- You link to a social bookmarking site, register, and receive a user name and password

- You download a little bookmarklet icon you can drag onto your browser's toolbar. Then whenever you are on a web, blog, or discussion page you want to save and bookmark, you can click that button to bring up a pop-up screen where you enter key data about the source. A couple of bookmark programs allow you to save just a portion or "clip" a part of the page, and even highlight a section.

- In that pop-up window, you also have space to enter tags to describe the page, as well as add some notes.

Those tags, your own notes, and the page's title are all available to you on that social bookmarking site. And if you chose to make your bookmarks public, they would also be available to other users.

Choosing a social bookmarking site

There are several well-known and popular social bookmark sites. By far, the most prominent and most popular site is del.icio.us (owned by Yahoo!).

You might find that using the biggest one is a good choice. Because del.icio.us has so many users, there is a greater chance that there will be a critical mass of users and bookmarks around whatever topics you may be following.

At the same time, don't overlook a few very good competitors, many which may offer special features not available on del.icio.us. (See Appendix B, Productivity Tools under Social Bookmarking Sites for a list of some of my own favorites.)

While many users of social bookmarking sites may be active taggers and users, from a researcher's standpoint, you don't really need to worry about having to upload sites and being an active user in order to get the benefit of these sites. Though being active can certainly be convenient for organizing and keeping track of your own web-based research, you will likely see the main benefit as finding the relevant sources bookmarked by other people.

Finally, if you find a certain tag on a social bookmark site that you find consistently linked to sources you want to track, most social bookmark sites will allow you to create an RSS feed for it. This will then automatically alert you to all new pages that are categorized with that tag, so you can be kept up to date right in your RSS reader. If you find an individual who stands out because he or she seems to be someone that is particularly insightful or regularly bookmarks great sources, you may even have the option to create an RSS feed of all of that person's tags, so you can be automatically alerted each time he or she adds a new one.

Here's an example of a search on del.icio.us for bookmarks categorized with the tag "GenY":

FIGURE 11.5

A search on the tag "GenY" on the social bookmarking site del.icio.us

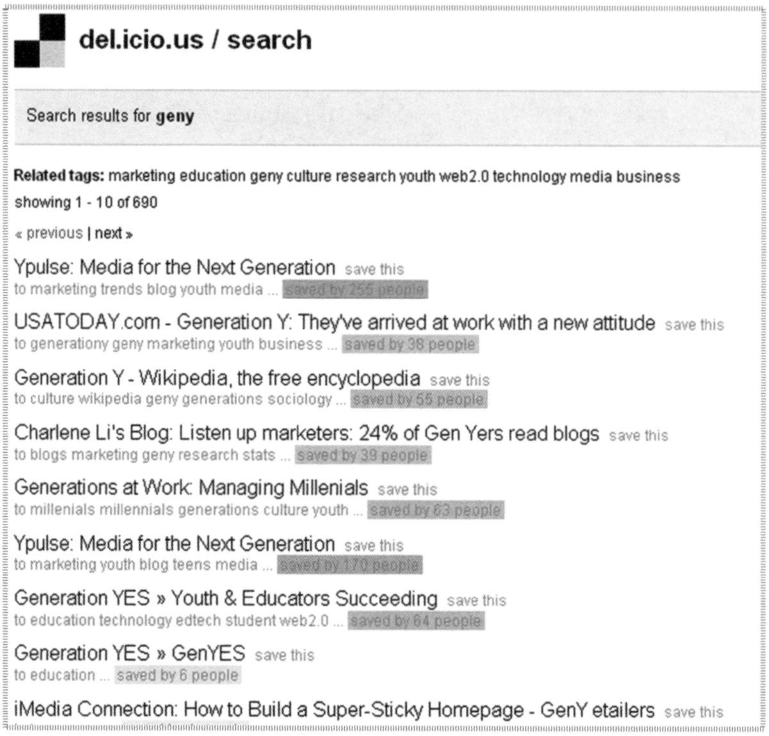

There is one other important question to address when discussing social bookmarking. These sites aggregate their members' favorite websites, but what about actual blog discussions. How do they capture these? Social bookmarking site users can and do save and tag blog conversations, and do so by saving the "permalink" of a particular blog posting. The permalink is the URL that points to a specific blogging entry, and is a valid live link even after that entry is no longer on the front page of that blog.

On the GenY tag search shown above, the fourth one from the top is a saved permalink blog posting by Forrester researcher Charlene Li ("Listen Up Marketers").

You can also discover useful information about a particular blog from a social bookmarking site. See for instance, the various useful bits of information (Figure 11.6) on the topic of changing libraries titled "The Shifted Librarian" and written by Jenny Levine. Included in the description is a cloudtag of the most common tags suggested by users to describe her blog, the comments left about the blog, a history of how the blog was tagged on del.icio.us, and more.

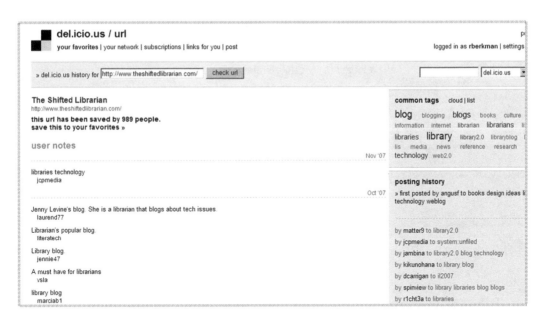

Social Networking Sites

FIGURE 11.6

The del.icio.us social book-marking site also provides information on specific blogs.

As discussed in Chapter 2, an increasing amount of online discussion is being held on what are called "social networking sites"—places online that primarily provide a social function, where users can communicate with current friends and colleagues, locate other people with similar interests, post and share pictures and videos, start and participate in special interest groups, organize online events, and more. The best-known purely business-oriented social networking site is probably Linked-In, and for more general social networking purposes, the major sites are MySpace (used primarily by younger people) and Facebook, (originally populated by younger people, but becoming increasingly popular for those over age 35) along with a newer entry in the field called Ning.

So how can you locate relevant discussions and content occurring on these kinds of social networking sites? The answer depends to some degree on the particular social networking site.

For example, if you want to search blogs created by users on MySpace, one convenient way to do this is by searching Technorati, since Technorati includes MySpace blogs in its own index. Technorati's advanced search page, under "This Blog URL" permits searchers to limit a search *just* to the MySpace blogs. Because there is so much purely chit chat, social and trivial type of discussion on MySpace, I'd also advise adjusting the Technorati "authority" filter up high to help further filter the MySpace bloggers to those that are often linked to by other bloggers.

FIGURE 11.7

Technorati permits searchers to limit results to MySpace blogs by entering <<blog. myspace.com>> into the "This blog URL" search box.

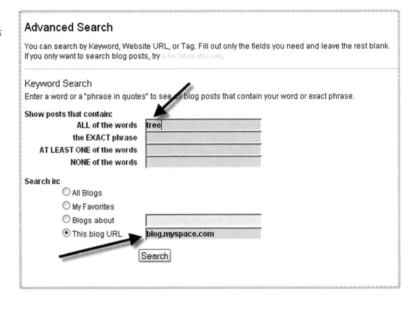

Another social networking site is Ning, a free web platform that permits anyone to start a social network on any topic. Thousands of social networks have been created on Ning, on topics ranging from European Independent Film Makers to 3D Designers to Australian warcrafts and so on. People join a Ning to talk, blog, share photos, describe new resources, and more.

You can find out if there is a community on a topic covering a topic of interest to your organization simply by searching the main page of Ning.com, and if you do find one, you can join the community and then you will have the ability to search an archive of the discussions that have taken place within that community. You might even consider starting up your own Ning social network. It's extremely easy, and you may be able to attract a community to discuss whatever topic you are most interested in exploring with others.

And then there's Facebook. There's no question that by 2007, Facebook was *the* hot social networking site, growing faster than all the others, and garnering the kind of buzz and momentum that made it perhaps the site to watch on the Net, even making it as the cover story of *Newsweek* ("Facebook Grows Up: Can it Stay Relevant?" August 20, 2007).

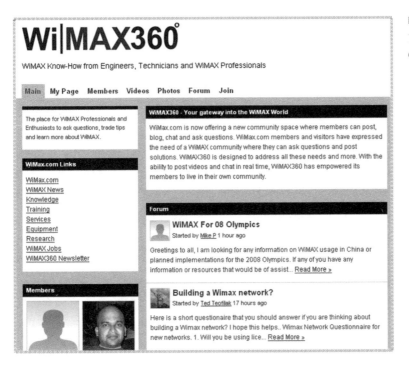

FIGURE 11.8

This Ning community discusses WiMAX.

Because Facebook continues to get so much attention and interest, I want to spend a little extra time discussing its potential for locating relevant market intelligence.

Although the best, and really only way to understand Facebook is to join it (it only takes a minute and it's free) I'll describe the key elements and aspects of Facebook.

The fundamental function of Facebook is "social networking" meaning the sharing of information between "friends." A friend on Facebook, as well as other social networking sites, is simply two people that have agreed to communicate with each other and allow the other person access to some level of their personal information and activities while on Facebook.

The way this works is that all members initially create a profile that normally includes a picture, some basic information about themselves (where they live, work, education, hobbies, interests, and whatever else they want to share). Members can then connect with other people on Facebook by sending a friend "request" to another person. If that request is accepted, the two parties can view each other's profiles, and will be alerted, via a regularly updated "news feed" to specified Facebook related activities that their "friends" have been doing recently (e.g., Joe Smith joined the Hitchcock movie lovers group;

or added a new photo; or added a new Facebook application). Friends can send each other private messages, write notes on each other's public "Wall," share web links, find out who their friends of their **friends are, and so on.**

In addition to sharing information between friends, members can also take advantage of certain Facebook features and functions. Probably the three most important are Applications, Networks, and Groups.

Applications are just mini software programs that can do something, and which Facebook members can add quickly and for free. There are thousands of these, ranging from applications for sharing movie preferences with friends, keeping up with friends' favorite blogs, creating surveys of Facebook members, creating a fantasy stock exchange, playing blackjack, sending virtual gifts to friends, reading their friends' RSS feeds, and so on. These applications, which are often created by ordinary Facebook users and not large firms, are one of the features that make Facebook stand out from other social networking sites.

Another key element of Facebook is the "networks." Networks are groups of people who share some kind of real affiliation—e.g., work at the same business; go to the same university; live in the same city. Facebook ensures that only people that really work at the same business or attend the same university can join the relevant network by requiring that they submit an email associated with that institution. Members are limited to join only one regional network, which can be changed only during limited intervals.

Finally, there are the "groups" on Facebook, which are thousands and thousands of special interest groups created by Facebook members who want to find people to share information on some topic or area of interest. Again, topics of Facebook groups runs the gamut, from Antique Typewriter Collectors to Web 2.0 entrepreneurs, with membership in groups ranging from 4 to 400,000+. Because these groups have discussion boards where people offer their opinions and share their experiences on the subject of that group, it is on the groups where there is potential for performing strategic listening. (Note that while there are private and restricted groups on Facebook, the majority are open to anyone)

How do you find and keep track of the relevant and meaningful discussions on your company, product, brand, or industry on a Facebook group? The first step is to join Facebook. Once you do you can try these strategies:

1. Start by simply doing a search on the target word or phrase in Facebook's own search box. While Facebook offers only the most rudimentary search engine, it does appear to be reliable, and will retrieve relevant personal profiles, applications, networks and groups where your keywords appear. Figure 11.9, for instance, is the result of the groups that Facebook identified based on a search on the word: Kitchenaid. The results appear to show consumer enthusiasm for its red and pink mixers.

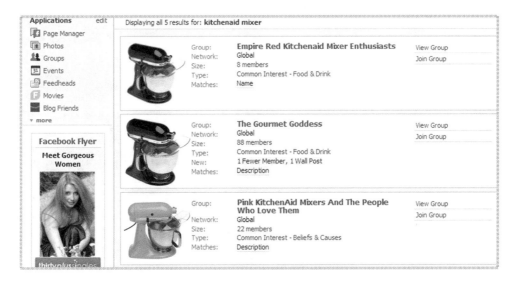

FIGURE 11.9

The results of a search on Kitchenaid on Facebook.

2. Once you've found one or more relevant groups on Facebook, you can simply click to join that group. When you do so, you have access to its conversational areas, including the "Wall" and discussion groups, which you can browse or search.

3. Another option is to create your own Facebook group. Organizations are permitted to "sponsor" a group, and then invite people to talk, share opinions, and hold a kind of customized online focus group. This is similar to the private hosted communities concept offered by some firms, and discussed in Chapter 8, but are a way to do this yourself. One firm that has been successful in doing this is Skittles, which set up a group for enthusiasts of the candy. Skittles even invites members to take surveys and polls, which it conducts off of the main Facebook site. Note that Facebook charges organizations to sponsor a group.

FIGURE 11.10

Once you join a group, you have access to the discussions (names and photos above removed for privacy purposes), as shown here in the group for enthusiasts of the Kitchenaid red mixer product.

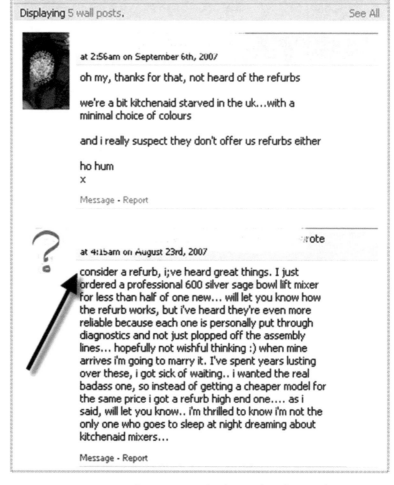

> **The Wall**
>
> Displaying 5 wall posts.   See All
>
> at 2:56am on September 6th, 2007
>
> oh my, thanks for that, not heard of the refurbs
>
> we're a bit kitchenaid starved in the uk…with a minimal choice of colours
>
> and i really suspect they don't offer us refurbs either
>
> ho hum
> x
>
> Message - Report
>
> ------
>   wrote
> at 4:15am on August 23rd, 2007
>
> consider a refurb, i;ve heard great things. I just ordered a professional 600 silver sage bowl lift mixer for less than half of one new… will let you know how the refurb works, but i've heard they're even more reliable because each one is personally put through diagnostics and not just plopped off the assembly lines… hopefully not wishful thinking :) when mine arrives i'm going to marry it. I've spent years lusting over these, i got sick of waiting.. i wanted the real badass one, so instead of getting a cheaper model for the same price i got a refurb high end one…. as i said, will let you know.. i'm thrilled to know i'm not the only one who goes to sleep at night dreaming about kitchenaid mixers…
>
> Message - Report

4. However, in November 2007, Facebook introduced a simpler, more fully featured and free version of its sponsored groups called "Facebook Pages." With Facebook Pages, members can set up a page that revolves around their firm, brand, or other commercial entity. And just as people with personal pages can find and connect with "Friends," creators of Facebook Pages can cultivate and attract what are called "Fans," and one's Fans' activities will be broadcast to their friends' news feed, just the same was as their other Facebook activities are reported to their Facebook friends.

5. If you can create a compelling and interesting Facebook Page for your firm or brand, you may be able to attract enough Fans so that

you can learn of their likes and dislikes, ask them your own questions, and attract other people you wan to connect with on your Page. As a way to promote awareness of your Facebook Page, you can also use another feature called "Social Ads," which broadcasts news about Facebook members' buying and selling activities to their friends. One interesting feature about Facebook Pages is that a non-Facebook member version can be accessed by search engines, making your Page available to be found not only by Facebook members but by anyone using an Internet search engine.

FIGURE 11.11

Skittles set up its own sponsored group on Facebook

Finally, what about the option of keeping track of specified discussions on Facebook groups, such as via an RSS feed? As of late 2007, a news feed from Facebook groups was not possible, and there were no applications available to facilitate it. However, my guess is that it's likely that this function will be developed either by Facebook or a third party in the near future.

Note that you can use Facebook for more traditional market research type applications. For instance, you can research information about people, find people who work at certain businesses or organizations, or conduct surveys and polls of Facebook users, either by Facebook's own "polls" application or by signing up with one of the third party's polling applications, such as Pollection's polls.

CHAPTER 12

Alerts and RSS: Letting Technology Do the Work

IF YOU HAVE a one-time need for a piece of information, or if you are not certain exactly how to describe the topics you need to regularly track, and you need to tinker and experiment with search words, an active search initiated by linking to a search engine or site may be what's called for, as we've discussed in the previous three chapters.

However, sometimes you already know the topics you want to keep up with and you will be better served by setting up a system that will alert you to these postings automatically. If you set up a system like this, you can be notified whenever there are new discussions and postings from bloggers you want to follow, and even get alerts when keywords that you've specified are mentioned anywhere on the blogosphere, or on other parts of the Internet.

There are primarily two ways you can set up this kind of automated monitoring: via email alerts or via RSS feeds. I'll discuss both options in this chapter.

RSS

Although email-based alerts have been around for several years as one way to enable automated notification, since around 2003 or so, this mode of keeping up with breaking news and blog postings has been surpassed by a new approach. That method is sometimes referred to as a news feed, or syndicated news, although it is still most frequently referred to by its technical acronym: RSS. We'll use that term, as well as news feed in this chapter.

No matter what label is used, the process works the same way. If you are already a regular RSS reader, you can skip the basic FAQ sidebar below. But if you're new or want a refresher, continue on.

RSS FAQ

Q. What is RSS?

The simple answer is that RSS is a way to automatically be notified on your desktop whenever a blog or other frequently updated site you follow has published new content.

Here's the more precise and technical answer. RSS refers to a specific variation of XML, a popular "markup language." A markup language is a way to describe the content of a piece of text, and XML is the markup language that is used on the web.

The RSS standard is employed to parse information from websites into clearly labeled sections: headline, summary, and the body of the text. It is used primarily by blogs and breaking news sites--as well as image sites, video sites, search engines, and others with frequently updated content-- that wish to distribute, or send content automatically to anyone who wants to subscribe to it. These sites act like syndicated services, similar to wire services such as AP, Reuters, or syndicated columnists, in that the information is sent out electronically, and can be read by anyone who subscribes. However, unlike a newswire, where users pay to subscribe and get the feed, on the Internet, anyone can subscribe to anyone else's news feed for free.

Note that there are two popular news feed standards: the most common news feed format is called RSS, but a competing standard is called Atom. These technical definitions and distinctions are not really important for users to understand in order to use it.

RSS in Plain English:
Amy Gahran

Q. How can I subscribe to a news feed?

In order to receive, view and read news feeds, it is necessary to use something called a feed reader or news reader. Although a few are fee based, and some reside on your PC, the more popular and common readers are available for free and accessible on the web.

Q. How do I find blogs and other sites that produce a news feed?

Look for orange buttons on the site. Sites that create a news feed will typically indicate it on the page with a small orange icon (orange is the industry standard for RSS), or have a link or orange button that says RSS or Atom. Most news readers also allow users to browse and search a collection of RSS feeds. Some readers and browsers will even automatically detect a site's RSS feed for its users when they are browsing a site. Websites usually make it easy to subscribe by providing a one-click function to add its RSS feed automatically to your news reader of choice.

RSS FAQ

Once you have located a feed from a news, blog or other site that you want to begin receiving updates from, you can just copy the URL of that feed, and enter it into your reader, and you will begin receiving feeds from that site.

Note that the actual URL for an Internet feed looks just like any other Internet address, except that it usually contains the letters, "rss," "atom," or "xml" somewhere in its string of characters. Internet feeds point to a file that contains summary information (e.g. title, author, excerpt) rather than the full content.

Q. Once I have a news reader, and have found a few blogs or other sites with feeds I want to subscribe to, what exactly will I see in my news reader?

It's easier to illustrate this with a picture than describe it in words. Below is an example of how Bloglines, perhaps the most popular free news reader, displays several incoming feeds that I subscribe to.

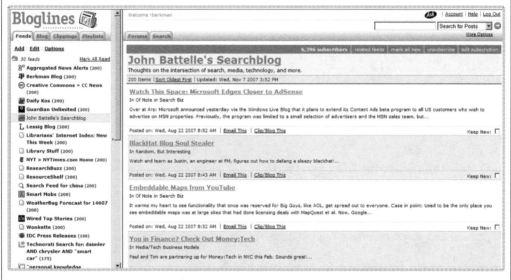

FIGURE 12.1

A listing of the feeds I subscribe to on Bloglines

Bloglines Beta

On the left hand bar are the names of the various blog and news feeds that I've signed up with. In the image, I've highlighted the feed from "J's Scratchpad," so that blogger's most recent postings are displayed on the right side of the page. I can then scroll up and down on that page to view her older and newer postings, and if I wanted to read an entire post, I could click on the headline. New postings are added on an hourly basis or so, depending on the reader.

Keyword Tracking via RSS

Although one primary use of RSS is to automatically obtain the latest postings from your favorite and trusted bloggers, another powerful way to use them is to get notifications of any new discussion in the blogosphere where a specific word, phrase, or search string that you've specified appears. You can enable this function by creating a keyword search on an RSS-enabled search engine, and then copying the RSS feed generated for that search and entering it into your reader. That feed will then automatically and regularly alert you to new results that match your keywords on the search engine.

Here's an example of what I mean. Some search engines, such as Technorati, allow you to run a keyword search, and then "subscribe" to that particular search via RSS. Below are the results of a search on Technorati for the terms "smart car" AND Daimler AND Chrysler. Note that there were 166 postings on that topic, and that we could choose to "subscribe" to that search by clicking on the orange icon.

FIGURE 12.2

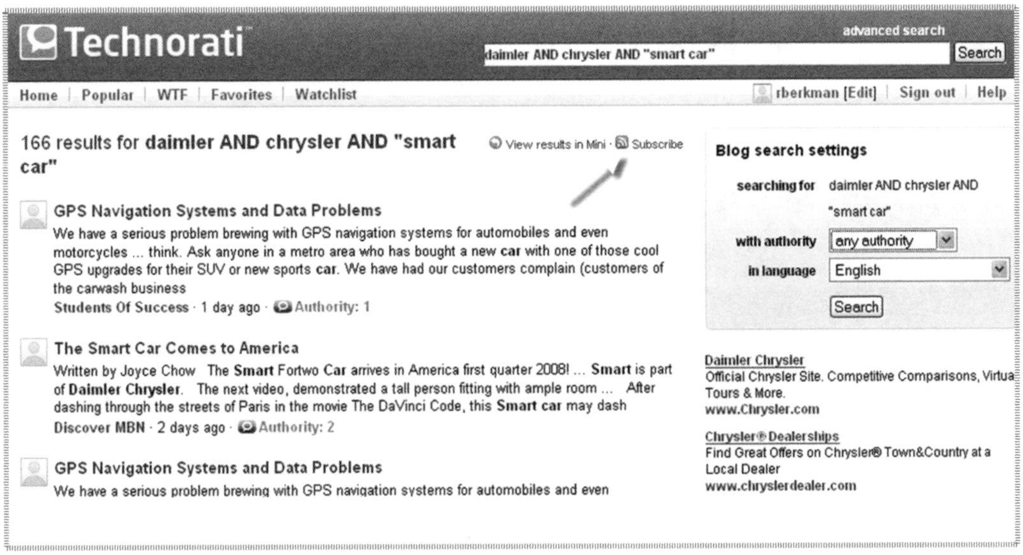

Here's what occurs after we click on that orange icon indicated by the arrow.

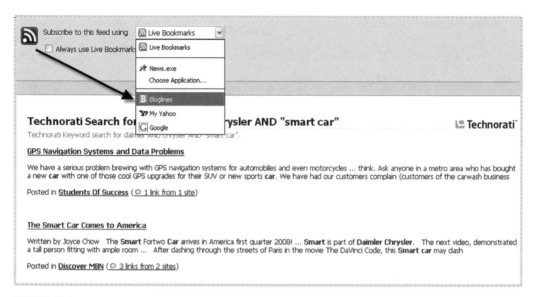

FIGURE 12.3

See how my Firefox browser then provides me with a variety of news readers to choose to add a feed. In this example, I've chosen Bloglines. Clicking
here automatically sends me to my Bloglines page, where I'm given a few
options on how I'd like to add that feed to my collection:

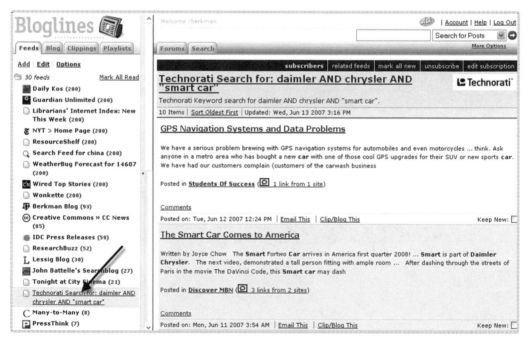

FIGURE 12.4

Once I click the "Subscribe" button, you can see in the image above how my Bloglines' list of news feeds has been updated to include this keyword search. I've also highlighted that feed in the left hand bar of my Bloglines home page, so that the latest feeds from that search now appear on the right side of the screen: ("The Smart Car Comes to America").

FIGURE 12.5

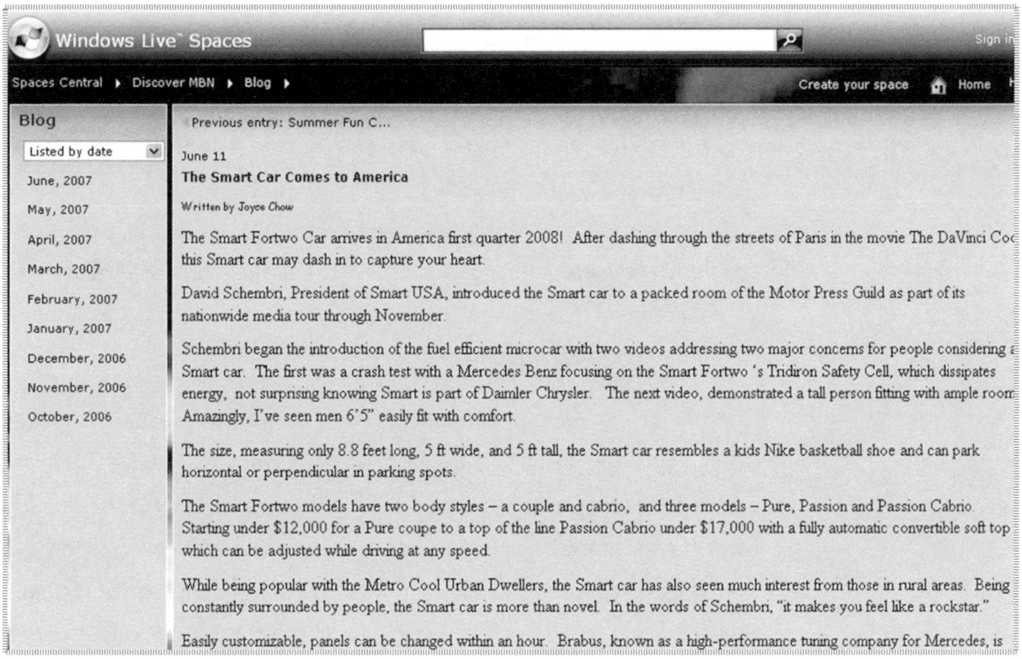

Finally, clicking on that second link "The Smart Car Comes to America" links to the original blog posting in full, as displayed above.

So now, whenever I link to my Bloglines news reader, not only will I be getting the latest postings from all the news, consumer media, and blogs whose feeds I have subscribed too, but I'll be getting headlines and summaries of just those blog posts that Technorati tracks that include the words: smart car, Daimler, Chrysler. This is a powerful way to keep track of emerging conversations!

Technorati is not the only search engine that permits you to set up keyword monitoring feeds. Other blog search engines that let you do this include Google Blog Search, BlogPulse, Yahoo! News (which includes blogs), and the Bloglines news reader itself, since it incorporates a blog search function. You can also set up keyword-based RSS feeds to monitor discussion forums on BoardTracker, the forum search engine discussed in the previous chapter. Also, the "public" Yahoo! Groups, as well as Google Groups, while not permitting keyword based RSS feeds from a search, do offer a feed for tracking the newest messages from specified groups. To find a Google group feed, you can go to the group's homepage and click the "About this group" link on the right-hand side of its homepage. To get an RSS feed from a public Yahoo! Group, just search or browse to a group you are interested in, and you can scroll down to an RSS icon to beginning receiving the feed.

> ▶ **TIP:** There are sites that permit you to create a keyword search against not one, but multiple blog, news and other search engines simultaneously, so that you can receive feeds from all of those sites in your reader. The one I recommend is a site called Kebberfegg, created by well known Internet research author and analyst Tara Calashain of ResearchBuzz.com and author of the excellent book on Internet research, *Information Trapping* (New Riders Press, 2006)

Although, as mentioned earlier, the technology for searching spoken words embedded inside a podcast or video is not fully reliable, there are other options for setting up a feed to track podcast and video sites about a particular topic. You can do so through the use of the meta information, like the tags and conversation that surround the actual content. For instance, YouTube offers several ways to get RSS feeds so users can be alerted to new videos, including:

* **Tracking videos by tags.** You can create a YouTube URL feed with the tag name attached. For example, if you wanted to track all videos on YouTube that were tagged IPhone, you would enter this exact URL into your reader: feed://www.youtube.com/rss/tag/iphone.rss

* **Tracking videos by specific YouTube users.** You can also create a feed to be notified of all new videos uploaded by a specific user. For instance, if there was a user by the name of "Ted Walsh" whose videos you wanted to track, you would enter: feed://www.youtube.com/rss/user/tedwalsh/videos.rss

Feeds for these and to other categories: http://www.youtube.com/rssls

YouTube also offers the ability to create RSS feeds for certain *categories* of videos. Some of these include "recently added videos" or "top rated videos" or "most discussed videos."

Note that you can also create RSS feeds on the multimedia search engine Blinkx, which I discussed in the previous chapter. Blinkx offers some particularly useful and valuable features for creating effective feed searches. For one, you can use an advanced search option to create more precise searches, using phrases, "all the words" and a "without the words" semi-Boolean search. Furthermore, you can even limit the videos in your search to only the consumer-generated ones if you so wish, which Blinkx calls its "Viral and Garage" videos. See the following screen shots for examples of how I set up an RSS feed on Blinkx to alert me to any "viral and garage" videos (which includes YouTube, as well as other popular consumer-generated video sites) that contained the word "freegan."

FIGURE 12.6 (top)

Here I've set up a search on Blinkx to search consumer videos that contain the word "freegan."

FIGURE 12.7

After the search was run, I could click on the RSS button to create a feed for this search. Once I entered that feed into my reader, I would be automatically alerted to any new consumer videos described with the word "freegan."

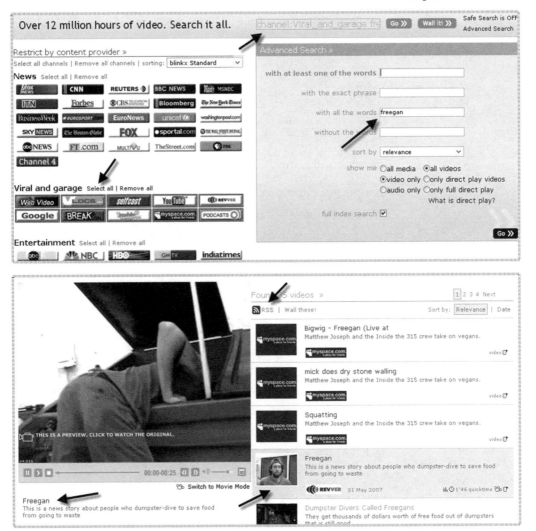

Finally, you can also set up an RSS feed to keep up with new sites high-lighted by people on the web that you've come to trust. You can do this if that user posts his or her favorite links and bookmarks on a social bookmarking site like de.licio.us. See the following image for the items saved by business librarian Laurie M. Bridges, one of my trusted sources on the topic of business information.

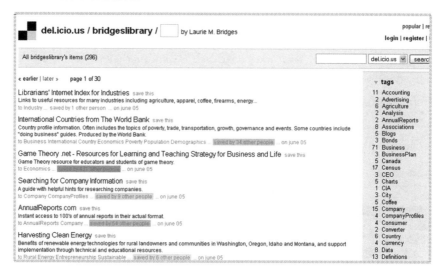

FIGURE 12.8

RSS Feeds can keep you up to date of favorite sites of people you trust on social bookmarking sites like del. icio.us.

Choosing and setting up a news reader

As mentioned earlier, there are lots of free news readers, and all will let you read incoming news and blogs and track keywords. Later in this section I'll discuss a few important differences among news readers, but for now, you should know that although the two biggest and most popular ones are Google Reader and Bloglines, the following are other worthy, and free, alternatives:

- Kinja
- Lektora
- NewsGator
- Rojo

I also want to mention one fee-based reader, NewzCrawler, which I will discuss a little later in this section.

How do you decide which of these—or any other—news reader is best? As I said, the basic function of any news reader is the same, and since these are all either free or dirt cheap, it's not worth much energy to perform extensive, detailed, time consuming news reader comparison exercises. Strictly from the business researcher's perspective, I'd say that the following features and capabilities are most important when selecting one:

- Clean, elegant, nice to look at interface

- Ability to filter incoming feeds with your own keywords

- Ability to view incoming feeds either as headlines only or headlines with excerpt

- Ability to save, tag, and search past feeds by keywords

- Ability to mark feeds that you've read as "already read;" and the ability to keep certain already read items as "unread"

- Ability to create folders so you can group similar incoming feeds together by topic or other category

- Ability to easily share your feeds with colleagues

News readers do offer different capabilities and advantages. In general, I'd say that the key differences and significant strengths among these readers are as follows:

Bloglines

- Integrates an advanced blog search capability

- Provides popularity rankings for feeds based on number of Bloglines subscribers

- Can perform a keyword search limited just to the feeds you are subscribed to

- Receive email content via RSS with a "disposable" email address

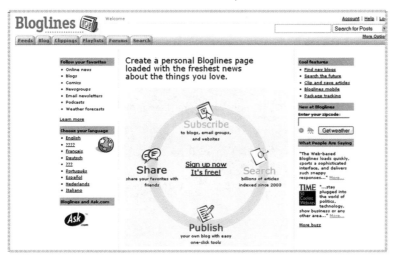

FIGURE 12.9

The Bloglines reader

Google Reader

- Elegant and intuitive interface
- Extensive keyboard shortcuts
- Connects with other Google services (Gmail, Google Notebook, etc.)
- Can mark feeds in bulk or individually
- Can easily email or share content via RSS
- Can flag items with yellow star for personal reference or sharing
- Can assign tags to items
- Can monitor your feed consumption trends
- Ability to read new items while offline with Google Gears

Google Reader:
Getting Started

FIGURE 12.10

The Google Reader news reader

Google Reader

🏠 **Home**	
All items (100+)	
☆ Starred items	
Shared items	
Trends	

Add subscription   Browse »

Show: updated - all   Refresh

- **businessandmarkets (65)**
  - **Blogspotting (19)**
  - **Fast Company Now (46)**
- **businessresearch (100+)**
  - **AlacraBlog (14)**
  - **business search resea...**
  - Christina's LIS Rant
  - **Intelligent Agent Blog (2)**
  - **John Battelle's Searc... (**
  - **Library Stuff (56)**
  - **Moreover Technologies..**
  - New Media 2.0
  - **panlibus (16)**
  - ResourceShelf's DocuT...
  - **Technorati Search for... (**
  - **Technorati Search for... (**

MediaShift (19)

Supernova 2007::Business Crowd Considers Web Users in Third Person [image: Supernova logo.jpg] SAN FRANCISCO — Anyone tired of Web 2.0 topics and discussion, and the current ...

Digging Deeper::TechDirt Builds Community of Bloggers to Offer Corporate Analysis [image: TechDirt Insight Community.jpg] In the world of technology research, firms such as Gartner, Forrester Research and ...

Your Take Roundup::'Cup Is Overflowing' for Future of Journalism [image: Digital Media Federation.jpg] If there is one overriding debate in the world of journalism, it's whether technology ...

See more from journalism (23) »

Creative Commons Blog (26)

Spoon to Headline Creative Commons Benefit Concert to Kick Off WIRED NextFest in LA We are very pleased to announce that Spoon, the Austin, TX based rock-quartet, will headline a benefit concert for Creative ...

FOSS + Creative Commons LiveContent for libraries Creative Commons is developing LiveContent, a project to connect and expand Creative Commons and open source communities. The ...

Where are the Joneses? Last Friday (June 15th), Where are the Joneses?, a "daily fictional interactive comedy shot entirely for the web", went live. ...

See more from copyrightdigitallife (26) »

Blogspotting (19)

Read this and hand it to four friends Mathew Ingram takes on the traditional media metric that says five people read the average newspaper or magazine. I agree, ...

Kinja

- Very simple to use; friendly, clean pre-filtered digests of feeds
- Nice interface
- Auto discovery of feeds on a Web page
- Can easily share feeds with others

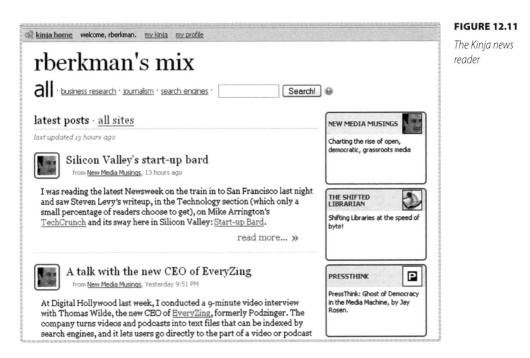

FIGURE 12.11

The Kinja news reader

Lektora

- Excellent folder creation feature for organizing feeds
- Can filter incoming feeds by keyword
- Can perform keyword search of past feeds

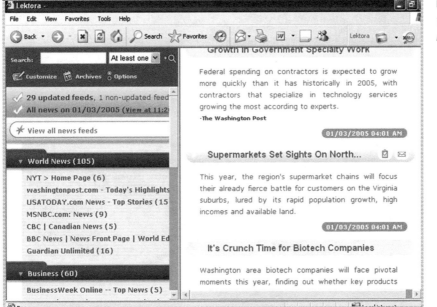

FIGURE 12.12

The Lektora news reader

NewsGator

- SmartFeeds for keyword searching of feeds
- Ability to integrate with Microsoft Outlook (on the fee-based Outlook Edition)
- Can sort feeds into folders

FIGURE 12.13

The NewsGator news reader

NewzCrawler (fee based)

- Outstanding at-a-glance interface for reading incoming feeds
- Can filter incoming feeds by keywords
- Auto discovery of feeds on a Web page

FIGURE 12.14

The NewzCrawler news reader

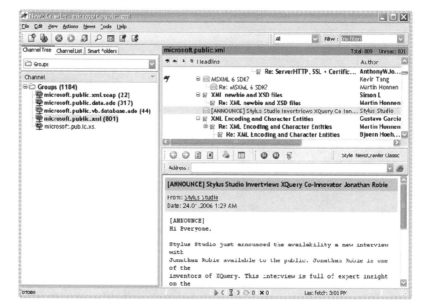

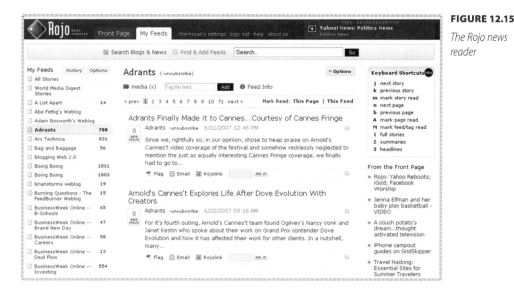

FIGURE 12.15

The Rojo news reader

Rojo

- Incoming items can be sorted by popularity, based on user voting
- Permits tagging of feeds

Setting up Your News Reading via Bloglines

Bloglines, along with Google Reader, is one of the two most popular news readers, so let's illustrate how this reader works in practice, and how you can use it to begin your news reading.

Some of Bloglines' special features include the integration of a top-notch blog search engine, a blog publishing tool, and an internal Internet browser. Bloglines also includes a few free services that are often considered premium, like keyword searches, URL citations (links), and disposable email addresses. It is also worth noting that Bloglines is able to add special functionality, like RSS popularity rankings, since it can draw on the subscription behavior of its sizable user community.

When you log into Bloglines, rather than being taken to your feed browser, you are first taken to Bloglines' homepage, which you will be required to navigate past in order to view your news feed content. Sticking with a news reader tradition of an email-inbox type interface, Bloglines has a two-column layout, and uses a tabbed interface to delineate the major areas of its application. The upper-left area includes a list of subscribed feeds, a personal blog, saved feed items, and feed "playlists." Links to modify the options for each of these areas are given at the top of the tabbed area selected. On the top-right, you'll find account settings links and a search box.

Finding and Adding Feeds to Bloglines

Bloglines' strong suit is its search function, and you can use it to easily locate new feeds to input into your reader. Bloglines allows users to search the blogosphere, find specific RSS feeds, or monitor conversations that are discussing a webpage. All of these searches can be performed via Bloglines' search box in the upper-right corner of every screen. However, just below this box, you can also access advanced search options similar to more powerful standalone search engine like Google Blog Search. Here, you can build Boolean queries, specify a language, and indicate a time period for when conversations took place. Separately, searches conducted via the "Search" tab in the main browsing window, will provide the option to search feeds, or exclude them entirely from search results. This option can be extremely handy for sifting out items that have already come across your radar, or for discovering entirely new conversations.

Search results can be sorted by other factors such as, relevance, date, or number of Bloglines subscribers for a specific feed or timeframe.

The look of the results page will naturally vary based on the query. A search for posts and post citations (links) will provide options to clip and email the articles, as well as preview and subscribe to an RSS feed. Hovering your cursor over the "More Info" link will reveal the number of Bloglines subscribers the feed has and the number of times the post has been cited. This can be useful information to determine how popular, if not authoritative or influential, a particular post has been.

FIGURE 12.17

Bloglines identifies how many subscribers a particular blog has on its own news reader.

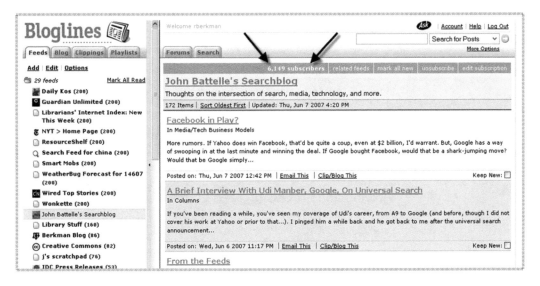

To continue to get results on a particular query, rather than having to repeat your Bloglines search again, you can just "subscribe" to it as a keyword-based search feed.

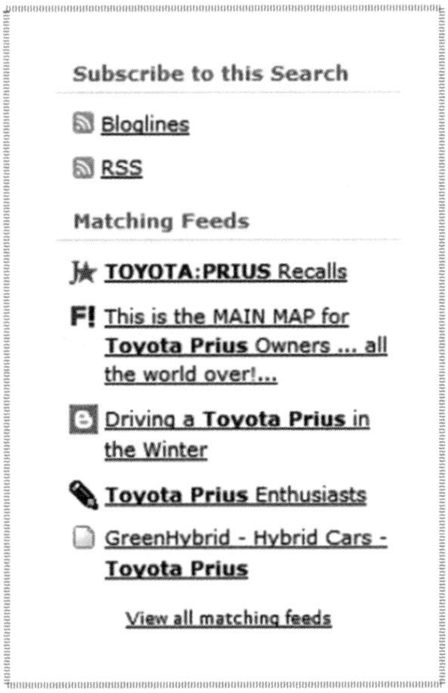

Once you have subscribed to a feed in Bloglines, you will be given the opportunity to add it to a new or current folder. Here, you can set up how you would like incoming feeds to be displayed (e.g., headlines only, summary, etc.) and whether or not the feed should be listed in your "public" listing of RSS feeds (a.k.a.

FIGURE 12.18

Bloglines permits users to subscribe to a search.

your "blogroll"). To get to the settings screen while browsing, click the "edit subscription" link at the top of the main window for each feed.

A few more useful options can be found by expanding Bloglines' "Additional Features" bar underneath your list of subscribed feeds. There, you can find feed recommendations based on your current subscriptions (again helpful for discovering new conversation sources) and a feed directory for the entire Bloglines community. Also listed is a Bloglines' bookmarklet to automatically subscribe to a website's Internet feed, as well as links to export your list of feeds and import someone else's.

Bloglines also includes a useful service not found in most news readers, which will help separate your research from your email inbox. In order to receive email newsletters and email alerts that do not also offer an RSS feed, Bloglines lets you create "email subscription" feeds. These email subscriptions allow you to view email as an RSS feed. You may want to use this feature to better manage an overflowing inbox, or as a way to receive email without handing out a private email address.

Viewing and Processing Feed Content with Bloglines

On Bloglines, it is simple to mark items as read. All feed items loaded into the main window will be automatically marked as read, saving users the trouble of having to individually mark each item or feed. You are also able to mark every feed read without viewing any feed content at all just by clicking the "Mark All Read" link in the "Feeds" tab. Conversely, to keep feed items "unread," you can check the "Keep New" box in the lower-right border of each item's expanded contents. You can also mark all items unread by clicking the "Keep New" link at the top of the page.

For a customized view of your feed folders, Bloglines allows the creation of individual "Playlists," which are collections of feeds that you can create for yourself and are not part of your main feed folder structure. Rather than change the groupings of your feeds by permanently changing the folder they are in, you can create a new context for a selected group of feeds.

Navigating Bloglines is also enhanced by the provision of a few keyboard shortcuts. Keyboard shortcuts, or "hotkeys" are listed at the bottom of the main browsing window. Keyboard shortcuts take some getting used to, but the ability to scan your feeds without having to reach for your mouse can speed up feed browsing.

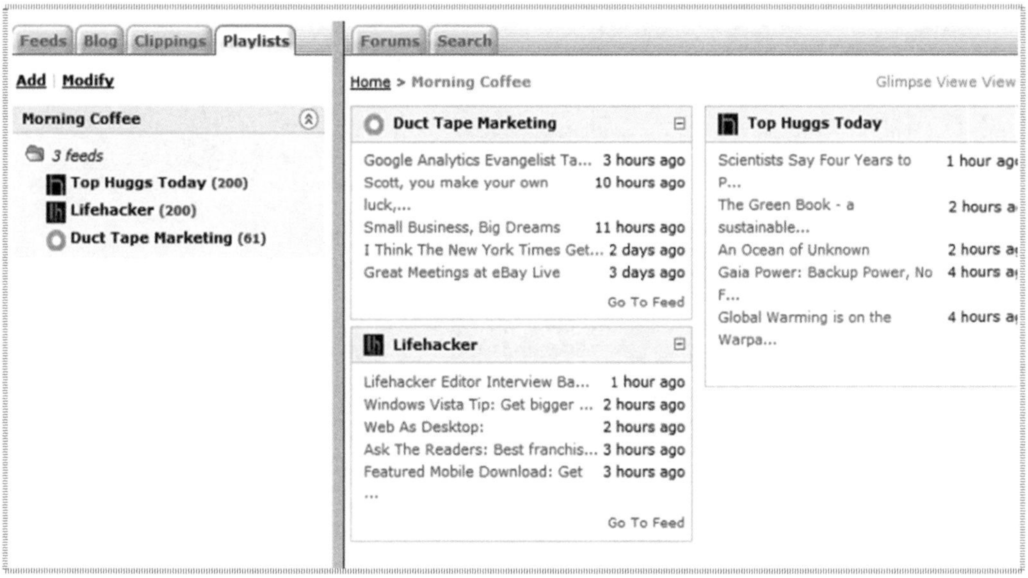

Sharing Conversations

Feeds that you have subscribed to and elect to make public can be shared via a personal "blogroll." A Bloglines' blogroll is just an editable list of your feed subscriptions. Your blogroll can be presented in a browsable Bloglines format, where others can export your list of feeds and import them into their own news reader, or it can be published as a much simpler list of links on a blog that you create. In both situations, you will need to make your blogroll public by "enabling" it via the options link in the Blog tab.

FIGURE 12.19

You can create customized "playlists" of associated feeds on Bloglines

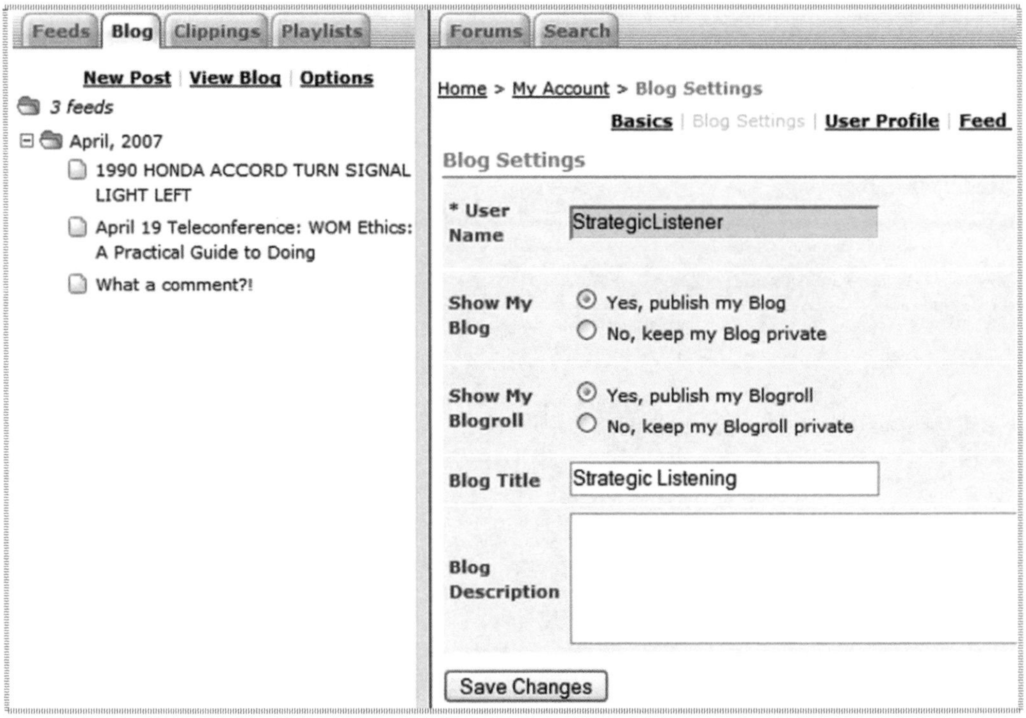

FIGURE 12.20

Bloglines lets users share their "blogroll" or collection of RSS feeds with other Bloglines users.

Clicking the "Clip/BlogThis" button below an item's contents will allow you to add comments to an item and then save it to your "Clippings" tab, or publish it to a personal blog. A Bloglines blog is the primary method for sharing posts with others. No coding experience is necessary; you can just click the "Blog" tab in the upper left and go to "options." In this screen you will be able to make your blog public.

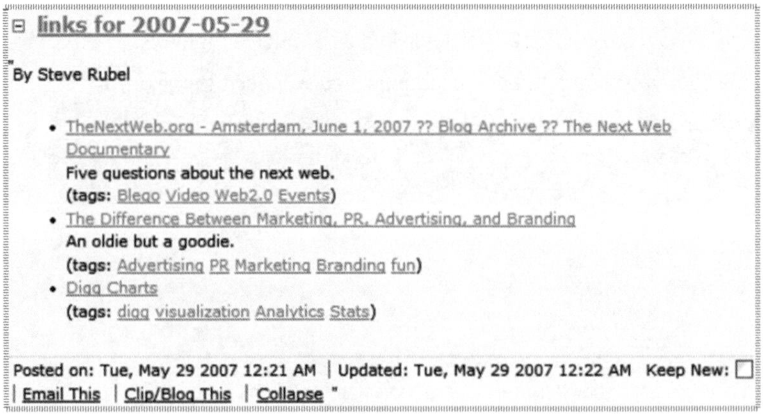

FIGURE 12.21

Bloglines provides options to clip or blog a particular posting below the blog post.

WHAT ABOUT TRACKING COMMENTS?

News readers will let you keep track of the latest entries from selected bloggers, as well as other bloggers out there who have posted something that includes your key words, but there is really no way to track the comments that readers leave on the blogs. At this point in time, the only way you can track and analyze comments is to hire one of the blog-monitoring vendors, such as those described in Chapter 6, since many of these, such as Umbria, will have the capability of setting up a comment tracking system.

There are a couple of specialized tools that can help with comments, such as co.mments. com. This site lets you keep track of specific comment threads on a particular post that is of interest to you. You copy the link to the post into co.mments, and future comments will be tracked there. You can even put the feed into your own reader as well.

Best Feed Reading Practices

Once you've chosen your reader, and selected your feeds, you will naturally spend some time getting accustomed to the features of your reader, and will likely be pleasantly surprised at all the relevant and interesting blog posts and keyword focused conversations and news that will be coming your way every day, every hour, even every few minutes. That's a good thing . . . right?

As you might have guessed, the great enthusiasm of new RSS users typically starts waning after a few weeks. The reason? As you begin to discover the convenience and power of getting information via your reader, you naturally begin to find and add more feeds, and quickly discover there is too much to keep up with. You begin to confront news feed overload.

This may seem somewhat ironic since setting up feeds is supposed to be a strategy for avoiding information overload. But these days, it is certainly possible to feel overloaded not only when you are being buried with irrelevant, trivial, and dubious information from a search engine or other open web research site, but by getting too much *good* information as well! And then you begin to feel that you "should" be reading all of this valuable and important information flowing into your reader, but of course, you simply don't have the time to do so.

Let's face it, you could probably spend 8 hours a day or more just reading all the news feeds that are coming your way, and there still will be important and valuable news, posts, and content that you won't be able to get to. So you do need to give up the idea of ever getting to it all. It's just not possible. It never was, and now in the age where there are no real barriers to keep anyone from publishing or broadcasting, and it's all instantly available 24 hours per day, it is not even remotely possible to keep up.

That's why I believe that the concept of "information overload," while it is real, is primarily a subjective and psychological matter. In other words, it is a *perception* and *feeling*—a real one to be sure—that can best be dealt with by a combination of practical and psychological strategies.

The following section is a guide, not a blueprint, to get you thinking about ways you might manage the information delivered to your news reader, and thereby minimize some of the pitfalls of using RSS. Let's discuss the practical strategies first.

Managing Your News Feeds and Feed Overload: Practical Tips and Strategies

One of the biggest reasons why it's easy to feel overloaded with RSS lies in the ease with which you can subscribe to feeds. With so many interesting conversations and resources available online, as well as the widespread adoption of RSS by bloggers, search engines, and other information aggregation sites, it doesn't take long to acquire a substantial list of feeds in your news reader. Exacerbating the problem is the fact that news readers display the number of unread items in your feed list so you will easily see the number of new items that arrive in your news reader. Unfortunately, as you see those "unread" numbers climb, your emotional discomfort can also increase. Here are some practical strategies for taking charge of your news reading habits.

Filtering content on your reader

A big help in dealing with too many feeds is to reduce unwanted information before it can take up your valuable attention. This is why it is so important to become familiar with the RSS filtering tools at your disposal.

Always take full advantage of a search engine's advanced search options that allow you to include and exclude words from your searches when you are setting up a keyword tracking feed. The advanced search options provided by blog search engines go beyond filtering keywords and allow you to restrict results to a single source or author, and even confine the items that come across your search feed to a date range or language. Then, once you copy the RSS feed generated by that search, you will be getting very precise blog conversations in your reader.

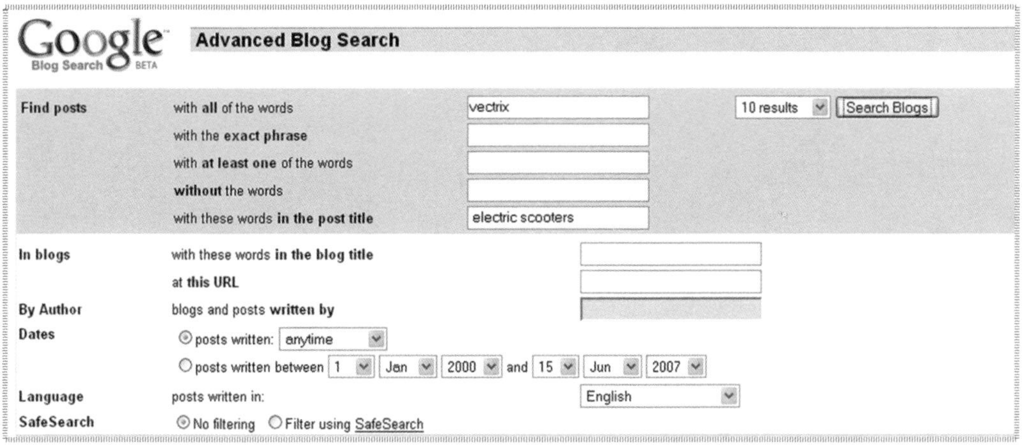

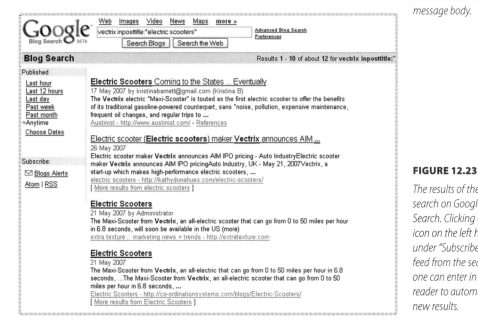

If the source of an RSS feed is not from a search engine, or your news reader does not provide keyword search filters, there are *standalone* RSS keyword filtering services you can turn to. Two leaders are FeedRinse and ReFilter, both of which are available online for free, and will do filtering for you. You just add your feed, and choose the phrase you would like filtered in or out. (See Figure 12.24)

FIGURE 12.22

*An advanced keyword search on Google Blog search restricts results to just those blog posts contain the words: electric scooters in the **post title**; and the company name vectrix somewhere in the post's message body.*

FIGURE 12.23

The results of the advanced search on Google Blog Search. Clicking on the "RSS" icon on the left hand bar under "Subscribe" creates a feed from the search, which one can enter in a news reader to automatically get new results.

FIGURE 12.24

FeedRinse will automatically filter your feeds to select or deselect those with designated keywords.

News reader developers are realizing the importance of adding keyword filtering functionality to their products, so it's likely that the need to use third-party services like these to provide this functionality will decrease over time. Bloglines already provides advanced filtering, and Google Reader will likely follow suit.

Managing Your Feeds

Another opportunity to "defend" your attention from too many incoming feeds is by taking some actions *after* you subscribe to a new news feed. Whenever you add a new feed to your news reader, consider adding it to an *"on probation"* type folder that you've specifically set up for collecting only new feeds. If after a few weeks, you find yourself reading this new feed frequently, you can add it to your permanent collection. However, if you are not referring to it, you should remove the feed entirely before it absorbs any more of your attention. Remember, there is absolutely no advantage to getting updates you feel might be useful in the future, but that you aren't using. You can always easily resubscribe to any feed if you need it in the future.

You should also consider adopting a strategy for *prioritizing* feeds as they come in to your news reader. Each bit of incoming information is not going to deserve equal parts of your attention and so doesn't deserve equal placement in your reader. For example, you may decide that feeds that you've set up to alert you to mentions of your company or product are going to be the highest priority. You can set up your news reader to reflect this priority. Here's one approach that relies on the use of feed "labels."

All news readers permit incoming feeds to be grouped into separate folders. Google Reader provides "labels" for its users to apply to distinguish incoming feeds. In Google Reader, "labels" are applied to each feed and every item that comes into your news reader via that feed will automatically be given whatever label you designate.

The way you assign labels to feeds in Google Reader is by first subscribing to the RSS feed, which brings up a view of the feed items in your news reader, and then assigning a label through the drop-down "Folder Settings" menu at the top of the page. Here you can select any number of existing labels for a feed or create a new one. Note that within this menu, you can also rename the title of the feed to help sort it within a folder, or for easier recognition as you are scanning your feeds.

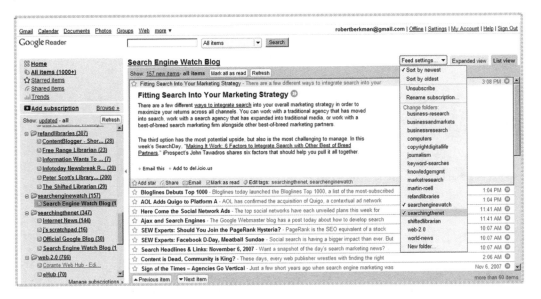

You can then use your folders (or "labels" as Google Reader calls them) to assist you in prioritizing and assigning value. One way is by numbering them. For example, the number 1 could be assigned to topics that should be monitored daily, the number 2 assigned to folders in need of a weekly glance, and a higher number for RSS feeds that can be monitored monthly or less. Numbering feeds will bring important folders to the top of your feed list and will help ensure that the most critical incoming information is always easily accessible.

For more general topics that can be monitored on more of an "as needed" basis, you may not want to assign a number at all. Such items can be grouped into non-priority folders that are treated more like a streaming newswire of news, rather than an "inbox" where each item needs its own attention. No

FIGURE 12.25

When adding a new feed to Google Reader you can apply a label to the new feed which can help you prioritize them.

matter how many unread items accumulate in these general folders, you can let the content flow by, as RSS pioneer Dave Winer puts it, like a "River of News," without worrying about keeping up with all that you may be missing.

As a final best practice for managing your feeds, you should regularly go through your list of feeds and clear out the ones you rarely find worthwhile. To make this easier, Google Reader provides some useful and interesting statistics regarding its users' RSS reading and subscription habits, which can be accessed by clicking the "Trends" link in the upper-left menu in Google Reader. These subscription trends show you how often each of your feeds is updated and the percentage of articles that you read from a particular feed. With Google Reader Trends, you can also discover feeds that are inactive, which feed's items you may be sharing most often, and even the times during the day you do most of your reading.

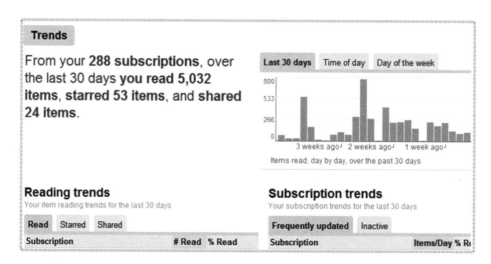

FIGURE 12.26

Google Reader's Trends function can help you quickly discover which feeds you read most often.

The Importance of Workflow

Once you apply a news reader to trap your research all in one place, you can apply some effective RSS reading and workflow processes. How do you get through your feeds without feeling overwhelmed? You can do this by breaking down the RSS feed review process into two smaller steps:

1. Scanning incoming feeds for interesting content, and

2. Separately following-up items that warrant closer inspection.

Incoming feed content can be displayed primarily by two different views: headlines only or headlines with summaries. First, you will want to decide which approach is most suitable for you. If your priority is to get through lots of content quickly, you might prefer the headline-only view. But if you find that this approach does not give you enough information about an item, or seems too dizzying, you may prefer a slower browsing mode where you see the summary of each item instead.

This matter of feed display is where I feel NewzCrawler does a particularly good job, in that the top of the screen is devoted to showing you all recent headlines, from all feeds, but when you highlight one, the summary of that item appears on the lower half of the screen.

FIGURE 12.27

NewzCrawler's interface makes it easy to browse incoming feeds.

Reader Shortcuts

If your reader offers them, you will want to take advantage of keyboard short-cuts, as these can also help you make your feed reading experience more efficient. For example, in Google Reader, keeping your fingers on the "J" and "K" keys allows you to move to the next or previous items in the RSS feed or folder without lifting your hand from the keyboard. Once you come across something in your feeds that warrants further follow-up, you can "star" it by hitting the "S" key.

FIGURE 12.28

If you would like to see all of Google Reader's keyboard short-cuts, hit, Shift + "?" to bring up a transparent cheatsheet.

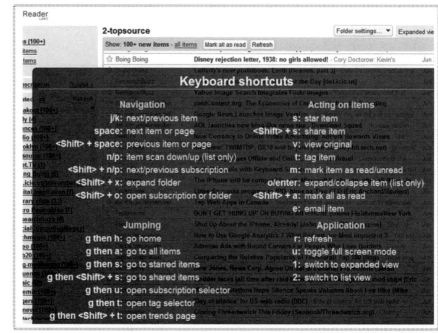

Once you've pulled (or "starred") items that seem to be of most interest, you can separately go over what you have selected by navigating to the "Starred Items" folder in Google Reader. The useful thing about starring items is that if you need to manage your time, you can always come back to your "starred" items later. They will always be there waiting for you until you remove the star.

Some feed content won't be entirely visible in your news reader and you will need to go to the original source. You can quickly do this on Google Reader by hitting the "V" key as you are viewing each item. You can also adjust how your Internet browser displays pages to make it easier to link to and read the original sources. I suggest using a "tabbed" browser, like Firefox, Netscape, Safari, or Microsoft's newest version of Internet Explorer. (Yahoo! Toolbar can add this functionality to older versions of IE.) Tabbed browsing allows you to click on links and open pages in a separate tab contained within the same browser window. So rather than hunting around the desktop looking for a browser window, you can just scan your toolbar tabs for the original items you have launched.

Importantly, tabbed browsing also allows you to completely "isolate" the process of scanning feeds. Once you have finished scanning your feeds, you will be able to close your news reader entirely, thereby shutting out any further distraction. You can now focus on your task at hand: digesting interesting feed content from your tabbed windows.

One more practical RSS tip: you might also want to consider dedicating a certain, bounded period of the day for accessing the feeds on your news reader. If you haven't realized it already, your news reader will consume as much time as you are willing to allow it.

Email Alert Services

Another option for automatically keeping up with your favorite bloggers or postings that include words that match your keyword profile is to sign up with an email-based alert service.

Alert services are a fine way to keep up with postings from bloggers and to monitor blog conversations. Before RSS began taking off, these kinds of alerts were the primary way Internet users kept up with timely and fast-changing information. And while alert services originally only updated users on the latest online *news* stories, alerts eventually came to include blog postings, as well as other timely information appearing on the Internet.

However, using an alert service to keep up with consumer conversations does suffer some drawbacks when compared to RSS. One big one is timeliness. Even if you set up your alert service to send your alerts to you on a frequent basis, you are not alerted to new items as quickly as you would be by your RSS reader. You also have to wait for the email to be delivered, and then you have to go to your email, open it, and read it.

Another drawback is that you may feel that you are already getting way too many emails, and you just don't want more coming into your in-box. Many of us feel we suffer from email overload, and don't want to sign up for anything that is going to increase the number we receive. (Note however, that if you do choose to use an alert service, your email program will likely permit you to create keyword filters and folders. In this way, all emails that arrive from your news alert provider can be automatically forwarded to their own folder to keep these from getting mixed up with your other emails.)

Another downside to email alert services is that you don't have the same ability to quickly browse and scan incoming information from multiple sources. RSS readers are optimized for fast browsing of scores of headlines as they flow in to your new reader, so you can quickly scan, read short excerpts, click on the full text, move on to the next item, skip an item, etc. An email is, well, just an email. Even an email that has more than one posting included in its body, with hotlinks to the original source is still not as optimized as a news reader for reading incoming news and blog posts.

Finally, all of the latest technology advances, features, and add-on tools that have been introduced over the last couple of years have been focused primarily on improving and enhancing RSS readers, and not email alert services. As a result, you can do many more things with a news reader than you can with an alert service.

Still, you might decide that you are more comfortable in using email as an alert service to monitor incoming blogs. One plus for getting updates via email is that your email program, if so configured, can automatically build a nice archive of the incoming items, which can serve as a customized searchable database. Most RSS readers typically only store incoming feeds for a few weeks or a couple months at the most.

If you decide you'd rather go with an email based alert system, there are really only two major players, Google and Yahoo!, and they take completely different approaches. Here are the details and how they differ.

Google Alerts

Google has offered a straightforward email alert for those who want to get updates of its latest web and news items for quite awhile, and when it launched its Blog search engine in 2005 it also began offering an email based alert for blogs. The process for creating a Google blog alert is simple:

1. Link to Google Alerts: www.google.com/alerts

2. Enter your search terms on the topics you would like to monitor. This is a critical step in the process. The quality of your alerts will be directly related to your ability to identify the best key words. See the earlier discussion on page 114 for some tips on how to identify the best keywords. One nice feature to Google Alerts is that it permits users to employ the same advanced search features and filters that are available on Google's advanced search page.

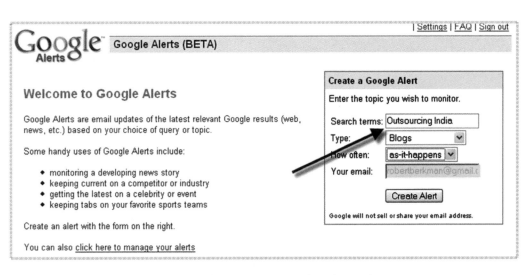

3. Choose "Blogs" from the "type" pull-down menu; and then choose the frequency of delivery: (once a day; "as it happens"; "once a week").

4. Enter your email address

That's it!

You will now begin receiving Google Alerts that contain postings from the blogosphere that include your key words, right in your email box. Below is an example of a Google alert email on the topic of outsourcing and India:

FIGURE 12.29

The Google Alerts page allows users to specify alerts from blogs

FIGURE 12.30

A sample of a Google Blog alert for postings that contain the words: Outsourcing and India

> ☆ Google Alerts <googlealerts-noreply@google.com> to m show details Jun 12 (6 days ago) ↩ Reply | ▾
>
> **Google Blogs Alert for: Outsourcing India**
>
> Offshore **Outsourcing**: What Side Are You On?
> By itmatchonline
> Advantages of offshore **outsourcing**. - Companies can exploit the lower labor costs in third world countries such as **India**, China, the Philippines, and Mexico. - It cost considerably less for companies to build facilities in third world ...
> Outsourcing in India - http://outsourcinginindia.wordpress.com
>
> **Indian** CIOs must consider offshore **outsourcing**: Gartner
> By Ramesh Natarajan
> **Indian** organisations facing the challenge of an IT skills shortage and "second-class" treatment from local service providers must consider offshore **outsourcing** to obtain high-end IT services, says Gartner Inc. "**India** is witnessing a ...
> Views and Thoughts of a Global Indian - http://fusions.wordpress.com
>
> Call Center Project - Travel Reservation- High end Customer Service
> By callcenterservices
> We are **India** based company looking for best center for inbound process. NO CONSULTANTS WILL BE ENTERTAINED- STRICKLY. Here are the brief details of the process would make you understand how it works. 1) Type of Project: Travel ...
> Outsourcing Call Center Services - http://callcenterservices.wordpress.com
>
> This as-it-happens Google Alert is brought to you by Google.
>
> Remove this alert.
> Create another alert.
> Manage your alerts.
>
> ↩ Reply → Forward ♡ Invite Google to chat

Yahoo! Alerts

The primary alternative to Google for email alerts is Yahoo!'s Alerts. However Yahoo! Alerts work differently than Google's. Rather than permitting users to create a customized keyword search to find blog posts from *all* bloggers in its database, when using Yahoo! Alerts, users need to specify *which* blogger's postings to monitor. To do this, you first link to Yahoo!, then choose a category called "blog/feeds." Then you must enter the RSS feed of a specific blog that you want to monitor via email.

FIGURE 12.31

Yahoo!'s Blog Alert set up page requires that the user enter the RSS of a blog or Web site.

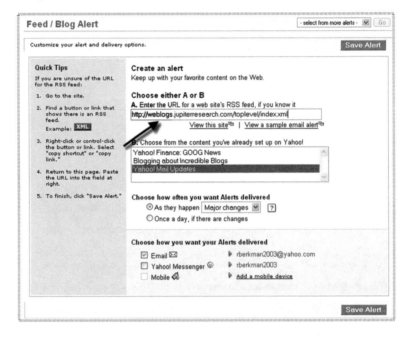

So while Yahoo! Alerts offers an email based alert service and you do receive new postings in your email box, it functions more like an RSS reader since you receive *all* postings from specific bloggers.

One noteworthy feature of Yahoo! Alerts is that in addition to getting your results via email, you also have the option of getting it delivered to a Yahoo! messenger or a mobile device.

Psychological Strategies for Dealing with Information and RSS Overload

Unlike some observers who say that there is no such thing as information overload, I believe information overload is real. However, I also believe that it is real in the same way that anxiety, frustration, worry, or any other emotion or perception is real. That is, it exists for the person who is experiencing it. Information overload is a feeling or perception, and so it is an internally created phenomenon, and not an external reality.

Therefore, there are internally focused, psychological solutions that can be used to help in overcoming the feeling of being overwhelmed with too much information

The approach I like best for helping avoid the negative feelings of anxiety, worry, and concern that can occur when you feel overloaded with information is derived from a type of cognitive therapy called Rational Emotional Behavioral Therapy (REBT), founded by the late renowned psychologist Albert Ellis. The basic principle behind REBT is fairly straightforward: we are not disturbed by things themselves, but by our thoughts about them, how we interpret them, and what we tell ourselves about those things.

So, if we tell ourselves that something we are dealing with is awful and that we just can't stand it, our accompanying feelings will likely be ones like dread, deep frustration, intense anxiety, and depression. If instead, we reframe the same phenomena that we're experiencing as "too bad" or inconvenient, or a pain in the neck, then rather than feeling all those intense negative emotions, our feelings are more likely to be resignation or disappointment, not necessarily positive, but not so debilitating either.

So it behooves all of us to specifically identify what it is that we are telling ourselves (explicitly or just beneath our consciousness) when faced with lots of information coming at us. Try to avoid thinking,

- This is an *impossible* situation.

- I'll *never* get to all of these critical pieces of information.

- It is *terrible* that I can't get to all of this.

- What a *disaster* it would be if I were to lose my job because I'm *no good* at keeping up the way I should be.

If you have a tendency to think like that, take a minute and analyze how you might be framing the situation of having lots of information to manage. You can see that you've chosen:

- To define the situation as "impossible"

- To tell yourself that you will "never" get to it all

- That all the information is "critical"

- That if you don't get to it, then it would therefore be "terrible"

- That you may lose your job as a result of all this; that you are "no good" at doing what you "should" be doing.

REBT trains its clients to find, identify, and isolate those kinds of "awfulizing" and catastrophizing statements that people often tell themselves. If you can examine whether what you're telling yourself is truly rational, reasonable, and healthy and you find that your statements may not be rational or healthy, you can determine if there are other, more legitimate, and more appropriate, realistic, and helpful ways to view the exact same phenomena.

For example, rather than defining the situation of having lots of incoming news feeds with the anxiety inducing word "impossible," wouldn't it be more appropriate to think it is difficult or challenging? Rather than moan to yourself that you will "never" get to it all, you can instead say to yourself that it's not humanly possible to get to everything, but you'll read the most pressing items whenever you are able to make the time. Rather than all the information being defined as "critical," it is more likely that most of the information would fall under the category of "useful, interesting, and helpful." And rather than defining the situation as "terrible" if you don't get to the information, you could more realistically call it "too bad" or "unfortunate, but hardly a disaster."

The larger point here is that you do have some control over how you define and interpret events in your external world. And we should apply that principle to any debilitating perceptions of information overload as well.

Vendors will continue to crank out and introduce all sorts of new tools, sites, search engines, and features that are going to purport to help us solve whatever may be our latest iteration of information overload. But technology problems are rarely solved by more technology. In fact, the irony is that because new technologies typically eliminate barriers to creating and disseminating information, they often result in *increasing* the amount of information that's available. So you can't rely on a technological solution to what is, ultimately and at its heart, partly a practical matter, but mostly a psychological and perception issue. And solutions to problems like this rest within you.

CHAPTER 13

Buzz Surfacing Tools

SO FAR the strategic listening strategies and approaches that I've discussed have described how to find conversations and consumer media about a *specific topic or keywords* that you've *predetermined* that you want to monitor closely. However, there is a different way that blogs and social media can help you identify what's important and worth your attention by finding out: what the hot topics and latest buzz are, what bloggers and other people are talking about the most right now, and what's getting lots of attention.

When you use these kinds of sites and tools, you aren't tracking conversations that conform to some topic, company, industry, or issue that you want to track, but instead you get a feel for the general buzz in the blogosphere. And just as there are sites and search engines that let you monitor defined topics, there are also sites and online tools that are designed to surface hot topics being discussed online. These sites and tools are called by different names, but one popular term is "Buzz Trackers." These tell you the buzz online, and purportedly help you identify the hot topics, and spot the latest trends.

In order to identify what's hot and the buzz online, these sites typically follow a philosophy or belief that's come to be called "the wisdom of crowds." That's an outlook that, under the right conditions, the smartest and most accurate decisions are made by large groups of people, acting independently. According to this philosophy in the blogosphere, if lots of people link to or click on a particular blog or a blog posting, this is a good clue that a discussion is significant, and worthy of your attention.

If your goal is to keep your finger on the pulse of what's on people's minds, these tools promise that they can help. However, although they can be fascinating and fun to use, they have limitations too. I'll get back to that issue in a bit, but for now, let's examine a couple of the leading buzz tracking sites and describe how they work.

There are a few types of buzz trackers. They differ primarily based on the different approaches they take in how they surface hot topics. I've organized them into the following broad categories:

Statistical Buzz Trackers

These sites track blog buzz primarily by relying on a counting method: counting words, links, or some other element to rank discussions online. Two of the big names that use this technique are Technorati via its "Popular" feature and BlogPulse. Some of these statistically oriented sites also allow users to enter their own terms, and generate a custom chart that identifies statistical trends of the popularity of those terms. Sites that provide this kind of customizable buzz tracking include Technorati's "Charts," BlogPulse Trends, and IceRocket's Trends.

Blogger Link Analysis

Another approach to surfacing hot topics in the blogosphere are sites that use their own algorithms to identify what stories are the hottest in the blogosphere, based on the linking behavior of bloggers. The leaders here are Memeorandum/Techmeme, and TailRank.

Community Vote Aggregators

These sites don't just count words or links, but integrate human input in some manner. They do so by setting up their site so people can vote (by clicking or via another mechanism) to express their preference on what discussion or item they feel is important and noteworthy. Those votes are then aggregated and counted up, and the ones with the most votes appear on the top of a list. A leader here is a site called Digg. A subset of this group are community vote aggregators that are customizable, where each user can get a listing of just what is most important to them. Some sites that offer this feature are BlogPulse's Trend Tracker, and IceRocket's Blog Trends.

Here's an overview of each of these tools, how they work, and how they might help you identify trends.

Statistical Buzz Trackers

Technorati: "Popular"

I've already discussed Technorati as a premier source for locating blogs and blog postings. Being the one-stop blog search shop that it is, Technorati also provides buzz-tracking features too. Its statistical-oriented, buzz-tracking service is a basic feature simply called "Popular." You can view Technorati's "Popular" feature by linking to: www.technorati.com/pop, and as illustrated in Figure 13.1, you can view not only the top blogs, but current information such as the top searches, and what news items, videos, and music bloggers are linking to most frequently.

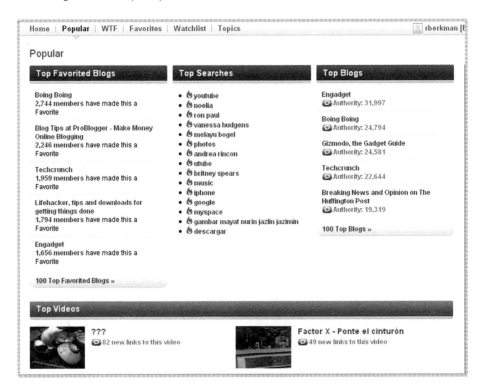

There are also other types of "what's hot" type rankings available from Technorati, though Technorati frequently updates and changes what kind of information it surfaces. If you browse the "popular" page on Technorati, you can see what's most popular in areas like movies, videos, blogs, tags, games and so on. These popular topics are derived by a simple *counting* method: Technorati adds up the number of incoming links to these items from bloggers to create its rankings.

FIGURE 13.1

Technorati shows the most popular blogs, searches, videos and other consumer content.

While Technorati's "popular" listings are interesting, what's being tracked is ephemeral, related to just one point in time, and is not really deep or robust enough to be considered a real trend-tracking tool. Many of the conversations, themes and postings surfaced would be better characterized as short-lived fads, rather than deep trends (I discussed the difference between trends and fads in some detail in Chapter 3.) These topics also are tilted towards entertainment, technology, the Internet, and personalities in the news.

Another statistically based buzz-tracking tool that Technorati offers is its customizable one, via its "charts" feature.

The "charts" feature is a straightforward aggregation of blog posts. You enter words or phrases, and then you can view a chart that displays the amount of discussion on that topic over a set period of time that you select. You can enable this feature by linking directly to www.technorati.com/chart/ (your keywords); e.g., www.technorati.com/chart/mortgages.

Once the chart is displayed, you can identify how much blog discussion there has been around your topic over the period of time of your choosing (7 days, 30 days, 90 days, 180 days, or 360 days). You can also look at a subset of this aggregation by specifying that you only want to view the conversations in a certain language or based on the popularity of a blogger as well as for similar or related terms. As mentioned earlier, blogger popularity is called "authority" by Technorati and measured primarily by the number of unique bloggers that link to a blog. See the chart and options made available for a search on iPhone in Figure 13.2.

FIGURE 13.2

Technorati charts the frequency of blog posts on words and phrases.

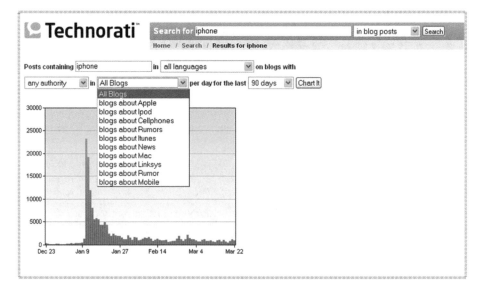

This Technorati charting function is pretty interesting. You can see in Figure 13.2 how bloggers' mention of the word "iPhone" took off on January 9, 2007, which was the day that Steven Jobs announced the new Apple product. You can also see how blog discussion of iPhone quickly dropped off.

Nielsen BuzzMetrics: BlogPulse

Nielsen BuzzMetrics is well known in the blog-monitoring industry as a vendor of fee-based blog tracking services, but also for its free web-based blog search and tracking engine, BlogPulse. Like Technorati, BlogPulse provides a range of statistically generated buzz surfacing tools, under the link on its home page titled "Analysis."

If you click "Analysis" you'll find several complementary statistical buzz tracking features:

- **Top Links.** The most popular links appearing in blogs (for a designated date).
- **Top Blog Posts**. The most-linked-to blog posts (by date)
- **Top Blogs.** The most linked-to blogs (by date)
- **Top News Stories.** The most linked-to news stories (bydate)
- **Top News Sources**. The most linked-to news stories (by date)
- **Top Videos.** The most linked-to videos (by date)
- **Key People.** Prominently features people across a designated date's blog entries
- **Key Phrases.** Key phrases and themes that are most frequently appearing on blogs for a specific date. Key Phrases are broken into two smaller categories: "Bursty Phrases" are phrases that have moved the most in the rankings; and "BlogBites" are stories and themes that have been the biggest movers.

FIGURE 13.3

According to BlogPulse, a spike in the word "freegan" occurred on blogs on June 21, 2007.

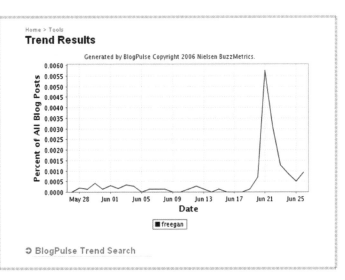

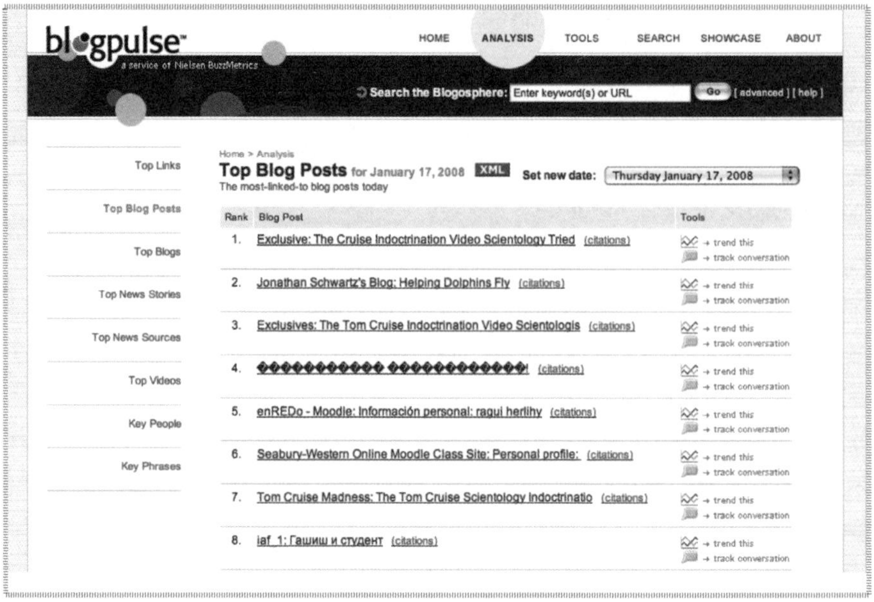

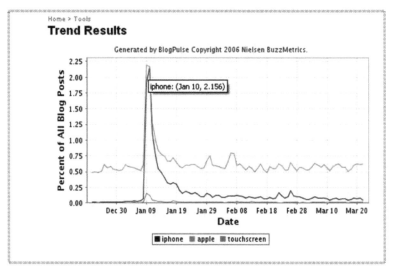

FIGURE 13.4

This page identifies what BlogPulse has calculated as the top blog posts for March 3, 2007.

As with Technorati's "Popular" feature, BlogPulse's charts only show the frequency of postings for a specific date, and not over a long period of time, so other than telling you what the buzz has been for a single day, it is not of significant value for discovering the emergence of a long-lasting trend.

However, like Technorati's "Chart" feature, BlogPulse also permits its users to create a customized chart to find out how frequently a particular word, phrase, or person, appeared over a longer timeframe, such as a period of months. BlogPulse takes this customized trending feature a step further then Technorati, and permits users to choose up to three different words or phrases,

FIGURE 13.5

BlogPulse permits users to track the level of discussion of up to three words or phrases over a period of months.

and then track these together over a period of time (1, 2, 3 or 6 months). It also creates its charts by calculating the percentage of all blog posts that included the user's words or phrases. See Figure 13.5 which identifies a 3-month frequency trend of how often bloggers mentioned any of three related words: iPhone, Apple, and touchscreen:

You can see how the graph clearly identifies the amount of discussion for these words over time. It also allows the user to mouse over a point in time on the chart to identify the frequency of blog posts for a specific date. In the example in Figure 13.5, by mousing over the chart, I could see that the peak date for blog discussion of iPhone was on January 10.

IceRocket Trends

Another blog search engine that offers a quantitative buzz tracking capability is IceRocket. Like Technorati and BlogPulse, IceRocket permits users to create customized charts to view how frequently specified words and phrases were discussed in blogs over a set period of time.

Figure 13.7 is an example of such a chart created on IceRocket. Notice that to create this chart, I was able to make a more complex comparison by entering more than one term or phrase in each search box (Figure 13.6). For instance, I entered terms in order to compare how often blog posts contained ALL the terms "delta and cancel," "usair and cancel," and "jet blue and cancel."

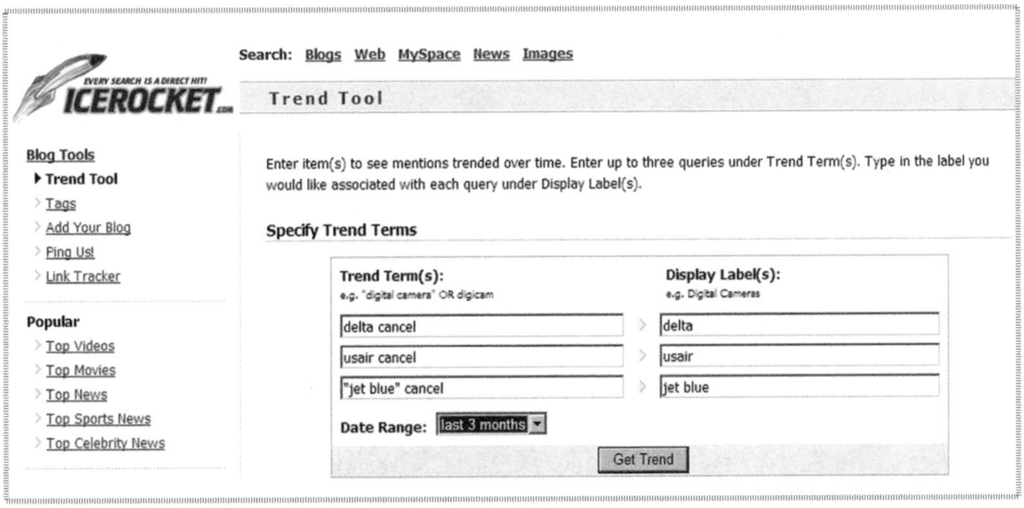

FIGURE 13.6

Setting up a trend search on IceRocket

And here is the result I received:

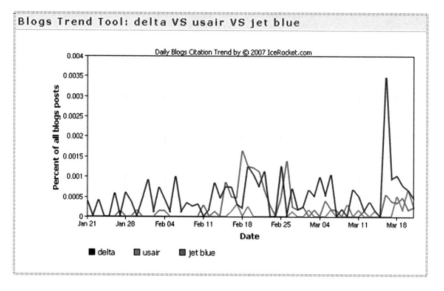

FIGURE 13.7

*The result of a blog trend
search on IceRocket.*

Figure 13.7 illustrates how the number of blogs that contained both the phrase "cancel" and "jet blue" were very low, particularly compared with Delta, until February 14, the day a major storm left many JetBlue passengers stranded on its airlines for 10 hours or more; then the number of blog posts with those two posts peaks and exceeds the others.

This is interesting information to view—but again, what can you do with it in terms of useful market intelligence? I'll discuss this later in this chapter.

Blog Link Analysis Sites

Another way that buzz trackers surface what's hot in the blogosphere is by analyzing how and what bloggers are linking to. One leader here is Memeorandum, along with its sister site Techmeme.

Memeorandum focuses on politics, and Techmeme covers technology. Like Technorati, IceRocket, and BlogPulse, they too surface what's hot in the blogosphere. As is increasingly true on the Internet, "news" is defined as almost any kind of timely and new content on the Internet—online newspaper stories, blog postings, and other kinds of media created by ordinary people.

The way the two Memeorandums identify the hot stories is by examining which bloggers are linking to whom, and to what sites. Every five minutes a new listing of the most popular (linked to) stories is generated. Figure 13.8 is an example of a front page on the technology oriented Techmemeorandum:

FIGURE 13.8

Techmeme's home page displays what it has calculated to be the hottest technology stories of the day.

You can see that the position and size of the headline is a key indicator of the story's importance. Note also how the site surrounds each item with a cluster of related stories and discussions.

These two sites are useful if you want to get a quick snapshot of what news, broadly defined, bloggers and others on the web think is most important at the moment. There is no way to look at trends over a longer period though.

TailRank

Another interesting blog buzz tracker is a site called TailRank. TailRank also surfaces what's hot among bloggers, and like Memeorandum, it does so by using its own algorithm that tracks conversations among blogs, looking at data like who links to who, the text surrounding those links, and what others are linking to and citing.

Note that TailRank includes only about 150,000 blogs in making its calcula-
tions, a small segment of the blog universe. It chooses these based on what it
deems blogs with "highly linked and discussed links and citations."

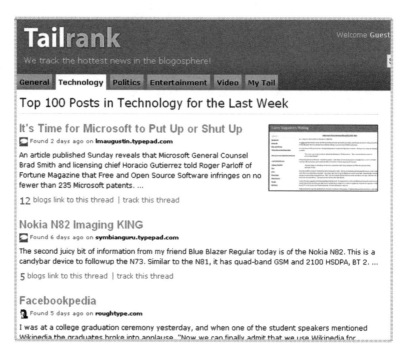

Community Vote Aggregators

Yet another approach to finding buzz relies on a community to cast its votes
for the most significant news items and content.

These sites aggregate the votes of hundreds or thousands of users. Users
are asked to click on a blog posting to actively indicate their preference or
endorsement of a particular item as noteworthy. The assumption with these
sites is that if you can discover which blog postings and discussions are being
chosen by others as significant, then these are worth your attention—relying
on that "wisdom of crowds" type of philosophy.

There are a few sites that offer this kind of community vote aggregation,
but as an example, I'll focus on the most prominent one, Digg.

Digg

Digg surfaces a wide range of content that its users have voted as noteworthy.
That content includes consumer-generated discussions and media such as

blogs, podcasts, and video, but also encompasses online news stories from mainstream newspapers and other publishers.

After registering as a member, a user of Digg can submit a news, blog, podcast or video item for the community to view it. Digg then places that content into a section called "Upcoming Stories." There, other Digg members can view it, read it, and if they like it, click on a "Digg It" link. The more members that click a Digg It link, the higher that story will appear on Digg's front page.

FIGURE 13.10

Digg's front page reflects the content that has gotten the most votes from its Digg community.

Digg offers a few interesting features. One is that users can locate the most popular stories from different time frames: currently popular, past 24 hours, past week, past month, or past year. You can also browse the most popular stories by categories. There is one for business and finance, for example (Figure 13.11):

FIGURE 13.11

The most popular business oriented stories on Digg for the past 7 days.

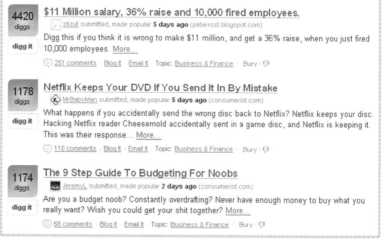

FIGURE 13.12

Clicking on the "Virgin America" link above displays this screen with more detailed information:

Digg is also doing interesting things in its lab, such as working on a visual map of hot items as they are being "digged."

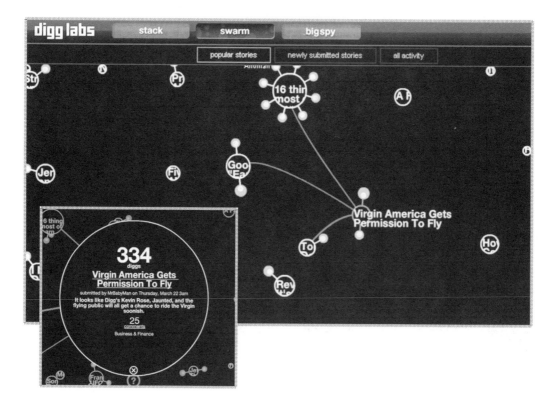

Finally, another significant feature of Digg is that you can perform a keyword search, and from that search, create an RSS feed for your reader. In this way, you can stay up to date with what the Digg community submits that relates to your topic of interest.

Because Digg is an influential site on the web that bloggers and even some mainstream journalists watch carefully, it can be useful to monitor when a relevant blog post, news story, or other content that discusses a topic of interest to you makes it onto this site. Often a high ranking on Digg will create additional buzz on the item that spreads to other forms of media, both online and offline.

Digg has become so influential that it not only reflects what's getting attention on the Internet, but also drives what becomes a hot news item. This makes Digg and others like it a powerful force in determining what stories and blog posts get attention. In fact, there are bloggers and others who will try to write stories in a manner that makes them more likely to get voted on in Digg. (These kinds of stories have been called "digg bait.") You may also notice that blogs and mainstream newspapers are increasingly providing a link to "Digg This!" near their content.

Where Does Google Fit In?

Finally, you'd think that with all the various services and options that Google offers, this king of online search would also have a blog buzz tracking feature. Somewhat surprisingly it doesn't. However, Google does offer a couple of complementary buzz tracking functions called Google Trends that are still worth noting. These are part of what Google calls its "Labs" site—projects that are still being worked on and developed.

When you link to Google Trends, you can enter a word a phrase, or multiple words and phrases (by separating the terms with commas) and then view some interesting results about the past history of Google's searchers. Figure 13.14 is example of a search on the word, hybrids.

As you can see from Figure 13.14, when you enter terms, Google reveals not only the overall frequency of searches on the words or phrases, but also breaks down the searches based on which cities, regions, and languages the terms were most frequently searched from. So in Figure 13.14, you can see that the word "hybrids" was searched for most frequently by people in Sacramento followed by three more cities in California. You can also choose what time period you'd like to see for the trends.

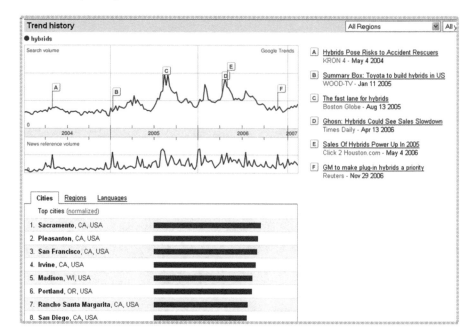

This regional breakdown adds some real potential meaning and value. For instance, if you were thinking of entering the carbon trading market, and wanted a lead as to what parts of the globe are most attuned to this concept and where people are looking for more information, this could be potentially valuable market information, as you'd get a sense of where people are talking about a topic, and presumably aware and attuned to it.

▶ **TIP:** The best words and phrases to use on Google Trends are those that are "packed" with a clear meaning (e.g., "sustainability" or "social networks" versus say, "business" or "computers") and where you could reasonably presume that searches on that topic imply that it's a hot topic, that people are thinking about it, or that there is some demand for learning more. You could do this for product names for instance.

Keep in mind, though, that because this Trends site is a "Google Labs" product, it means that it's still in an early stage of development, and so you can't really count on what you discover as something to take to the bank. However, I think it's intriguing to consider as one more input when doing initial new market research

Again, Google Trends identifies searches, not blog or consumer media con‐
tent, but does reflect some interesting overall online behavior.

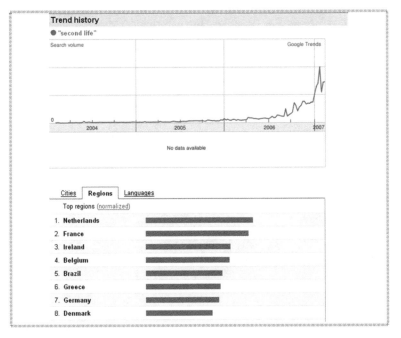

FIGURE 13.15

*A Google trends search
on the term "second life"
shows not only its increase
in frequency but where in
the world searchers have
searched on that term most
often.*

Finally, Google also offers another broad search trend surfacing feature
it calls "Zeitgeist." In Figure 13.16 Google surfaces the most popular searches
overall, categorized by time period and into broad categories.

FIGURE 13.16

*Google's Zeitgeist identifies
the most popular search
queries.*

Google™	Zeitgeist Archive

Week Ending **April 28, 2007**	**Top 10 Gaining Queries**

1. earth day
2. blue angels
3. katie price
4. jessica lynch
5. skybus

6. pokemon diamond
7. coachella
8. mike penner
9. new planet
10. mother's day

Week Ending **April 21, 2007**	**Top 10 Gaining Queries**

1. virginia tech
2. Cho Seung-Hui
3. boston marathon
4. 420
5. nbc news

6. columbine
7. kate middleton
8. Ismail Ax
9. alec baldwin
10. shia labeouf

You can look at Google Zeitgeist on a year-end basis, a monthly basis, or a weekly basis, and most intriguingly, I think, on a country-by-country basis. For example, if you wanted to know the fastest gaining search terms in the countries of Netherlands, New Zealand, and Norway for April 2007, Google would provide this (see Figure 13.17).

FIGURE 13.17

Google's Zeitgeist also breaks down popular queries by countries around the world.

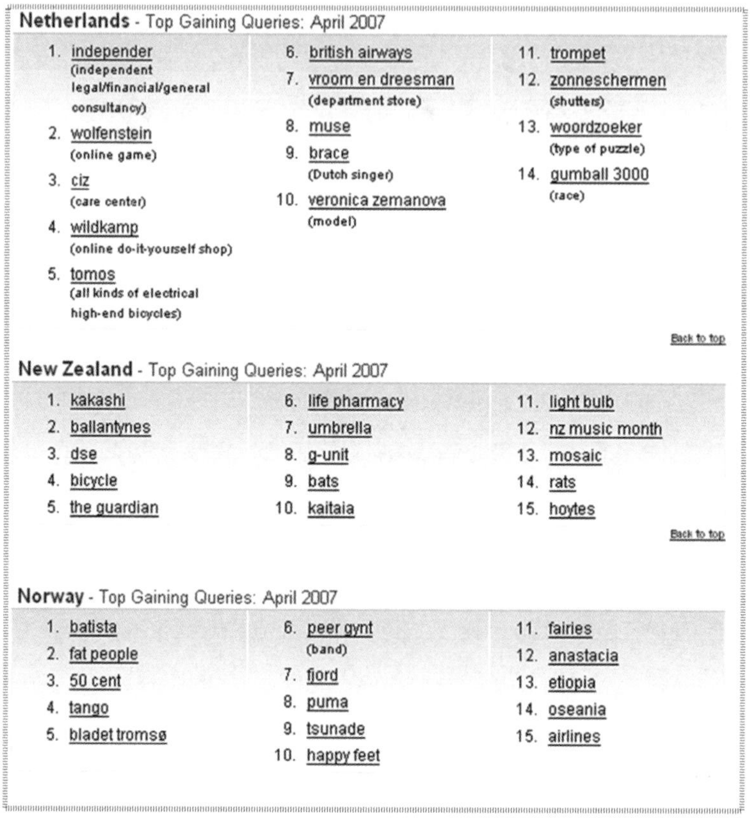

Netherlands - Top Gaining Queries: April 2007

1. independer (independent legal/financial/general consultancy)	6. british airways	11. trompet
2. wolfenstein (online game)	7. vroom en dreesman (department store)	12. zonneschermen (shutters)
3. ciz (care center)	8. muse	13. woordzoeker (type of puzzle)
4. wildkamp (online do-it-yourself shop)	9. brace (Dutch singer)	14. gumball 3000 (race)
5. tomos (all kinds of electrical high-end bicycles)	10. veronica zemanova (model)	

Back to top

New Zealand - Top Gaining Queries: April 2007

1. kakashi	6. life pharmacy	11. light bulb
2. ballantynes	7. umbrella	12. nz music month
3. dse	8. g-unit	13. mosaic
4. bicycle	9. bats	14. rats
5. the guardian	10. kaitaia	15. hoytes

Back to top

Norway - Top Gaining Queries: April 2007

1. batista	6. peer gynt (band)	11. fairies
2. fat people	7. fjord	12. anastacia
3. 50 cent	8. puma	13. etiopia
4. tango	9. tsunade	14. oseania
5. bladet tromsø	10. happy feet	15. airlines

CHAPTER 14

Identifying Trends and Evaluating the Credibility of Social Media

AS YOU CAN SEE from the previous chapter, buzz tracking sites are pretty cool tools. It's always fun to generate sharp looking graphs with dramatic spikes and drops illustrating the movement of some phenomena. And these buzz trackers do provide an interesting snapshot of what's caught the attention of many bloggers at the moment or in the recent past, providing some sense of what news items and postings are getting attention in the blogosphere.

But how much stock can you put on whether what you discover from these sites reflects significant discussions or a true trend that merits your close attention? And how do you know how much trust to put into what you've discovered on a blog, uploaded video, or some other consumer media-oriented sites? This chapter will provide some practical tips and advice both in identifying real trends, and assessing credibility of social media.

Say one of those buzz trackers shows a large and dramatic spike in the volume on a topic important to you. Certainly it would be prudent to at least consider the spike to be a lead that "something" may be going on that strongly suggests you take note and do some further investigation. For instance, if you follow the business media industry, and all of a sudden the highest ranking and most popular terms on these buzz tracking sites is Thomson Corporation, then it's worth finding out what's going on.

But I'd say that these buzz trackers are less valuable for performing true business and social trend tracking.

While Buzz trackers can provide a quick and rough snapshot of what bloggers and Internet users believe are currently the most important and interesting stories, this information is too ephemeral, superficial, limited, and even of iffy reliability to provide any kind of deeper understanding of a long-lasting trend. After all, identifying trends is a subtle art and science, and is much more than a summary chart of the most links, votes, and so forth.

Furthermore, it is not even completely clear that the data you get from these buzz trackers is as clean as it is presented in those neat little charts. Blogs and web-based discussions are messy, and you can either wade through them to get a sense of what's on people's minds or you can try to quantify them by looking at word occurrences, link occurrences, and other quantifiable measurements. Even sites like Digg that rely on users' submissions and votes are ultimately basing their results on a quantitative counting process among what might be a tech savvy and younger demographic.

But even if we give these sites the benefit of the doubt, and say that its method does provide accurate representations of what's hot in the blogo-sphere, it is also not clear about the *larger meaning* we can or should try to derive from this kind of quantitative measurement. Some research has suggested that to gauge the impact of word-of-mouth online, it's not only important to find the volume of buzz on a topic, but perhaps more important is figuring out how *widely dispersed* the conversations are within different communities. The study, conducted by Harvard professor David B. Godes to predict the potential success of new television shows by analyzing online con-versations on USENET groups, found that once comments began spreading outside of one or a few specialized groups to different types of communities, they will spread more quickly and have more influence.

See Godes, David, and Dina Mayzlin. "Using Online Conversations to Study Word of Mouth Communication." Marketing Science 23, No. 4 (Fall 2004): 545-60 available online at: http://www.people.hbs. edu/dgodes/womfinal.pdf

Furthermore, looking at data generated from buzz trackers like these do not answer the important question of "*why*"—*why* are so many more people searching for x this week rather than y; or discussing this blog post, or link-ing to that blogger?

As the late educator, author, and media critic Neil Postman wrote in *Con-scientious Objections,* a compilation of his essays (Vintage Books, 1992), trying to "do" social science by applying natural science methodologies is prob-lematic. To illustrate his point, Postman distinguished how we might study "a blink"—a natural biological phenomena that can be measured, versus a "wink," a socially initiated phenomena that is less amenable to being pinned down and analyzed numerically. There's a lot of subtle "blinking" going on in the blogosphere, and this is why I'd advise that you rely on the more quali-tative, analytical approaches examined in this chapter. Then perhaps you might check the data presented from these buzz-tracking sites to confirm, supplement, or provide leads for further research. In other words, use these as one interesting input, but hardly as "the answer" to what people are truly concerned about.

Tips on Tracking Trends Online

Choosing Your Conversational Sources

One of the first decisions you're going to have to make in scanning online conversations and social media is determining *which* conversations on the Internet you should be scanning and reading. You will have to consider whether your selection should be based on a topic, the nature of the conversation, or perhaps the influence of the online speaker.

Let's tackle the question regarding influence first, since it is a fundamental issue.

Marketers often try to determine who in a particular industry or sphere is considered influential, since what those people say can have an impact on the behaviors of customers in that market. Indeed, Jon Berry and Ed Keller based their book, *The Influentials: One American in Ten Tells the Other Nine How to Vote, Where to Eat, and What to Buy* (Free Press, 2003) on that premise.

Keep in mind, though, that while experts and influential people may have a wide audience and a certain level of authority, you also need to be careful in assuming that their opinions and behaviors will reflect what's going to happen in the future; instead these persons may just reflect *the status quo*. For instance, author and management guru Oren Harari says that he has worked in Latin America where certain individuals who have a corrupt relationship with government officials certainly *do* have power and influence. But these people don't point to where the future is going. Another example: Music companies had enormous power in the 1980s and 1990s, but today they are huge hulks trying to salvage something and don't represent trends in media and music use. As mentioned earlier, it is those on the fringe who are more likely to represent where things are heading.

But there can still be other reasons why you'd want to figure out who the influential bloggers and opinion makers on the Internet are. This is discussed further in this chapter on assessing credibility. For trend-tracking purposes, what's most important is not necessarily to find the most influential individuals, but to locate the most influential or key conversations.

The Key Conversation

I'd define a key conversation as one where involved, informed, and dynamic individuals in a particular industry are actively discussing and pushing their field forward and helping it evolve to a higher state. I'd say that key conversations also display the following characteristics:

- There is a lot of activity—meaning lots of postings daily

- There is a lot of energy—you can almost feel excitement and real interest from the members

- There is a lot of passion—you can tell that many of the people care a great deal about the topic

- The group is plugged into early developments and the latest news—and members share it with others

- There is a sense of history and community—many people know the others who participate

- There is little or no spam—that's a sign of a closely watched and cared for forum or blog

- There are a few leaders—often there are one or more persons who take on leadership roles and pull together the threads of the discussion, providing larger context and referencing some history.

When you are plugged into a key conversation, you can learn not just what *anyone* is doing or thinking, but you will be keyed into the opinions and behaviors of people that are most informed, involved, and care deeply about the matter.

Sometimes key conversations revolve around the blog of a well-known figure or leader in the industry. If you are already aware of the leaders in your field, you can check to see if the person has a blog and look for key conversations there. Or if you've been doing research on a topic, and have observed that a particular person or persons' names are cited regularly as a kind of authority or respected leader, you should begin following and monitoring that person's blog, and any important conversations that are occurring around it.

But if you are unaware of where key conversations might be found, here is one suggested method for locating them.

1. Make a First Cut

You might start your research by locating the most well-known, popular, and linked-to blogs and forums, as these would represent *potential* places where you'll find key conversations. For this first cut, you might try to locate 50 such conversations, by using the sites and tools below.

- **Technorati:** Do a keyword search on just the blog search section (search.technorati.com), and set the authority filter to "some" or "a lot" to surface just bloggers who are linked to most frequently by other bloggers.

- **Google Web Search:** Do a keyword search, attach the word "blog" and see which blogs come up towards the top of the returned listings, indicating a high ranking on Google.

- **Google Blog Search:** Do a keyword search, and see which blog posts Google ranked the highest.

- **Yahoo! Groups:** Search and look for the most active groups; these are groups with the most members and with the highest number of posts.

- **Traditional media:** Read articles in newspapers and trade journals to see which bloggers are cited by mainstream reporters. This way you are leveraging the work that journalists have already done. When reporters quote a blogger as an authoritative source, they will typically quote one that is considered a leader in the field or has something significant to say

2. Make the Next Cut

After you've turned up this initial batch of potential key conversations, spend a week or so just browsing and scanning the postings on those blogs, forums and groups. Doing this will help you make your next cut, where you choose between 7 to 10 key conversations to read and monitor regularly.

To make this cut, you'll need to have a certain level of introspection and self-awareness while you are reading and scanning the discussions. Note which conversations you end up getting "sucked into," and spend the most time on. Which are most intriguing and thought provoking? Which make you want to join in and participate? Which ones challenge the way you have always thought about your industry or customers, and give you a fresh perspective? Which ones articulate something you've been thinking to yourself? These are all indicators that what you are reading may qualify as a key conversation.

Also, when you are doing this initial reading, be attuned to other important themes. Are particular bloggers or people continually cited, in a matter of fact way that implies that others in the discussion know that person or blog, even though you don't? If so, it's a good sign that the cited blogger is a respected and important person. If that person's blog did not make your "first cut" you should consider reviewing it and adding it to your list. And if you find that a particular person or couple of people consistently seem to make the sharpest, most relevant, insightful, and articulate remarks, you should pay close attention to who *they* cite often, and then add any blogs or discussions where those people are leaders or major contributors.

After a week or so of immersion in this initial batch of conversations, you should try to choose roughly 7 to 10 that you feel meet all the above evaluation criteria, are relevant to your research, and simply just feel right to you, from your own intuition. Ideally, this final selection would also include some built-in diversity, drawing on a fundamental principle of pre-Internet trend tracking, which is to read a wide variety of news and information sources. To achieve that diversity you should try to integrate:

- At least one, or preferably two or three blogs and forums where the members are mostly people who live outside of your country

- One that seems to be on the fringe and whose views are less accepted by mainstream thinkers in the field

- One that has a loyal and dedicated following, but whose overall perspective or outlook you disagree with

- One that would be considered the most influential mainstream conversation, which will give you a good reference and benchmark for the generally accepted thinking for this field

- A couple whose focus is outside of your field, but where the conversation relates to issues where you think there may be some overlap and potential future influence. For instance, if you are in an industry that promotes healthy foods in school cafeteria, you might also include a key conversation on good parenting. If you are introducing fuel cells for home energy use, you might include a conversation on sustainable home building.

You should then consider creating an RSS feed for each of those conversations and adding it to your reader, as described in Chapter 12. I'd advise adding one general buzz surfacer or meme tracker too, like one of the ones mentioned in Chapter 13. Although I am skeptical of their value for true trend tracking, they can still be added to your collection of conversation browsing sources, as long as you use them for quick snapshots of the online buzz of the moment and don't give them undue emphasis.

Your final collection of key conversations will necessarily be imperfect and incomplete. There is no way that you can monitor all possible key conversations occurring online around the world! And although these can represent your core sources to monitor for trends, you should supplement that list by doing an occasional keyword search on Google, Google Blog Search, and Technorati. That's to ensure that you reach out beyond your initial preferred selection, and get exposed to new discussions you didn't originally locate. This will give you the opportunity to refine your core set of conversations, perhaps selectively adding new ones now and then, and weeding out others that you determine did not provide that much insight after all.

Once you have your key conversation sources to monitor for trends, it's time to discuss some strategic reading techniques so you can actually make sense out of all the Internet chatter coming your way.

Creating the Right Context and Mindset for Browsing and Reading

Once you have your key blogs and forums lined up, your next job is to begin to prepare how you will delve into all this material. That preparation means creating the right context and mindset so you'll be in the best position to detect the significant information from all the noise you are bound to encounter.

By creating the right context, I mean having a clear but flexible idea of just what you want to find out from your reading, and why. You'll use that personal understanding as a kind of overarching filter to guide you during your reviewing of these online conversations.

TRACKING TRENDS BY MONITORING CONFERENCE BLOGGERS

One of the best sources that savvy businesspeople look to for discerning trends are professional and trade conferences. After all, it is there that the movers and shakers in a field give presentations that reflect the latest thinking, and where exhibitors display and demonstrate state-of-the-art products. Not insignificantly, it is also at these events where gossip and networking between attendees serves as a source for less official, but often even more valuable insider news.

Over the last few years, an increasing number of conference attendees have begun blogging their notes, observations, and experiences. This has created a potentially valuable source of timely and substantive information for finding the latest news, developments, and trends discussed at these events. Bloggers sometimes do their posting in near real-time, too, and will jot down remarks from keynote speakers, create podcasts of presentations, and just offer their own opinions and observations on what they think is the key news and significant events coming out of the conference.

Here are some strategies for locating conference bloggers for events that interest you most.

1. The simplest approach to finding conference bloggers is to enter a conference name in Google Blog Search or Technorati. You should also add the year of the event to avoid finding older blog posts of past conferences. If this method doesn't work well in narrowing the results, try appending the current year's keynote speaker's name to your search string (put the name in quotation marks) to further filter and qualify your search.

2. A more precise way to find out who is blogging a particular conference is to see if there is a descriptive "tag" being used by the bloggers at the conference to identify and describe posts specifically related to that year's event. If there is a tag, you can do a tag search on Technorati (as well as a couple of other blog search engines, such as IceRocket), and by doing this you are insured that virtually all posts you retrieve will be about that conference. Note that the trade off in using a tag search is that even though your retrieval will be more precise, you won't retrieve postings from persons who blogged the event but did not use that tag to describe their postings. This could be the vast majority of people who are blogging the conference.

3. The best way to find that correct tag is to browse some initial relevant blog postings to see if the same tag or tags are being used over and over, and then use them in your next search. Or you can link to the conference's home page (almost all have one and you can find it with a simple web search) and see if the conference organizers have suggested a

TRACKING TRENDS BY MONITORING CONFERENCE BLOGGERS

specific descriptive tag for bloggers to use. Not all conferences do this, but for those that do, it will likely make your research easier. You might also discover an official conference blog, which can be quite useful, though you're not going to get the level of critiques, nor perhaps the level of detail that you may get from independent conference bloggers.

I should note that although I do believe conference bloggers represent a superb source of news and trend information for business researchers, they are not a replacement for going to an event. You can't replicate those all-important hallway conversations by reading a blog post. You also have no guarantee that the bloggers will cover the sessions most important to you, nor will you know how accurately the blogger transcribed what he or she heard and saw. And you can't browse the exhibit hall either. However, the point is that even if you can't get to all the events you'd like to attend, conference bloggers become, in a sense, your own correspondents taking notes for you.

FIGURE 14.1

A search on the official conference tag "il2006" retrieves bloggers who wrote about the 2006 Internet Librarian conference.

Here's an example of what I mean. Say your firm is a supplier to the home-building industry, and you wanted to get a sense of what kinds of housing retiring baby boomers need if they move out of their longtime home into a new one. Once you have this mission as your framework, you will not just be aimlessly absorbing the variety of conversations you encounter, but will continually be checking what you are reading against that framework to assess whether or not it is relevant.

There also may be a couple of important sub-contexts too that you keep in the back of your mind during your reading. Say, for instance, that you hear that "going green" is important for baby boomers, but you aren't sure what that means in practice. Perhaps it is also important for you to know if there is going to be more emphasis for retiring baby boomers on city vs. country living. With those additional contexts in mind, you can read through the conversations, discarding any that are clearly irrelevant, and focusing on those that have some kind of potential impact on these questions.

As with all research though, it's important to revisit your initial context and assumptions at various stages along the way, so you can make necessary adjustments. Using this example, suppose after several days of reading key conversations that you determine that going green is indeed an important factor for older baby boomers, and that there are concerns that materials used in building homes are being culled from endangered forests. Then you might adjust your scanning antenna to try to pick up more detailed conversations just on *that* matter. Or you may determine that something you originally assumed was important to look for turned out to not have much resonance after all. In that case, you may decide to stop scanning for conversations around that issue.

So your overarching context and framework will always be present to help you organize and filter what you're reading, but it will be flexible enough to change and be updated throughout the course of your research.

In addition to having this overarching context, you also need to have the right *mindset* and *attitude* before you begin. That means having a clear and open mind, which requires that you leave your own prejudices behind. You don't want to look for only those discussions and opinions that conform to what you think they *should* be, and ignore those with which you don't agree. Research, like a river, will take you where it wants to lead you.

Peter Schwartz, in his outstanding book on strategic information gathering and scenario building, *The Art of the Long View*, advises businesses that to do effective research, it is necessary to know your "filter"—biases, belief systems, points of view, and so forth—and then to "suspend judgment" during research. In fact, Schwartz even advises researchers to *actively seek* disconfirming information.

The Art of the Scan

It may seem that knowing how to scan and review information is self-evident. It's certainly true that this is something anybody can do. But like many activities, there are also ways to make a simple job more effective, and most of us can benefit from a few tips.

In general having a knack for noticing new trends and emerging issues requires cultivating a broad but observant view of the world, a kind of alert and peripheral vision that lets you see what's going on around you, even as you do your day-to-day work. It's the kind of peripheral vision discussed in the book, *The Intuitive Manager,* that the author Roy Rowan said basketball star Bill Bradley had when playing his game. By looking closely at what was in front of him, but also rapidly scanning the environment around him at the same time, Bradley was able to detect slight movements in his peripheral field that gave him a head start in making a successful move.

Cultivating this kind of alert, attentive orientation is extremely valuable when reviewing printed materials, but when it comes to blogs and consumer conversation on the Internet, this capability is even more important since the material is so voluminous, unfiltered, and has such a high noise-to-signal ratio.

So what does it take to be really good and efficient at scanning information, particularly conversational information on the Internet, with the end goal being to identify and surface trend data? Here are some suggestions:

Zoom In and Zoom Out

I like to think of the scanning process as similar to having the zoom lens of a camera in front of you as you do your reading. You start with a wide angle so you can expose yourself to as many sources and broad themes as you can and absorb as much as you can. Futurist Oliver Markley, who previously directed the graduate program in studies of the future at the University of Houston, Clear Lake, has advised, "Don't try to reduce the (information) nozzle—let yourself be hosed." By immersing yourself in as much information as you can, you help increase the odds that you'll be exposed to important information and conversations.

However, there are times when you need to go deep, and then you turn that zoom from wide angle to telephoto. Now you can move in closer for a better view of what you spotted in the wider view. And then you may adjust back again, for the wide view, then go back in deep, and so on.

Most of the time it's best to start broadly by *browsing* items like head-lines, blog post titles, and summaries of news and conversations with that wide-angle lens, and as you are doing this 20,000 foot type scan, you pick up some of the broad themes and get a general sense of the big picture. But when something catches your eye, or you begin to read a conversation that is right on target and speaks to just what you want to know, it's time to zoom in and slowly absorb all the important details.

Sometimes, when reviewing your feeds in your RSS news reader, you can also adjust your lens to a "medium" view if you set the browser to show you feeds as a headline accompanied by an excerpt of the full piece.

This summary level of information can be helpful because there's more detail than just a headline (and headlines can also be misleading), but not as detailed as full text, where you'd have to wade through the whole posting to identify key points. When you are able to review summary excerpts, you can more efficiently look for relevancy, quickly determine if the full posting is likely to be valuable, and if so, zoom in by clicking on the link and go to the full text for more detail.

Talk Back to Your Sources

In addition to getting the hang of the zoom in-zoom out approach to scan-ning, another valuable technique is to cultivate the art of "talking" to what you are reading. I put the word talking in quotation marks here, because I don't necessarily mean verbally speaking back to what you are reading (though there's nothing wrong with doing that either). I'm talking about constructing and creating a mental dialogue with the sources you encounter as you read through them.

When you read something that prompts you to wonder about what the author said, or provokes an emotional response, or raises important questions in your mind, don't let that reaction of yours just float away. Capture it somehow. Any kind of back and forth dialogue (even if it's just you and a print-out) means that you will be clarifying what you've read, and you'll be helping the discussion evolve to a higher, more refined level, meaning it will be addressing harder and therefore more fundamental issues.

To create a dialogue with conversations on someone's blog, you can usually just post your comment, and often, though not always, you will get a response back from the blogger, or from another reader. By doing this you are, in a sense, customizing this conversation so that it meets your own specific needs and concerns.

If you are not actually on a blog, but are just reading something in your RSS reader or in some other non-interactive format, you need to do something else to create that dialog. In the past, whenever I read some particularly thought-provoking book or article in print, I would jot down my responses, reactions, and questions in the margin of the work.

That's a lot harder to do with digital information displayed on your desktop PC, but it's not impossible. You can, for example, print out a particularly enlightening conversation, and when reading it in print, add your own comments and reactions on the print out, next to the relevant comments. There are also programs that allow you to attach a kind of "sticky note" annotation to websites where you can add your comments, and then whenever you return to that site, you will view the comments you added (my favorite of these is the social bookmarking site Diigo).

Don't underestimate the value of asking questions. Remember, you can compel the answer you seek by asking the right question. Questioning is a powerful research tool that can be used to create a customized set of information, on demand, that corresponds to what you need to find out. The late Neil Postman said that question asking is the most significant intellectual tool human beings have.

One Personal Approach

I'd also share one other more personal approach on what to pay attention to, which has helped me discern trends. It starts with cultivating basic awareness, or at least *having the intention* to pay attention.

Be mindful enough to observe and be attentive to what is happening around you in your own life, and what others are saying and doing, offline and online. By doing so, you avoid operating on automatic pilot, like driving on a well-known road and not really noticing what is going by.

Once you accept the importance of awareness, and you are alert—like Bill Bradley on the basketball court—and not mentally sleeping, you are better able to notice little anomalies—something that stirs some feeling of surprise, dissonance, or recognition.

Here's a popular example of how being aware and paying attention can help spot an emerging trend: Did you happen to see the 1997 film *As Good as it Gets,* with Helen Hunt, who played a mother with an asthmatic son? When she railed against HMOs, the theatre audiences cheered her on with relish! This was a good example of a surprisingly powerful emotional response that reflected a new, but not quite fully articulated popular rage against a poorly run and unpopular healthcare system. Anyone in the healthcare industry that was at this movie and experienced the audience's reaction, but did not see it as an early sign of things to come was *really* not paying attention.

Some clues are a lot more subtle and could include, for instance:

- A new word or lingo ("Hmm, a *freegan,* what's that?")

- A behavior ("Hmm, these young people don't seem to care what they reveal about themselves online.")

- An attitude ("Wow, I never heard so much anger directed at universities before.")

- An activity ("Gee, look at all those urban couples buying a farm and farm animals up in the hills.")

- A new perspective on something ("Hmm, it used to be everyone had their PDAs while on vacation, now it seems that everyone wants to keep them off.")

Other tip-offs on what to pay particularly close attention to:

- Something unusual

- Something surprising

- Something that makes you say to yourself, "*Aha!*"

- Something that takes you aback and makes you say, "Huh?"

- Something that makes you excited

- Something that makes you angry

Finally, be particularly attentive when something fits into the above list AND comes from someone whom you've learned to trust as particularly knowledgeable and insightful. For example, a couple of years ago I regularly read two key bloggers who wrote about information technology and research. I liked them both because they consistently wrote in ways that expanded my understanding of the topic. One of the bloggers began raving about a new PDA she was using, called Treo, which at that time was quite new and not well known. I was struck by her enthusiasm for it, and remembered it. Then I discovered that the other blogger was using it and talking about it as well. This caught my attention, and I was in a heightened state of awareness for other important mentions. By the time I saw a third mention in a short period of time, I was convinced that this product was likely to be a big hit among the "digerati," and indeed within about a year to 18 months it was.

The key is to notice and remember what you observed. That way, if you notice, hear about, or read of that odd or noteworthy event happening again, it will resonate with that existing memory. You've seen something unusual or noteworthy happen twice. This does not mean you've spotted a trend, but it puts you on a "higher alert" so that you will be sure not to miss it, if you come across this phenomenon again. If you do come across the phenomenon a third time, I think that there is a pretty decent chance that it represents a pattern, which might reflect some kind of emerging trend.

Of course, this casual method for spotting trends—paying attention, remembering, and looking for additional confirmations—won't withstand any kind of scientific or academic scrutiny as a way to determine anything whatsoever. It is purely subjective and anecdotal, and can easily be challenged on lots of levels. But remember that good reporters, researchers, marketers, and others who need to rely on a combination of gut instinct, experience, and being well-informed to decide what is significant and worth paying attention use a variation of this unarticulated method all the time.

Ultimately, we are talking about probability. That is, when relying on this "noticing 1/2/3 times" method, all I am really saying is that it seems more likely than chance that X phenomena represents a meaningful new pattern and therefore is worthy of some attention.

Then should come all the reality checks: additional research, talking to people, seeking out disconfirming information, and so forth. These checks will either increase or reduce to a more assured level the probability that this observed phenomena is a real trend.

You also need to put any potential trend through another "rinse" so to speak. This is a filter that will help you distinguish if the phenomena you're considering as a trend may be truly important and meaningful. You need to check whether:

- It is something that is *truly new*

- It has the potential *to impact many people*, or at least a certain key segment of the population

- It will be something that matters to people—they will *care* about it

- It resonates with others, particularly key demographics, generational, or other segments of the population

- A lot of what you can pick up that signifies a meaningful new trend often begins offline just from casual conversations with friends and family who are expressing a concern or problem. For instance, maybe people you know are talking about obese children or why their flights are always being delayed. If you are observant and begin *noticing* the frequency of their concerns you can assume that if those concerns have some power and energy behind them and are matters that a lot of people *care* about, "something" is likely to happen as a result.

- What might that be? You can begin to make some educated guesses. Perhaps family restaurants will begin advertising that they offer *smaller,* rather than large portions; or that consumer groups will begin lobbying Congress to do something about the airline delays. So if and when these changes occur, you need to begin considering what it will mean for your industry and organization.

Again, trend spotting is not so much a matter of arriving at a definite yes or no, but of probabilities. If you are well informed, use good sources, have attuned your mind and are prepared, mindful, and self-aware, you can begin feeling a level of confidence in making an educated judgment on when there is a higher probability that the pattern you've detected signifies a trend.

One final important component to identifying trends is cultivating the ability to trust yourself. Many of us, when we notice something unusual, might dismiss it as not meaningful, perhaps thinking that we viewed the situation incorrectly or did not understand what was truly happening, or use some other rationalization to dismiss the importance of our observation. It is always possible that we misinterpreted something, but rather than automatically resorting to this as the default analysis of our observation, it is better to respect and acknowledge the likely legitimacy of what we noted and especially how we felt. Don't short circuit what could be a meaningful line of thinking about something you think is noteworthy.

Processing and Filtering the Conversations

Even if you've managed to do all of the strategic scanning and reading, you still need a way to process, filter, organize and make sense of the material you've been collecting.

One of the primary ways that I've recommended you track online conversations is by setting up an RSS reader. There are also some broader general principles that can help make your scanning process more organized and productive. Here are a few guidelines:

1. As you begin to identify valuable information, try to identify similar items and then sort what you feel is worth retaining into logical categories. This can help provide some initial structure to this mass of conversations, and help you begin to make sense out of them.

2. Once you have some of these conversations organized into categories, it's an excellent idea to look for patterns and trends within them, to see if there are larger implications. For example, if you are discovering that lots of people are talking about their frustrations when flying and others are expressing anger at airlines, you might begin wondering if new federal regulations will be coming next to penalize airlines more severely for losing luggage or delays that are their own fault. Then you need to think about how these implications can impact your own industry.

3. As you pull together these threads to look for patterns and identify implications, it's also extremely helpful to do this activity with other people, as a kind of informal brainstorming session. Who you decide to pull in to do this will vary on how your organization has

decided to perform trend tracking and blog monitoring. However it is done, it's important to get other people's input, opinions, and analysis.

4. As you and your colleagues begin looking at these organized conversational threads, be sure that you think about the potential impact on your own industry, company, competitive landscape, products, services and product features.

5. Finally, the last stage is deciding what, if any, *action* you are going to take. Here is where the rubber meets the road, and you have to be prudent about what you are going to do based on what you've found. Remember, when we're talking about trends, we're talking about the future—and that means we're basically guessing. So again, we're working in the realm of likelihoods and probability. As Yogi Berra was reputed to have said, "It's hard to make predictions, especially about the future." As usual, Yogi was right.

Because of the inherent uncertainties in predicting the future, you may want to hedge some of your initial conclusions too, by viewing what you found online not so much as an "answer" but more as a kind of "lead" worth pursuing. You can narrow down what you think are three to five of the most significant trends that will likely have an impact on your industry and firm, and then do a reality check, by performing some traditional focused research. This can shore up your confidence in the accuracy of what you detected, or perhaps you'll discover new information that makes your initial assumptions appear less likely to occur after all.

If you get to a point where you feel you are as confident as you can be about something like the future, then of course you'll have to decide what to do. One of the final considerations, of course, will be deciding if you can build an economic case for whatever action steps you are considering taking.

Presenting Your Conclusions

A significant aspects of the full trend tracking process is deciding how to present what you've found and to whom to make your recommendations. Of course, this will vary depending on your organization's structure, culture, and other individual factors. However, if you are the person that needs to make a formal presentation to others in your firm on whether and how to take action based on what you located, you need to do this mindfully too. Here are some tips:

- Be cautious about using the word "trends" or "trend tracking" or "future trends." As I wrote earlier, for many people, the word trend (and thereby the whole concept of tracking a trend) sounds dated. So you might think about another way to frame your work, such as "monitoring change," or "anticipatory management," or "proactive decision making," or, even better, a more straightforward plain English description of the activity that is likely to elicit a more receptive reaction in your organization.

- When you do make a presentation, don't be abstract, but be sure to identify how what you've discovered has a direct link to a key company goal, mission, or plan. This is critical for success. You need to identify just how and why some proposed action will have a real impact on something the firm has already articulated, ideally explicitly, or at least tacitly, as very important to its success

- Provide the needed context and speak the right language. If you are in information technology or a library function, for example, you don't want to assume that the people in marketing already know about blogs, RSS, and other buzzwords or tools that might be obvious to you. You don't want to use lingo from your own discipline. Understanding your audience means knowing what their assumptions are, what their knowledge base is, and what words they use. Try to present what you know in a language and context that will be of greatest meaning to that group.

The above is an abbreviated and much more informal process of an activity that many Fortune 1000 firms, governments, and large entities engage in when they want to be sure they are prepared for the future. That much more formal process is called scenario planning. To learn more about formal scenario planning, I recommend getting a copy of Peter Schwartz' book, *The Art of the Long View* (Currency, 1991).

CHAPTER 15

Evaluating Blog and Social Media Credibility

IN ADDITION to knowing how to strategically research and read so you can identify significant trends, you will also want to know how to evaluate the credibility of what you do come across. I noted in Chapter 4, that in the blogosphere, the metric that has become a kind of default in making a determination of credibility has related primarily to popularity—that is how many links to a particular blog—as well as to the slipperier matter of influence. This chapter examines some of the ways you can assess the popularity, influence, or other measures of credibility of the blog or source you come across on the Net.

There are primarily two different types of situations where you'll want to make a determination about a blog's credibility. One is when you are reading a *known* blog; the other is where you want to *discover* credible bloggers. Let's discuss the latter situation first: how to *find* the most credible ones.

Finding Popular and Influential Bloggers

Although I've discussed how ranking blogs by the number of incoming links is not truly a good measure of authority or influence, these are still a good measurement of plain old popularity, and so perhaps could serve as an indicator of a blog that is authoritative or influential. Indeed, in many ways, counting incoming links has so far been about the best the open web has been able to come up with for trying to approximate how academics have performed scholarly citation analysis for many decades.

So although the following strategies will help you find popular bloggers, keep in mind that this criterion is still an imperfect measurement to establish true authority or influence. New bloggers on the scene, or those that are in a niche area that have fewer links-in may indeed be authorities and hold quite a bit of influence in their own field, but because they don't have lots of links or traffic you may not find them.

I am going to provide you with some sources and strategies for locating these popular—and perhaps influential—bloggers. But I'll provide additional strategies on how to actually surface those that are more likely to be truly influential as well, and offer research strategies that go beyond just counting incoming links.

Free Tools and Sites

There are a few options for identifying the most popular bloggers on the open web.

- Google: Web Search/Blog Search
- Technorati: Authority Filter/Blog Directory/Favorites

Google

As mentioned in Chapter 9, you can locate blogs on Google by searching both its regular web search engine, as well as its more specialized blog search engine. Both kinds of searches can be valuable for identifying the more popular, and perhaps even influential bloggers.

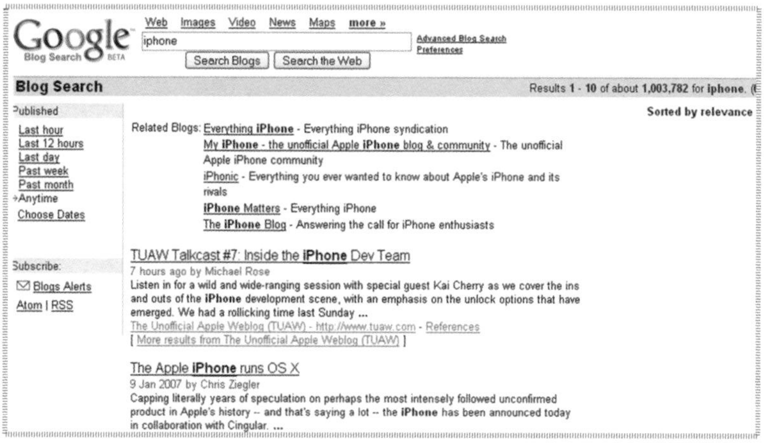

FIGURE 15.1

A search on Google Blog Search identifies not just blog posts but key blogs.

Although Google's Web Search is not restricted to blogs, it does include blogs in its standard Web Search. Google's web page ranking method heavily emphasizes incoming links to a page, so only those blogs with pages that have relatively large number of incoming links will receive a high ranking in the list of returned pages, since they must not only be high vis-a-vis other blogs, but also in a sense, "compete" against all the non-blog web pages to get that high ranking in Google's Web search. A highly ranked blog page on Google's Web page is likely to indicate that the page it was derived from is probably highly linked to, from other highly linked to sites and blogs.

If you choose to use Google's blog search directly you will only be searching blog posts (actually, technically you are searching on the blogs' RSS feeds).

To locate popular blogs themselves, you should not only look at the highly ranked posts, but also look at Google's "Related Blogs" feature, which appears at the top of the screen after running a search. This will alert you to the names of other key blogs identified by Google, which again are likely to represent the "popular" ones.

GOOGLE CUSTOM SEARCH ENGINE: FOR SURFACING PRE-QUALIFIED BLOGS

In 2006, Google launched what it called its "Custom Search Engine," which permitted users to come up with their own a list of specific sites, (which could include blogs) on which to run a Google search. The idea was that rather than searching the entire web on a topic, a user could pre-qualify which sites he or she wanted Google to search by limiting the search to a collection of favorite, trusted, quality sites.

By definition, all of the results retrieved from a Google Custom Search could be from what the user pre-determined to be trusted sites. One could even consider adding his or her own incoming RSS feeds as an item to search against.

Technorati

We discussed using Technorati for locating blogs in Chapter 10, but let's revisit this search engine to examine a couple of its key features that can help you identify the most popular blogs, if not authoritative and influential ones.

The metric that Technorati uses to rank its bloggers is called "Authority." Authority is simply the total number of other independent bloggers that linked to a particular blog over the preceding six months (multiple links from the same blog still count as one link). Each blog is given an authority score, which is simply the number of those blogs that have linked in during that time period. So a blog that has an authority score of 50 means that 50 bloggers, over the last six months, have linked to that blog.

It's easy to disagree with Technorati's use of the word authority, but it is a rough measure of blog popularity and interest from other bloggers, and again, although popularity and influence are not synonymous, it stands to reason that at least a share of popular blogs are also likely to be influential. So Technorati's free tool is certainly better than nothing.

Here's how to use Technorati's authority filter:

1. Link to Technorati's Blog only search at: http://search.technorati.com

2. Enter your search terms and select a language

3. Choose a level of authority: none, a little, some or a lot. Technorati's definition of authority levels are as follows: Low: 3–9 blogs linking in last 6 months; middle (10–99); high (100–499); v. high (500+).

4. Run the search

5. View your results, and make any necessary refinements in the authority level

FIGURE 15.2

The results of a search on Technorati for bloggers with "some" authority who have discussed "finger lakes" and vineyards.

Remember, that when using Technorati to look for popular (or "authoritative") *bloggers* on a particular topic, you should click on the "blogs" tab. If you do this, you'll see an ordered listing of blogs, ranked by two of Technorati's key ranking criteria—authority and "favorited by," which is a measure of how many other people have listed that blog as a favorite one.

You can create an even more useful indicator that is closer to calculating actual influence on Technorati by setting up a search of a pre-defined community of bloggers, which would be more topically relevant to your area of interest. By creating your own set of "Favorites" you can create a set of blogs that you choose to be able to view and search separately. Like Google's Custom Search Engine, doing this will enable you to search a more pre-qualified listing of bloggers.

It's simple to set up your favorites. You need to register with Technorati, and you will then be guided on how to input your own favorite blogs. From there, your home page will show you the latest posts from your favorite bloggers, and importantly, you'll be able to restrict a blog search just to your own favorites. See the image below for an example:

FIGURE 15.3

A search on the words Technorati and Google retrieves a small, filtered set of posts from bloggers who I've already determined are influential and of high quality.

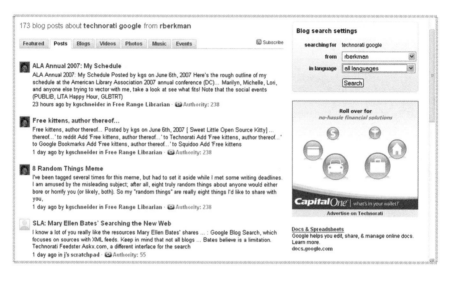

Fee-based Services

Depending on your budget and how critical it is that you locate influential bloggers, there are vendors that promise the use of advanced algorithms, along with a human review, to do a better job than automated search engines in surfacing bloggers that are more likely to be influential and not just popular. BuzzMetrics, which was profiled in Chapter 6 is one firm that promises it can do this.

Another is Onalytica, which performs social network analysis for large organizations and governmental agencies in the U.K to identify influential sites, including blogs. Onalytica founder Flemming Madsen told me that his clients generally want to locate the influential stakeholders, in order to "make decisions, project trends and compose better models of their 'worlds.'"

Onalytica published a paper that demonstrated how its theory works in practice titled "Who are the Most Influential Authorities on Business Blogging" (See Appendix C for URL)

Some Research Strategies

In addition to using these tools and sites, here are a few softer research strategies I recommend for finding influential bloggers on the web.

- Be as familiar and knowledgeable as possible with the area you are researching. This is a basic principle for virtually all types of research. The more you know about any topic, the better position you'll be in to assess the quality and credibility of the discussions and bloggers you come across. Sometimes, of course, having this knowledge isn't possible. Typically the reason you're doing research is because you need to learn about some topic. But the point is, when it comes to deciding what sources to believe—which are of highest quality and most trustworthy—you'll likely do a better job in determining the best sources once you've been immersed in the field for awhile.

  Once you are a little familiar with a field, you'll eventually notice bloggers and others referencing the work, sites, and opinions of the same people over and over. It will become fairly clear that those cited people are influential—no need for some fancy search algorithm or expensive vendor to tell you that—and you can start attending to what those people are saying, by reading their blog or whatever medium they use to communicate, as you've observed their influence on others for yourself.

- If you are starting out with very little knowledge on a field, here is a shortcut to help you zero in on the best bloggers:

  Use the above free popularity surfacing tools (e.g., Technorati's Authority filter) to do some initial searching. Consider what you locate from these tools as good *leads* for locating potentially influential sources, or perhaps as sources that will lead you to the influential ones.

Onalytica outlines its method and provides a sample result in a free report it published called **Who are the Most Influential Authorities on Business Blogging,** *available at: http://www.onalytica.com/ Who_influence_the_debate_ on_Business_Blogging.pdf*

Note that your keywords can be prominent individuals in the field. If you use persons whose work you already like and trust, using their names can serve as a kind of customized filter where you will then retrieve only bloggers (or just web pages or other content) that knew of those people and cited them in some manner.

REPUTATION SYSTEMS

Newly evolving "reputation systems" such as those used by sites like Amazon, NetFlix, and Epinions among others, where users get rated and ranked by other users, represent another way you can get a sense of the expertise or trustworthiness of unknown persons, and these have proven to work pretty well. If you are on a site that includes a reputation system scheme for rating unknown persons, you should give it some credence. One caution, though, is that in recent years there has been increasing concern about users who try to artificially manipulate or "game" the system, though the sites typically are able to counter those attempts by making some adjustments on their end.

Identifying the Credibility of Known Bloggers

The strategies discussed so far will help you figure out which new bloggers you encounter are popular, and perhaps influential too. But if you are already reading commentary by a particular blogger, and wondering about his or her popularity, authority, or influence, there are additional free tools on the web you can use to help you find the answers.

*Another ranking site called **AttentionMeter** allows users to view the popularity of a particular URL as determined by combining several other site traffic rating sites.*

There are sites and tools that provide quantitative "Nielsen-like" ratings of how often a blog is accessed, viewed, or linked to by its "audience," or what is typically called a blog's "traffic." The leaders here include Bloglines, Alexa, Compete, and Quantcast. Each takes a different approach in determining a particular site or blog's audience.

Bloglines, which is owned by the Ask.com search engine, is one of the most popular RSS news readers, and covered in detail in Chapter 12. Bloglines will reveal the total number of subscribers to a particular blog's RSS feed, which is a pretty clear indicator of its popularity.

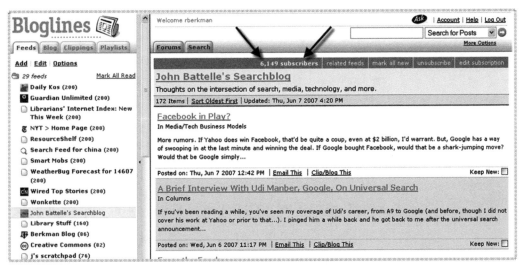

Alexa allows you to enter the URL of a blog (or any web site for that matter) and it provides a traffic ranking, as well as a graph with trend data over time for sites or blogs that are in its top 100,000. The traffic data is derived by combining page views and number of users, averaged over time. This viewing and user data is derived by aggregating the data from the millions of persons who have downloaded and use Alexa's toolbar when searching and browsing the web. Alexa shows what it calls reach, rank, or page views, and can graph results for time periods ranging from a week to five years.

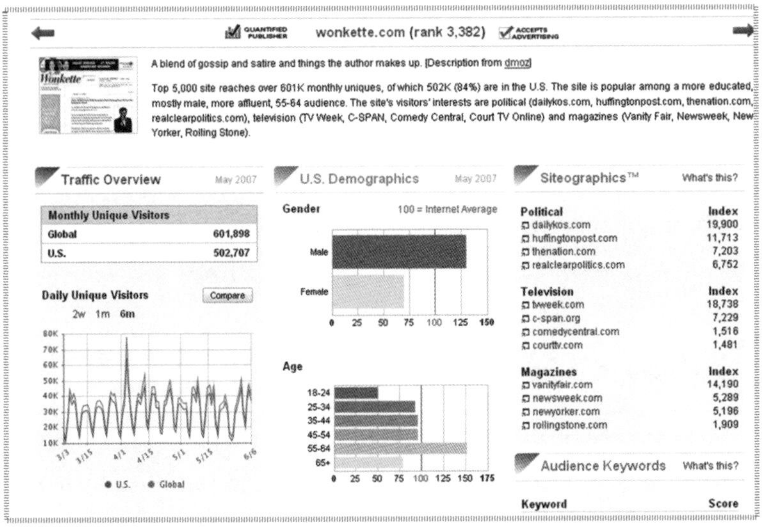

FIGURE 15.4

Here I can see that John Battelle's Searchblog has 6,149 subscribers on Bloglines

FIGURE 15.5

Quantcast shows the daily reach of the Wonkette blog over a period of three years.

Another tool called Quantcast not only provides free data on the number of estimated monthly unique visitors, but also surfaces a variety of other related data of potential value for marketers, such as demographics, other sites visited, commonly used keywords, and similar audience. See the figure above for Quantcast's summary of the popular Wonkette blog.

Be cautious in using these tools, though, particularly those that try to create detailed extrapolations from a small initial data set. Unless you're looking at something very straightforward, like the number of Bloglines subscribers, or links-in, a lot of this derived data can be very iffy. Audience measurement in the Internet world is an extremely young and evolving area, so you can't take this data as gospel by any means.

Assessing Factual Accuracy, Knowledge, and Experience

As discussed in Chapter 4, another measurement of credibility of blogs and social media is simple factual accuracy. If you are reading blogs primarily to find and track complaints, compliments, experiences of product use, and consumers' dealings with a company, you are going to be particularly concerned that what you are reading is accurate, objective, and honest. After all, what's the point of paying attention to a blogger who is railing against a terrible experience he's had with a car rental company, if you're not sure whether to believe what you're reading.

Of course, there's also no certainty that what you read in an article in *The Wall Street Journal* or *The New York Times* is always going be accurate either, but those kinds of sources do have traditional editors, fact checkers, and proofreaders that review copy before publication. A blogger or ordinary consumer can write whatever he or she wants to, without anyone reviewing the material ahead of time.

There are things you can do to check on the factual accuracy and objectivity of a blog posting. While these strategies aren't 100 percent foolproof, they can and will increase the odds that you are getting the kind of information you seek:

1. Assessing Factual Accuracy

It's only partially true that bloggers don't have editors. In fact, blogs, particularly the most popular ones *do* have editors—thousands and thousands of them—their readers. For blogs, the editing process occurs *after* publication, when their readers will point out errors or misleading statements.

This process of after-publication reader editing and fact checking of blogs typically works quite well. Other bloggers and regular blog readers are very good, to a fault some might say, at spotting factual inaccuracies, and will pounce on the blogger who has made a mistake.

So one way to increase the odds that what you've just read on a blog is accurate is not to rely on information the day it's posted, but wait a few days (or for the really well read blogs, just a few hours). Then read through the responses and consider the accuracy of what the blogger said in the comments you read, and the bloggers' response to any corrections or criticisms.

This reader-editing process, which again reflects the "wisdom of crowds" philosophy that has become something of a mantra and guiding principle in the blogosphere, can and does work surprisingly well. But it's not perfect either, and how well it works in practice for a particular blogger will depends on certain factors.

The biggest factor is probably the size of the blog's readership. With a blog with lots of readers there's a greater chance that an error or misleading statement will be challenged right on the blog. This also touches on the matter of accountability. Accountability means that one must answer for what one says or does. So, if say, *The New York Times,* or *The Atlantic* magazine, or MSNBC, or some other traditional large media source states something that's clearly factually incorrect, it will almost certainly be called on it. The media outlet, knowing that this will likely occur and that they may be held accountable for any errors, will therefore feel some external pressure to try to make sure that its information is accurate when it is published.

When you are reading a blog, you should also consider: just how accountable is this blogger? As a rough rule, the larger and more prominent the blog's audience, the more likely it is that it will be held to account for what it states, and so will be more careful (with the exception of a site like the Drudge Report, which while having a very large readership, is unusual in admitting to not caring if it publishes a degree of inaccurate information). Obscure bloggers might feel freer to pass along questionable information, since it is unlikely that anyone will spot it and challenge their accuracy.

For the same reason, anyone that blogs or posts anonymously has virtually zero accountability, and there is little reason to trust the information.

In the natural world, MIT professor Judith Donath has stated that animals show their intention by the use of *signals,* and that the "costliest" signals are the most believable. For instance, she explains that the antlers of a moose or the feathers of a peacock are costly to that animal in terms of the resources they require and so they are more likely to be real (e.g., antlers can be counted on to represent strength). Newspaper editors have the reputation of their paper at stake, so they are highly motivated to check the reputation of their writers, particularly newer writers. But bloggers also need to figure out how to put out believable, costly reputation signals. There are "cheap" signals—if someone lies on their site and says, "I'm a great singer," there is no real cost. Visitors to these sites need to be able to look for costlier signals so that they can assess the underlying quality of the information provider. Donath has published an article outlining her analyses, titled "Signals in Superness," (*Journal of Computer-Mediated Communication* 13(2), October 2007).

So Donath raised the question: How can bloggers risk their own reputations so that there are real repercussions if they are not credible? That's a question for bloggers to think about, but for now, though, the burden for establishing accuracy of what they read is on the information seeker. Here are a few tips on how to do so by following some of the tried and true methods that reporters have used for years. Here are the two most important ones:

- **Go to the source yourself.** A basic reporter's rule that works quite well online, is to never accept a second- or third-hand description of a document, conversation, or other event or source material, but to go to that original source and review it yourself. This is a particularly important rule when reading a summary or a paraphrase from another source on a blog, as it is quite easy for anyone to get numbers wrong, misinterpret something, or mangle what someone actually said. Often if the original source is a document or statement of some kind, you can find that original source or statement right on the web with a simple keyword search on Google.

John Hinderaker, the creator of PowerLineBlog has said that this capacity of readers to track down original primary sources makes his blog more credible. He says that the reason that his blog and others have high credibility is because he links to sources so that readers can judge for themselves as to whether what he said is accurate and his interpretations are valid.

- **Get a confirming source.** This is another fundamental reporter's rule. Don't accept what you hear from one source as necessarily accurate. Always confirm with a second, or even third confirming source. Donath made this point too when she stated that to determine credibility,

"We can look for convergence, like a poll. If all the newspapers say, 'It's cold in Boston,' we can feel more confident about it."

This rule of getting a confirming source has gotten a bit trickier on the web, though because of the propensity of the Internet to replicate *all* information, good *or* bad! So getting an additional source does not mean finding more than one website or blogger that's repeating the same statement. It means finding two or more completely *independent* sources where one party is not just repeating the statement from another. This requires a little more work. One way to approach this would be to try to make your confirming source one that is an *offline* source (e.g., a hard copy directory, print journal, or personal phone interview).

The Problem of Paying Bloggers to Post

The recent trend for some firms and sites to pay bloggers to post about their firm or product has been gaining momentum and become more organized. While the payment to a blogger can be made directly from the company, more commonly it is being paid by a middleman that creates a website to attract and match up advertisers with bloggers who wish to write reviews and commentary about products for cash. While the original and most well known of these middleman sites is called PayPerPost, others with similar business models for paying bloggers have emerged as well, including SponsoredReviews, LoudLaunch, and ReviewMe.

Blogging for money from companies raises clear ethical issues. Some bloggers dismiss these as unimportant while others strongly condemn them. In my view, bloggers are indeed violating ethical standards if they blog for money about products and companies if they are not up front about it. It presents several ethical problems including a further commoditization of human conversation, the potential deception of the reader of the blog (despite the small icon that PayPerPost bloggers are supposed to display on their site), and a diminishment of the Internet's role in helping facilitate authentic conversation and enhance our knowledge and understanding. Blogger Jeff Jarvis puts it this way: "Credibility is the cake you can't have and eat, too." Even the FTC weighed in on this matter. In December 2006 it ruled that ties between word-of-mouth marketers and their sponsored consumer must be disclosed, and that it would be watching for any cases of deception.

But for the purposes of *this* chapter, the ethics issue is not of primary concern. What is of immediate and more practical concern to the researcher is whether you may be misled by encountering bloggers who are saying overly positive things about a company and its products because they are being paid to do so.

FIGURE 15.6

Some bloggers are getting paid by firms like Pay Per Post to blog about specific products.

This is a tough question to answer. The first thing we would need to figure out is how prevalent paid blogging is, and it hard to do that. According to an article on the pay per post phenomena published in March 2007 by the *Los Angeles Times*, "thousands of bloggers are writing sponsored posts."

This sounds worrisome, but consider that with tens of millions of blogs, even if 100,000 bloggers are being paid to blog, this would still represent a tiny percentage of the entire blogosphere. Furthermore, even if you do encounter a pay-per-post blogger, you won't necessarily be misled. If you have your antenna up, you may also be able to spot that it is a paid blogger. Does the person sound just a bit too chatty and enthusiastic about how much he or she loves xyz product? Do her words sound like marketing talk? If so, then just follow some of the above advice on determining credibility, such as finding confirming sources. If you are suspicious about a particular blogger, you may also be able to do a search on the blog and find out who else has cited that person and if there is any conversation about that particular blogger's credibility. Other bloggers have been good at "outing" fraudulent bloggers, and you may get some help here from the larger blogosphere.

In summary then, to help ensure the likelihood of factual accuracy and honesty on a blog:

1. Wait for comments to appear after the blog is posted.

2. Consider that an error on the larger blogs might be more likely to be found and corrected than on the smallest ones and that larger bloggers might be more careful than in checking what they publish.

3. Use the reporter's rules of going to an original document yourself and getting confirming sources.

4. Keep attuned for bloggers that may be overly enthusiastic about a product and do a little more research on any that seem suspect.

5. What about evaluating a blogger's knowledge and expertise? Remember that from a market research standpoint, evaluating knowledge may not always be so critical since a blogger's complaints and opinions could be worth listening to on their own merits, and if a person has lots of readers, his or her views—informed or uninformed—may have an impact on other customers. But when you *do* need to assess a blogger's actual level of expertise, there are steps you can take to make such a determination. Here are a few strategies, excerpted in part from a book I wrote a few years ago, titled *The Skeptical Business Searcher: The Information Advisor's Guide to Evaluating Web Data, Sites, and Sources* (Medford, N.J. Information Today, 2004).

   • Where did you locate this person? Was he or she referred to you by another trusted source?

   • Where else has this person presented his or her views? In forums other than an Internet discussion group?

   • Who else has cited the views of this person? Are these people considered reliable and trusted sources?

   • Does the person demonstrate some familiarity and knowledge of this area? For example, does he or she know about existing sources and information, or others who are in the field?

   • How does the person present his or her views? Is it in a clear, logical, thoughtful, and organized manner? Is he or she open to alternative views? Is he or she open about the methods used to come to conclusions? Does he or she offer backup or evidence for claims?

- Does the person have hidden biases that you should know about? Does he or she work for an organization with a specific agenda? What could be his or her motivations for providing this information?

- Has this person kept up with changes and new developments in the field?

Other, more subtle, indicators of a good source include:

- Writes in a fresh, lively manner that displays caring and enthusiasm about the topic

- Cites others' work and knowledge in the field and demonstrates understanding of a larger context

- Offers a high level of detail in descriptions and analyses

- Explains to you something you have been thinking about but had not been able to articulate

- Expands your understanding of a topic to a higher level

- Provides insight and an "aha" feeling as you read their writings

There are also some standard active steps researchers have been able to rely upon to assess an individual's knowledge and expertise:

- Find other sources to confirm what the person is saying

- Do some research: enter the person's name into a search engine to see where else he or she has spoken or written.

- Contact the individual yourself by phone or by email and ask your own follow up questions. This will give you a much better feel for the extent of his or her knowledge.

These guidelines apply quite well for evaluating bloggers' knowledge and expertise. One possible modification, though, is that, as mentioned earlier, because the blog culture is more accepting of emotional and even angry discussions, you should be more tolerant and open to some level of ranting than you might in other cases.

CHAPTER 16

The Big Picture and Future Trends

THIS BOOK is based on the premise that it's important for organizations to pay close attention to discussions on blogs and other forms of social media, and I've outlined the reasons why the information can be of such high value.

But like any tool, technology, or activity, there are cases where relying on some new method will serve you well, and there are other cases where the approach is not helpful or appropriate. So it's important to point out the situations where monitoring blog and social media will not be to your benefit, and some of the pitfalls that can occur if you focus too much on watching the blogosphere to the detriment of engaging in other kinds of research-related activities.

There's no question that the conversation and content sharing that's occurring on blogs and other social media is *not* a fad. While the *forms, tools, and sites* of how people communicate and share information online will undoubtedly change over time, the basic human desire to communicate with others, voice one's opinion, create and share information is certainly here to stay. The digital trail that these conversations leave represents new and potentially valuable sources of market intelligence, and spending some time gathering them, as long as you have well-thought-out and ethical strategies for effectively locating the relevant and insightful discussions, should be considered an important aspect of market-related research.

But there's also some hype, and there are lots of opportunities to be led astray. Here are what I see as the main areas where you need to be wary and cautious:

The Tyranny of the Now

By its nature, the Internet is a medium focused on speed and real-time information. This has been a great boon for searchers who want to find breaking news, financial data, and other information where being up to the minute makes a real difference in its value. But for market research purposes, what's happening "right now" has its own limitations.

When you are engaged in a medium that stresses immediacy, it's easy to get caught up in a kind of state of artificially induced urgency. As an example from another medium that places an over-emphasis on speed, we can look at cable news, and how *CNN Headline News'* endless string of red "breaking news" and "developing story" scrolls are designed to create in its viewers a reaction approaching near crisis, and clearly as a way to capture and hold the viewer attention. If you listen carefully, too, you'll notice that one of the reason that CNN's anchorperson Wolf Blitzer is so compelling is that no matter what he is discussing, his voice contains a level of urgency, again conveying the message that "I have some very important, and urgent information for you, so you had better listen"

This is the message of the blogosphere too—less consciously created, but still in its nature. Good market intelligence means attending to trends and behaviors that develop over some period of time. Not everything that is happening on the web is urgent, and you should be on guard not to let your valuable time and attention be fooled this way.

The Tyranny of Quantification

Just as the nature of the Net is to emphasize the "now," it is also true that because so much of what occurs on the Net can be rather easily counted (how many links; how many clicks; how many users), there is an emphasis on quantification as the method to answer questions and provide new insights. For the most part, this is a good thing, because having access to this data can provide some very useful and interesting information: (e.g., today there are XX number of blogs; XX are in the language Farsi; XX of bloggers post every day: XX of consumer-generated videos have tags).

However, the use of counting and quantification methods again is just one tool, and you can't obtain real insights and understanding of larger trends by relying only on numbers, without the kind of softer immersion, analysis, probing, questioning, and human interpretation that is needed to figure out more complex phenomena. We discussed this a bit in the chapter on tracking trends, in that you don't want to rely just on buzz tracking sites that rely on counting. In the same way, you don't want to rely just on quantification for generating insights for your market intelligence.

The Tyranny of Technology's Tools

Technology, as well as the vendors and programmers who create technology tools today, rules the Internet. We can only do with what we are given: without search engines we could not effectively find information on the Web; without news readers we could not gather news and blog posts to our desktop; without blog and video hosting sites, we could not find and read blogs.

So we are dependent on information technology experts, vendors, and increasingly, enthusiasts, to create for us the tools *they* think we need (or think will bring in revenue), and those tools tend to define what we think we can and should do while on the Internet. Of course, when it comes to searching and filtering blogs and consumer content, thousands of vendors of new technologies promises that they have come up with "the solution"

However, if we can only react to the mindset of the information technology vendor, we are not actively thinking about what we truly need. Neil Postman has suggested that any time we are shown a new technology we should ask the vendor "what is the problem, to which this is the solution?"

The Tyranny of the Internet

We all love the Internet, and it is truly an amazing technology. But it is still not "everything." Although going on the Internet has become synonymous with doing research, performing research is not the same as going to the Internet, and certain basic principles of research and market research have not changed.

Perhaps the biggest drawback and pitfall of the Internet itself is to encourage a certain level of passivity. You can't just do a few keyword searches, or set up a few news feeds and assume you're doing effective market research, or any kind of research for that matter. Just because information comes easily to your desktop, that doesn't mean it's all you need to do. Somewhat paradoxically, although we all know how the Internet seems to provide us with too much information, at the same time, relying on information from the Net can also serve to narrow our focus on the world. Most of the world's knowledge is still in offline sources like books, journals, and importantly, inside of people's heads, (and most of those people don't have blogs!)

> **Bottom line:** What you ultimately want to achieve for any market research endeavor is understanding and insight. Blogs, forums, user videos, and the rest of consumer-generated content will get you some of the way towards this end, but not the whole way. Use them, but use them with caution!

Some Future Trends

While things change so fast in this arena that it's dangerous to make predictions, I feel on safe ground in noting these trends, which will have implications for market research and social media:

- **Blurring of types of consumer-generated media and content**

    There are various forms of content created by consumers: news, blogs, images, video, and so forth. While the distinctions are not going to go away, these forms will increasingly be combined, and the sharp definitions that now exist between them will become less clear. Search engines like Google and Technorati are already combining results from these different forms in a single search, rather than offering a separate news, blog, image, or video search, and will likely do more of this kind of integration.

    A few things are driving this trend including more content creation in multimedia, and more tools that make it easier to do so. Another key force: increasingly searchers don't care too much what kind of format they get, as long as what they find answers to their questions.

    The implication: I think this trend will make searching more, not less complicated. Good researchers know that different forms of content have distinct origins and characteristics, and so usually prefer to focus their searching on a particular type of format.

- **Blurring of consumer-generated content with traditional professional content**

    Yahoo! has already decided to include blogs as part of its general news search. Like the above trend, this one is also blurring boundaries, but this one blurs the distinction between content produced by traditional information sources like professionally created online newspapers, journals, newswires, with that of blogs, user-generated videos and other consumer content and media. RSS readers combine all types of sources in a reader, treating all the same, and flattening distinctions. Again, this trend is driven partly by searchers not really caring that much about the origin and derivation of the content. However, it is also spurred by the movement among some consumer media aggregators, such as YouTube, to begin paying or compensating its contributors in some manner, blurring the difference between the amateurs and the pros.

The implication: This trend will likely make it more difficult to ascertain the credibility of a particular source of information, as it will remove one of the clear markers we have now in making our assessment of an information source—is it from a professional or an amateur? I don't mean to imply here that this means we would always say a source from a professional is necessarily more credible than one produced by an ordinary citizen, just that we will lose one more indicator in understanding the origin and nature of a source.

- **More emphasis on locating non-English language blogs and other social media**

  Other than the technical hurdles of indexing spoken words and images on podcasts and consumer videos, the next big issue to be tackled by search engines like Google and Technorati will be to make it easier to locate blogs and other content that are not in the English language.

  The implication: As new methods and tools are introduced to search and understand bloggers and other consumers who post in languages other than English, global market intelligence that previously was only available to firms that could hire expensive PR agencies with human translators will be opened up to ordinary businesses and researchers.

- **More emphasis on real-time information exchanges**

  With the advent of live chat platforms like Twitter, it is clear that the desire, particularly among young persons, to easily chat at any moment about virtually anything and to do so in real time is a strong one. As such, we are likely to see even more digital tools developed to help people share real-time information. Perhaps soon it will become quite common for users of advanced cell phone devices like the iPhone to be casually sending and transmitting short videos to their friends and to their video blogs as a way of communicating what they are doing at the moment.

The implication: On the downside: more information overload, and more concerns about determining the real value from instant consumer videos. Also, more issues regarding how to truly search real-time information, particularly real-time video. All of this will make navigating the world of digital consumer content more complicated, will generate more search, filtering, and aggregation tools and methods, which itself will likely spur the creation and dissemination of more real-time information.

On the positive side, from a market research perspective, if one can cultivate the skills and ability to effectively pinpoint and review or search real time videos as they are being transmitted, it would represent an as yet unprecedented opportunity for gathering market intelligence (e.g., "I see that some of the customers of our new magnetic induction cook tops are not using it properly—perhaps we should add a new feature to make it easier"). However, this capability also raises new and difficult ethical and perhaps legal issues related to matters like surveillance, intrusion on customer privacy, and concerns about overly aggressive and intrusive marketing.

FIGURE 16.1

Twitterment allows users to input a keyword and view up-to-the-minute statistics and excerpts from Twitter users who have used that word or phrase.

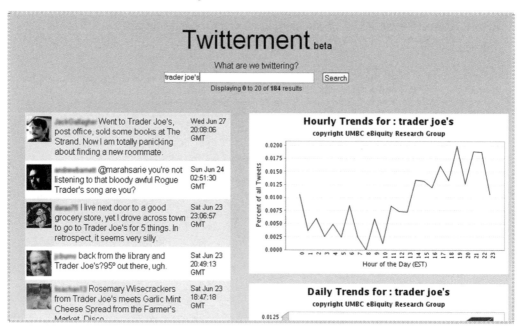

Finally, the virtual world Second Life is still in its infancy but continues to grow extremely rapidly and firms have been establishing a presence there to play a role and reach possible customers. Reuters even set up a news bureau to report on what's happening in Second Life. While doing market research by tapping into occupants of this virtual world was beyond the scope of this book, it would behoove market researchers to begin learning about the kinds of activities consumers engage in while there, and look for opportunities to identify possible forms of market intelligence. To learn more, I recommend checking out "Business Communicators of Second Life" at http://freshtakes. typepad.com/sl_communicators/

Appendix A

Suggested Reading

THE FOLLOWING LISTS of sources is a selective compilation of books, blogs, and other sources on the topic of marketing, research and social media that I've read and can recommend or have been highly recommended by others in the field.

Books, Journals, Papers, and Associations

On Wikis, Crowds and Social Media

Morville, Peter, *Ambient Findability: What We Find Changes Who We Become,* (O'Reilly Media, 2005)

Rheingold, Howard, *Smart Mobs: The Next Social Revolution,* (Perseus, 2002)

Sunstein, Cass, *InfoTopia: How Many Minds Produce Knowledge,* (Oxford University Press, 2006)

Surowiecki, James, *The Wisdom of Crowds: Why the Many Are Smarter Than the Few and How Collective Wisdom Shapes Business, Economies, Societies and Nations,* (Doubleday, 2004)

Tapscott, Don, *Wikinomics: How Mass Collaboration Changes Everything,* (Portfolio, 2006)

Weinberger, David, *Everything is Miscellaneous: The Power of the New Digital Disorder,* (Times Books, 2007)

On Blogs and Journalism

Gillmor, Dan, *We the Media: Grassroots Journalism by the People For the People* (O'Reilly Media, 2004)

Marketing/Word of Mouth Marketing/Consumer-Generated Marketing

Berry, John and Ed Keller, *The Influentials: One American in Ten Tells the Other Nine How to Vote, Where to Eat, and What to Buy* (Free Press, 2003)

Gillin, Paul, *The New Influencers: A Marketers Guide to the New Social Media* (Quill Driver, 2007)

Kozinets, Robert V., "The Field Behind the Screen: Using Netnography for Market Research," Available at: http://research.bus.wisc.edu/rkozinets/printouts/kozinetsFieldBehind.pdf

McConnell, Ben and Jackie Huba, *Citizen Marketers—When People are the Message,* (Kaplan Business, 2006)

Prahalad C.K. and Venkat Ramaswamy, *The Future of Competition: Co-Creating Unique Value with Customers* (Harvard Business School Press, 2004)

Seybold, Patricia, *Outside Innovation: How Your Customers Will Co-Design Your Company's Future* (Collins, 2006)

Psychological Strategies for Adapting to Information Overload (or other frustrations)

Ellis, Albert and Robert A. Harper, *A Guide to Rational Living* (Wilshire, 3rd revised edition 1975)

Online Information and Credibility

Berkman, Robert I. "The Skeptical Business Searcher," (CyberAge 2004)

Bruzzese, Len; Houston, Brant and Steven Weinberg, *The Investigative Reporter's Handbook: A Guide to Documents, Databases and Techniques* (Bedford/St. Martins 4th ed., 2002)

Harrison Smith, Sarah, *The Fact Checkers Bible* (Anchor 2004)

Trend Tracking

Schwartz, Peter, *The Art of the Long View: Planning for the Future in an Uncertain World* (Currency, 1996)

Research and Online Searching/Books

Calishain, Tara, *Information Trapping: Realtime Research on the Web* (New Riders Press, 2006)

Business Research and Online Searching/Journals

The Information Advisor (Information Today, Medford, NJ) www.informationadvisor.com

Blog Monitoring Industry

Peter Kim's Report Wave

The Forrester Wave: Brand Monitoring http://www.forrester.com/Research/Document/Excerpt/0,7211,39442,00.html

Other: Young People and Digital Information

Montgomery, Kathryn C., *Generation Digital: Politics, Commerce, and Childhood in the Age of the Internet* (MIT Press, 2007)

Blogs, Web Sites and Online News Services

Blogs/Trends in the Blogosphere

Technorati: State of the Live Web http://technorati.com/weblog/2007/04/328.html

Blogs/Marketing and Consumer-Generated Media

The Net Savvy Executive: Nathan Gilliat http://net-savvy.com/executive/

ConsumerGeneratedMeida.com: Pete Blackshaw http://notetaker.typepad.com/cgm/

AttentionMax: Max Kalehoff http://www.attentionmax.com/

Groundswell: Charlene Li and Josh Bernoff (Forrester Research)
http://forrester.typepad.com/charleneli/

Marketing Vox: http://www.marketingvox.com

Seth Godin: http://www.sethgodin.com/sg

Church of the Customer: http://www.customerevangelists.typepad.com

Word Of Mouth Marketing Association (WOMMA): http://www.womma.org

WOMMA Code of Ethics: http://www.womma.org/ethics/

Blogs/Web 2.0

MicroPersuasion: Steve Rubell http://www.micropersuation.com

Library Clips: http://www.libraryclips.blogsome.com

Read/Write Web: http://www.readwriteweb.com

Digital Inspiration: http://www.labnol.blogspot.com

Social Computing Magazine: http://www.socialcomputingmagazine.com

Blogs/Citizen Journalism

BuzzMachine: Jeff Jarvis http://www.buzzmachine.com

Dan Gillmore's Blog: http://www.dangillmor.com/

PressThink: Jay Rosen http://journalism.nyu.edu/pubzone/weblogs/pressthink/

Research and Online Searching

Intelligent Agent: Robert Berkman http://www.ia-blog.com

ResearchBuzz: Tara Calashain http://www.researchbuzz.com

FreePint: http://www.freepint.com

Search Engine Watch: http://www.searchenginewatch.com

Blogs/Productivity

LifeHacker: http://lifehacker.com

Lifehack: http://lifehack.org

43 Folders: http://www.43folders.com

David Allen: GTD http://www.davidco.com

Trend Tracking

TrendWatching: http://trendwatching.com

The Blog-Monitoring Industry

The blogger below keeps a continuing updated list on firms that monitor and measure social media sources

http://www.web-strategist.com/blog/2006/11/25/companies-that-measure-social-media-influence-brand/

Sentiment Detection/Scholarly Papers

Sanjay Sood, Kristian J. Hammond, Larry Birnbaum, Sara Owsley "Reasoning Through Search: A New Approach to Sentiment Classification" http://www.cs.northwestern.edu/~pardo/courses/EECS395-22-MachineLearning-Winter07/papers/sentiment-classification.pdf

Lee, Lillian, "A matter of opinion: Sentiment analysis and business intelligence"

IBM Faculty Summit on the Architecture of On-Demand Business, May 17–18, 2004 http://www.cs.cornell.edu/home/llee/papers/ibm-facsum04.html

http://domino.research.ibm.com/comm/www_fs.nsf/pages/20040609_facsuminfoint.html/$FILE/lillian lee.pdf

Pang, Bo, Lillian Lee, and Shivakumar Vaithyanathan, "Thumbs up? Sentiment Classification using Machine Learning Techniques" *Proceedings of the Conference on Empirical Methods in + (EMNLP)*, pp. 79–86, 2002, http://www.cs.cornell.edu/home/llee/papers/sentiment.home.html

Turney, Peter D., "Thumbs Up or Thumbs Down? Semantic Orientation Applied to Unsupervised Classification of Reviews" Institute for Information Technology, National Research Council of Canada, Ottawa, Ontario, Canada, K1A 0R6 http://acl.ldc.upenn.edu/P/P02/P02-1053.pdf

Soo-Min Kim and Eduard Hovy Kim, Soo-Min and Eduard Hovy, "Automatic Detection of Opinion Bearing Words and Sentences" Information Sciences Institute, University of Southern California http://www.isi.edu/~skim/Download/Papers/2005/ijcnlp_cameraready_letter.pdf

Social Networking Sites

While there are thousands of articles, discussions, and Web links on the topic of social networking sites, to get an overview of some of the major issues I highly recommend a series of articles published in a special issue of the *Journal of Computer-Mediated Communication*, October 2007 (Vol 13, No. 1). That issue, which is available online for free, contains several in-depth articles from leading experts in the field, including danah boyd. For the full issue, link to: http://jcmc.indiana.edu/vol13/issue1/index.html. Although it is a scholarly publication, it is also quite readable and accessible for the lay public.

I also highly recommend browsing danah boyd's own blog at: http://www.zephoria.org/thoughts/.

APPENDIX B

Productivity Tools

THERE ARE COUNTLESS sites and tools on the Web that can help you improve your searching, blog monitoring, Net navigation, and assist you in organizing the results of your research. This appendix provides a listing of what I think are the best general productivity tools that you could use to make all of your blog and consumer content searching and monitoring more effective and productive. I've grouped these under the following categories:

- Browser plug-ins

- Bookmarklets

- Widgets

- Note Taking and Organizational Aids

- RSS Productivity Tools

- Do it yourself directory: Search Engines, Blog Search Engines, Buzz-Trackers,

Browser Plug-ins

Browser plug-ins allow you to add functionality to your web browser, whether the browser is Internet Explorer, Firefox, or another. Here are several of the most interesting and relevant for research purposes:

Firefox Addons

You can add the ability to search Technorati or other search engines in the Firefox toolbar by browsing Firefox Addons: Search Engines: https://addons.mozilla.org/en-US/firefox/browse/type:4

as well as at MyCroft:
http://mycroft.mozdev.org/

The links in this section are active in the digital edition of this book.

Firefox Bookmark Synchronizer

This site lets you keeps your bookmarks synchronized if you use Firefox on more than one PC:

https://addons.mozilla.org/en-US/firefox/addon/2410

Sage

Sage is a lightweight RSS reader that integrates directly into Firefox
https://addons.mozilla.org/en-US/firefox/addon/77

StumbleUpon

A collaborative surfing tool for finding and sharing sites:
https://addons.mozilla.org/en-US/firefox/addon/138

Other add-ons

You can find hundreds more add-ons for Firefox at Mozilla Firefox at: https://addons.mozilla.org/en-US/firefox/.

These subcategories of the most popular extensions can also help you pinpoint the most useful add ons for Firefox: https://addons.mozilla.org/en-US/firefox/browse/type:1/cat:71/sort: popular https://addons.mozilla.org/en-US/firefox/browse/type:1/ cat:22/sort:popular

https://addons.mozilla.org/en-US/firefox/browse/type:1/cat:13/sort: popular

Bookmarklets

A bookmarklet is a tiny snippet of Javascript that you can drag to your browser's toolbar. Once clicked on, a bookmarklet will perform a search or other function on the page you are currently viewing. Here are a few worth checking out:

TalkDigger Bookmarklet

http://www.talkdigger.com/tools/bookmarklet

TalkDigger can look up what conversations are taking place that link back to the page you are currently on by searching across the top blog search engines at once. It is a sparse database, because it depends heavily on user submitted conversations, but it is interesting as it combines the benefits of comment tracking, like co.mments, and link tracking, al la Technorati, in one place.

Technorati This

http://technorati.com/tools/favelets.html

This bookmarklet searches what blogs have linked to the page you are viewing, but with the added functionality of Technorati. You can highlight text on any page and Technorati will search its blog index for just those words as well.

Email This! Bookmarklet Extension

https://addons.mozilla.org/en-US/firefox/addon/3102

Email This! will send your recipient the link, title, and highlighted text of the page you are viewing. This works for GMail, Google Apps GMail, Yahoo!, Hotmail, and standalone programs like Outlook Express.

Widgets

Widgets are mini applications that are added to your desktop. Rather than launching your browser or navigating to a webpage, desktop widgets allow you to conduct search queries, among other things, directly from your desktop.

Technorati Dashboard Widget (Mac OSX)

http://www.apple.com/downloads/dashboard/blogs_forums/tech-noratisearchwidget.html

You can install this widget to add a Technorati search box to a Mac OS X desktop.

Desktop Widgets   http://widgets.com

Web Widgets   http://desktop.google.com/plugins

Note Taking and Organizational Aids

Here are a few of my favorite tools for Internet-based note taking and for storing important pages and conversations as you navigate around the web and a wide variety of social media sites.

Furl
http://www.furl.Internet

Furl not only permits you to save the URL of any Web page you come across, but also lets you save the full text, add your own notes, and then store all of this on Furl's server so you can conduct a keyword search of your notes and the full text of the saved pages to retrieve just what you need.

Clipmarks
http://clipmarks.com/

Clipmarks allows you to easily grab text and pictures to annotate and share just by clicking on different sections of a webpage.

Google Notebook
http://www.google.com/notebook/

With Google Notebook and its accompanying bookmarklet, users can share web pages of annotated webpage and blogpost information. Although not as advanced as some other clipping services, if you already have a Google account, it can be convenient to stay within the Google suite of applications.

 An Introduction to Zotero

Zotero
www.zotero.org

Zotero is a "research manager" that is designed to help collect, manage, and cite sources you've encountered on the Web.

RSS Productivity Tools

The following tools and sites are all designed to improve your RSS news feed reading experience:

Browser Extensions
There is usually an extension available that will more closely integrate your RSS reader with your browser, no matter which one you use. In Firefox, for instance, the "GreaseMonkey" extension allows users to change the overall appearance of Google Reader, as well as add functionality not currently included in that news reader. To find

the most popular RSS-related extensions for the Firefox browser, you can link to this site:

https://addons.mozilla.org/en-US/firefox/browse/type:1/cat:1/sort:popular

Browser Bookmarklets

One Pipe—Utilizing Yahoo!'s development "Pipes" platform (see below), Marjolein Hoekstra of CleverClogs.org (she's Dutch) has created a bookmarklet that will create filtered Internet feeds of the websites you visit on the fly.

http://www.cleverclogs.org/2007/03/onepipe_the_sin.html

Feed Filtering/Remixers/Mashups

Use the sites below to remix, filter, and mash RSS feeds the way you like:

FeedRinse—Filters keywords in or out of your RSS feeds.

FeedBlendr—Turns many feeds into just one, easy to manage feed.

Yahoo! Pipes, which is a bit more technically oriented than the tools and sites in the rest of this book, offers a way Internet savvy users can combine and filter rss feed content and then provide these RSS feed "mashups" to anyone interested in using or copying them. Here are instructions to build a pipe that will translate RSS feeds into the language of your choice

http://www.webware.com/8301-1_109-9731147-2.html

And here's one that searches several video search engines.
http://pipes.yahoo.com/pipes/pipe.info?results=100&search=schwab
&=Run+Pipe&_id=AHkR4ai42xGlKUilZFUMqA&_run=1

This one will setup a persistent search at Bloglines, Findory, Google Blog Search, Google News, IceRocket, MSFT Live News, Technorati, and Yahoo! News: http://pipes.yahoo.com/pipes/pipe.info?_id=fELaG mGz2xGtBTC3qe5lkA

RSS Feeds Generators

The following sites allow you to build keyword-based feeds for multiple search engines, all in one place.

TagJag [tagjag.com), creates a feed on multiple blogs and search engines, and does so by specifically searching only the tags created by the users.

Kebberfegg [www.researchbuzz.org/tools/kebberfegg.pl] is a recommended site covered earlier in the book.

MonitorThis [http://alp-uckan.net/free/monitorthis/] With MonitorThis you can subscribe to 22 different search engine feeds at the same time.

Personalized Start Pages

Rather than sign up with a dedicated news reader, you can also sign up with a personal start up portal on the web, where you can get your feeds along with other personalized information as a kind of home page on the web. These sites use the Ajax technology to make a fast and elegant presentation of the data.

FIGURE A2.1

The NetVibes Portal permits users to create a keyword search over multiple types of consumer content.

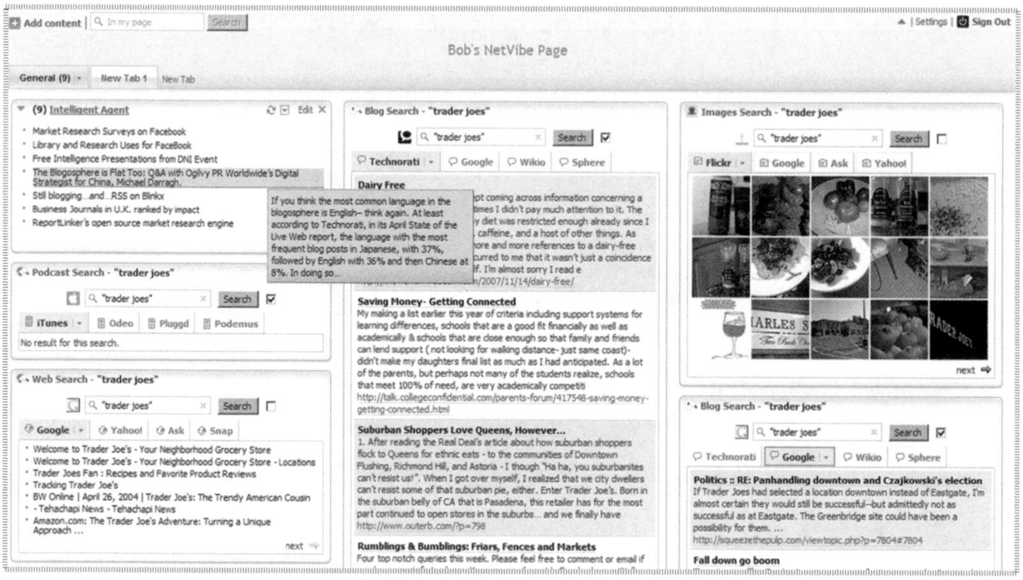

NetVibes	http://www.netvibes.com
PageFlakes	http://www.pageflakes.com

RSS Feed Presentation

You don't actually have to use a news reader to read RSS feeds. Here are some alternatives

Rmail [www.r-mail.com] With RMail, you can get your RSS feed content delivered to you via email

DodgeIT [www.dodgeit.com] Go the other direction and have email delivered via RSS feed.

RSS2PDF [rss2pdf.com] Read and share your RSS feed content offline.

More on News readers

About.com: Windows RSS Feed Readers/Aggregators

http://email.about.com/od/rssreaderswin/Windows_RSS_Feed_Readers_Aggregators.htm

CNET Review of news readers:

http://www.download.com/News readers/3150-2164_4-0.html?tag=dir

An RSS Compendium:

http://mashable.com/2007/06/11/rss-toolbox/

Appendix C

URLs of Key Sites

The following listing, by chapter, provides the URLs for selected sites, blogs, and other important Internet-based sources mentioned in this book. **These links are active in the digital edition of this book.**

Chapter 1

Technorati	http://www.technorati.com
Brandimensions	http://www.brandimensions.com
Biz360	http://www.biz360.com
Converseon	http://www.converseon.com
Factiva	http://factiva.com
FAST	http://www.fastsearch.com
Monitor 110	http://www.monitor110.com
MotiveQuest	http://www.motivequest.com
Nielsen Buzzmetrics	http://www.nielsenbuzzmetrics.com
TNS/MI Cymfony	http://www.cymfony.com
Umbria	http://www.umbria.com

Chapter 2

Planet Feedback	http://www.planetfeedback.com
Complaints.com	http://www.complaints.com

Chapter 7

OpinMind	http://opinmind.com/

Chapter 8

BuzzLogic	http://www.buzzlogic.com
Communispace	http://www.communispace.com
Hosted Conversations	http://www.newsgator.com/Business/PrivateLabelPlatform/Default.aspx

Chapter 9

Google	http://www.google.com
Google Blog Search	http://blogsearch.google.com/
LiveDoor	see Wikipedia entry at: en.wikipedia.org/wiki/Livedoor
2 channel	see Wikipedia entry at: http://en.wikipedia.org/wiki/2channel
Baidu	http:// ir.baidu.com/
Hao Hao	http://www.haohaoreport.com/
Intelligent Agent	http://ia-blog.com
OhMyNews	http://english.ohmynews.com
Technorati Japan	http://www.technorati.jp/
BabelFish	http://babelfish.altavista.com/
Google Translate	www.google.com/translate_t
Global Voices Online	www.globalvoicesonline.org

Chapter 10

Technorati	http://www.technorati.com
Ask.com	http://www.ask.com
Feedster	http://www.feedster.com
IceRocket	http://www.icerocket.com
Sphere	http://www.sphere.com
Clusty	http://clusty.com
Serph	http://www.serph.com
Zuula	http://www.zuula.com

Chapter 11

BoardTracker	http://www.boardtracker.com
Google Groups	http://groups.google.com/
Yahoo! Groups	http://groups.yahoo.com/

Email-based Mailing Lists and ListServs

Topica	http://lists.Topica.com/dir/?cid=0
EveryZing	http://www.everyzing.com
Blinkx	http://www.blinkx.com
del.icio.us	http://del.ico.us
MySpace	http://www.myspace.com

Facebook	http://www.facebook.com
Ning	http://www.ning.com

Chapter 12

Bloglines	http://www.bloglines.com
Google Reader	http://www.google.com/reader
Kebberfegg	www.researchbuzz.org/tools/kebberfegg.pl
Kinja	http://www.kinja.com
Lektora	http://www.lektora.com/index.htm
Newsgator	http://www.newsgator.com
Rojo	http://www.rojo.com
NewzCrawler	http://www.newzcrawler.com
Co.mments	http://co.mments.com/
FeedRinse	http://feedrinse.com
ReFilter	http://re.rephrase.net/filter/
Albert Ellis Institute	http://www.albertellis.org/aei/index.html
	rational emotive behavior therapy (REBT)
Google Alerts	http://www.google.com/alerts
Yahoo! Alerts	http://help.yahoo.com/l/us/yahoo/alerts/

Chapter 13

BlogPulse	http://www.blogpulse.com
IceRocket	http://www.icerocket.com
Memeorandum	http://www.memeorandum.com
Techmeme	http://www.techmeme.com
TailRank	http://tailrank.com
Digg	http://digg.com
Google Trends	http://www.google.com/trends
Google Zeitgeist	http://www.google.com/press/zeitgeist.html

Chapter 15

Google Custom Search Engine	http://www.google.com/coop/cse/
Ad, Marketing and PR Blog Search Tool	http://www.google.com/coop/cse?cx=010639246631309871017%3Axfkc4nc_55e

Onalytica	http://www.onalytica.com/
"Who are the Most Influential Authorities on Business Blogging"	http://www.onalytica.com/Who_influence_the_debate_on_Business_Blogging.pdf
Alexa	http://www.alexa.com
Quantcast	http://www.quantcast.com
PayPerPost	http://www.payperpost.com
Sponsored Reviews	http://www.sponsoredreviews.com
LoudLaunch	http://www.loudlaunch.com
ReviewMe	http://www.reviewme.com
AttentionMeter	http://www.attentionmeter.com
Twitter	http://twitter.com

Index

Editor's note: Index does not include links and resources found in the appendices.

About the Author

ROBERT BERKMAN, editor of *The Information Advisor,* an international monthly journal for business researchers that he founded in 1988, has authored several books on research, technology, the media, and the Internet. He serves as Associate Professor at the Department of Media Studies & Film at the New School in New York City where his focus is on emerging media technologies. Berkman has given workshops and seminars on effective research  techniques for Eastman Kodak, Accenture Research, the European Journalism Centre and many other companies and organizations. He has an MA in Journalism, and lives in Rochester, New York.